On the Brink

The environment is our only life-support system. As we approach the twenty-first century, however, there are indications that we are severing this life line.

Canada, like many other countries, has implemented State of the Environment (SOE) Reporting. Written for Canadians interested in their environment, SOE Reporting takes many forms: fact sheets, reports, newsletters, data base, and a five-year national report, to be published in 1991. SOE is a partnership that will increasingly involve federal, provincial, and territorial governments, private industry, academia, nongovernmental organizations, and you, the individual citizen.

Careful, objective analysis and interpretation of data will monitor conditions and significant trends in the health of our environment. Of equal importance are the explanations for these trends and the actions we are taking to sustain and enhance the natural environment. By increasing awareness of the state of our life-support system, we should be stimulated to protect it through better decision making and management.

On the Brink: Endangered Species in Canada is one indicator of the health of our country. If you are interested in obtaining more information on SOE Reporting, please write to:

State of the Environment Reporting Branch
Canadian Wildlife Service
Conservation and Protection
Environment Canada
Ottawa, Ontario
K1A 0H3

On the Brink

Endangered Species
in Canada

J. A. Burnett
C. T. Dauphiné Jr.
S. H. McCrindle
T. Mosquin

◆

Foreword by
Candace Savage

Western Producer Prairie Books
Saskatoon, Saskatchewan

Canadä

Copyright © Minister of Supply and Services
Canada, 1989
Western Producer Prairie Books
Saskatoon, Saskatchewan

Catalogue number EN40–366/1989E

Published by Western Producer Prairie Books in
co-operation with the Canadian Wildlife Service,
Conservation and Protection, Environment Canada,
and the Canadian Government Publishing Centre,
Supply and Services Canada.

Jacket and interior design by John Luckhurst
and Sandra Hastie/GDL
Front cover illustration, detail from "Disturbed Day
Dreams – Eastern Cougar," by Herbert Pikl
Back cover photographs: sea otter by Tim
Fitzharris/World Wildlife Fund; giant helleborine
by Donald R. Gunn; burrowing owl by Gary Seib
Credits appearing on page 173 are hereby made part
of this copyright page.

Printed and bound in Canada
96 95 94 93 92 91 90 89   8 7 6 5 4 3 2 1

Western Producer Prairie Books is a unique
publishing venture located in the middle of western
Canada and owned by a group of prairie farmers
who are members of Saskatchewan Wheat Pool.
From the first book in 1954, a reprint of a serial
originally carried in the weekly newspaper *The
Western Producer*, to the book before you now, the
tradition of providing enjoyable and informative
reading for all Canadians is continued.

The publisher wishes to acknowledge the support
received for this publication from the Canada
Council.

Canadian Cataloguing in Publication Data

Main entry under title:

On the brink: endangered species in Canada

Includes bibliographical references.
ISBN: 0-88833-298-X

1. Endangered species – Canada. I. Canada.
Conservation and Protection.
QL84.24.06 1989   639.9'0971   C89-098117-5

Contents

About the Authors

Although this book represents the combined efforts of many individuals and organizations, the four people responsible for writing the text deserve special mention.

James A. (Sandy) Burnett,

the book's principal author, is a writer and naturalist. A graduate of the University of Toronto, he has worked as a park naturalist and high school teacher in Ontario, and spent fifteen years with the National Film Board in Montréal and the Maritime region. He now lives in Sackville, New Brunswick. His columns on nature and conservation appear regularly in newspapers in the Atlantic provinces. He also writes for magazines such as *Equinox* and *Atlantic Insight*.

T. Charles (Chuck) Dauphiné Jr.

has a master's degree in forest zoology from the New York State College of Environmental Science and Forestry. He began his career with the Canadian Wildlife Service (CWS) in 1965, working in the Arctic studying caribou. He has also worked in national parks, primarily with large mammals. Chuck is now the endangered species co-ordinator for CWS. He is a member of the Committee on the Status of Endangered Wildlife in Canada (COSEWIC) and scientific advisor for the Convention on International Trade in Endangered Species of Flora and Fauna (CITES). Although Chuck worked on all aspects of the book, his main contribution was the concluding section on recovery programs.

Sheila H. McCrindle

graduated from the University of Guelph in 1983. She has been with the State of the Environment Reporting Program since its inception, and before that worked in the Environmental Protection Service of Environment Canada. Sheila managed the conception and production of the book, in addition to participating in its writing and editing.

Ted Mosquin

obtained his Ph.D. in botany from the University of California, Los Angeles. He worked as a research scientist for Agriculture Canada for eleven years and now runs his own consulting firm, which specializes in ecosystem restoration. Ted is active in many conservation and environmental preservation programs, and is the president of the Canadian Parks and Wilderness Society.

Foreword

Friends of mine, who are in their eighties, save everything. Plastic milk bags, odd bits of hardwear, buttons and pins — it's all carefully sorted and stored for reuse. One day, when I was packing a box of china for the mail, I discovered that they had even tucked away the wadding from their vitamin pills. They had bags of it, which I gratefully used; but I have to admit that I laughed at them.

I share this homely detail because it brings us close to the underlying subject of this book — ourselves and the choices we make in our everyday lives. The animals, birds, fish, and plants described in these pages are being crowded off the Earth and overwhelmingly, as the authors make clear, human beings are the cause. In Canada, where we have about 1,800 species of vertebrates in all, approximately one in 40 is endangered or threatened. Globally, we are losing several species a day, and the rate of loss continues to accelerate. If this macabre rhythm is to change, we must change ourselves, both individually and collectively. This will mean rediscovering the virtues of reuse and recycling, and sometimes choosing to act in ways that others may find ridiculous.

New modes of behaviour presuppose a new vision. The concept of the Earth as an integrated, self-regulating system, in which everything is linked to everything else, is now quite familiar; but for most of us it remains abstract. When we leave lights on or buy more appliances, we are not inclined to think of an increased demand for electricity, new hydro dams, and the loss of fish-spawning grounds. When we construct office towers, we tend to forget the impacts on migrating birds. If we toss out a pair of worn socks, we aren't reminded of the songbirds and peregrine falcons that were inadvertently poisoned to grow the cotton in the first place. However round-about and remote the linkages may be, the consequences of our actions are devastatingly real.

On the Brink is a landmark publication, the first concerted attempt to inform the public about the impending loss of wildlife in this country. Its power lies in permitting us to visualize, clearly and specifically, how we are affecting certain vulnerable species and, by extrapolation, the rest of the biosphere. There is nothing vague nor conceptual about the effects of oil spills on sea otters or of habitat loss on burrowing owls. Chapter by chapter, case after case, it becomes evident that human ignorance, waste, and mismanagement translate directly into death. The message is unambiguous, the challenge unmistakable.

If this book calls us to change personally, it may also inspire us to act politically. At a minimum, we have a responsibility to ensure that our research and conservation agencies are adequately financed. The scientific effort that went into creating the information presented in these pages is almost inconceivable. For years, biologists have been sighting, counting, weighing, measuring, settling details of taxonomy, estimating populations, wrangling over policy. Yet, as the authors make clear, much remains uncertain and unknown. Maintaining consistent support for environmental research should be high on our list of national priorities.

Few of us want to live in a world without whooping cranes, beluga whales, or any of the species whose names will be added to the danger roll in succeeding years. We may be able to avoid this fate, but, as this book makes plain, it will not happen automatically. Perhaps, in the end, it is we who are on the brink, of a new way of life.

Candace Savage
Yellowknife, N.W.T.

Acknowledgements

Many thanks to COSEWIC, its chairman, Bill Munro, and the subcommittee chairmen who reviewed the text: Dr. R. C. Campbell, fish and marine mammals, Dr. F. Cook, reptiles; Dr. E. Haber, plants; Dr. M. Shoesmith, terrestrial mammals; and Dr. R. James, birds.

Several research scientists put a great deal of effort into the species accounts and they, too, deserve mention: John Ambrose, University of Guelph; Lu Carbin, Geoff Holroyd, Ernie Kuyt, Frank Miller, and Hal Reynolds, CWS; Bill Koonz, Manitoba Wildlife Branch; Barbara Minish, Environmental Protection Service; and Alex Peden, Royal British Columbia Museum.

Photographs of endangered species can be difficult to obtain. We were helped by: John Ambrose, George Argus, Vivian Brownell, Daniel Brunton, George Califf, Barb Desrochers, Connie Downes, Mel Falk, Ernie Gollop, Dave Gray, Mike Oldham, Don Sutherland, Neville Winchester, Robert Watt, Allen Woodliffe, and the World Wildlife Fund Canada.

We also want to thank Dr. F. Cook, Dr. D. McAllister, Dr. H. Ouellet, and Dr. C. Van Zyl de Jong of the National Museum of Natural Science for their advice on the illustrations.

The range maps are the creation of Rick Allen, Heather Dewar, and Karen Lloyd, all with Environment Canada. They received information from wildlife biologists across the country.

David Love, of the World Wildlife Fund, Theresa Aniskowicz, of the Canadian Nature Federation, and Luba Mycio-Mommers, of the Canadian Wildlife Federation, provided valuable help with the contents and illustrations. Mary Bogaard and the resources of the Dorothy and Edgar Davidson Collection of Canadiana at Mount Allison University's Centre for Canadian Studies were a great help with historical references.

Special thanks to the staff of the SOE Reporting Branch who were there at the beginning to help get the project off the ground: Patricia Food, Darrell Piekarz, Mark Richardson, and Peter Rodgers. Special thanks also to the staff of the Canadian Wildlife Service (Atlantic Region), and especially Tony Erskine, Al Smith, Debbie Harris, and librarian Jean Sealy.

Because it is a joint production between a government agency and a nongovernment publisher, the project was fraught with some added challenges. Thanks to Nora Russell and Jane McHughen at Prairie Books, and to Wendy Simpson-Lewis and Susanna Erasmo at Environment Canada for the time and effort they spent in getting this book to press.

Introduction

This is a State of the Environment Report — one in a series of books published or sponsored by Environment Canada as a means of informing Canadians and other nations about some of the most pressing environmental issues facing this country today. That such publications are being given priority reflects an awakening of public consciousness to the fact that our world is a more vulnerable place than we had long supposed.

Scarcely a day passes without the release of some disturbing announcement about the environment. Our everyday speech has become flavoured with a new glossary of terms: acid rain, deforestation, impact assessment, ground-water pollution, ozone depletion, soil erosion, toxic waste. We learn that tropical forests are being destroyed at a rate of 11 million hectares per year; that there is a net yearly loss of 26 billion tonnes of topsoil from the world's crop lands; that several thousand plant and animal species become extinct annually. And yet, there is hope in the very fact that this litany of ecological damage reaches so many people. It helps to motivate a public and political determination that something should be done to reverse destructive trends before it is too late.

This book addresses one of those trends: the extinction of wildlife species. It examines some of the reasons why we should be concerned that human activity is making life impossible for many of our fellow creatures on this planet. It summarizes the situation of several dozen species of Canadian wildlife faced with the very real possibility of extinction. It discusses the official efforts that are being made to bring about their recovery, and outlines some of the practical steps that individuals and groups can take to assist in the work of preservation.

On an international scale, a large part of the impetus for this sort of concern has been stimulated by the International Union for the Conservation of Nature and Natural Resources (IUCN). This affiliate of the United Nations has initiated programs to monitor and report on the state of the global environment through a series of "Red Data Books," which have become standard reference works among people working for wildlife preservation around the world. IUCN projects have led to global agreements such as the Ramsar Convention, which provides a means of protecting internationally important wetlands, and the Convention on International Trade in Endangered Species of Wild Flora and Fauna (CITES), which aims to regulate a pernicious and long-ignored global trade in endangered wildlife and wildlife by-products.

In Canada, the responsibility for determining the status of wildlife species has been assigned to the Committee on the Status of Endangered Wildlife in Canada (COSEWIC), a joint committee of wildlife conservation agencies of the federal, provincial, and territorial governments and three environmental groups: the World Wildlife Fund Canada, the Canadian Nature Federation, and the Canadian Wildlife Federation. COSEWIC commissions status assessments on a wide range of species each year, and at an annual meeting assigns an appropriate classification to those that merit concern. The ecologists and wildlife biologists who advise COSEWIC base their status recommendations on a variety of factors that govern species viability. Specialized ecological requirements, reductions in range, loss of habitat, low reproduction, small or declining populations: all these indicators can help to pinpoint a species that may be at risk and also to determine the urgency of its situation.

Across Canada, several provinces have enacted their own legislation concerning the identification and management of endangered species. In some instances, particular local conditions or conservation goals may lead a province to designate a species as Endangered when it is not considered to be at risk nationally. For purposes of consistency, the present report refers only to the status assigned by COSEWIC.

Technically, Extinct and Extirpated are the most negative status designations that can be assigned to any life form. Extinct indicates that the plant or animal in question has ceased to exist anywhere on earth, while extirpated means that it no longer exists within a particular part of its range, i.e., within Canada, in the case of species so designated by COSEWIC.

Aside from Extinct and Extirpated, the most serious designation granted by COSEWIC is Endangered. This term refers to any native species whose existence in Canada is threatened, due to the actions of man, with immediate extirpation or extinction throughout all or a significant portion of its range.

The designation Threatened indicates a species whose status is only slightly less at risk. It is assigned to any indigenous species of fauna or flora likely to become endangered in Canada if factors affecting its vulnerability are not reversed.

Until recently, Rare constituted the fifth category recognized by COSEWIC. This was occasionally a source of some confusion, however, as a species might well be rare, in the sense of few in number, without its survival being at risk. At the annual meeting of the committee in 1988, it was agreed that Vulnerable would be a more precise term. It is applied to species which, because of declining numbers, restricted range, or some other reason, are potentially at risk in Canada, but not threatened directly. Many species that are common in more southerly countries, for instance, occur in Canada only at the extreme northern edge of their ranges. In such cases, the Vulnerable category effectively acknowledges the fact that the natural division of the world into ecosystems is seldom reflected by the political boundaries of nation-states. During 1989–90, species previously classed as Rare are being reviewed to determine whether they should be reclassified as Vulnerable, upgraded to Threatened or Endangered, or dropped from the list entirely.

Although the priority for preparing assessment reports is placed on species thought to be at risk, some species assessed by COSEWIC are found to be in no danger. Such species are listed as Not in Any Category, until such time as an updated review may indicate a reason for changing their status. Meanwhile, the time-consuming process of assessment and designation continues. Most of the mammals and birds, and many of the fish whose status in Canada might be in doubt, have now been considered at least once by the committee. The status of a great many plants remains unverified, as does that of a large proportion of the reptiles and amphibians and virtually all the insects and other invertebrates. This

Species Reviewed by COSEWIC but not Threatened, Endangered, or Vulnerable

Mammals

American Badger
Beluga: Beaufort Sea
California Sea Lion
Fox Squirrel
Gray Whale: Northeast Pacific
Grizzly Bear
Hooded Seal
Mountain Beaver
Narwhal
Northern Elephant Seal
Polar Bear
Stellar's Sea Lion
Walrus: Eastern Arctic
Woodland Caribou: Newfoundland
Woodland Caribou: Northeastern

Birds

Bald Eagle
Black Tern
Double-crested Cormorant
Eastern Screech-owl
Golden Eagle
Greater Sandhill Crane
Gyrfalcon
Merlin
Prairie Falcon
Red-necked Grebe
Sharp-shinned Hawk
White Pelican

Fish

Bloater
Blueback Herring
Green Sunfish
Hornyhead Chub
Lake Sturgeon
Longear Sunfish
Redfin Shiner
River Chub

Plants

False Mermaid

reflects the fact that wildlife biology traditionally concerned itself primarily with the conservation and management of species that were prized as game. Fewer scientists and resources were devoted to the field study of species in other kingdoms, orders, and classes. Nowadays, as the science of ecology encourages consideration of whole systems rather than of species in isolation, this bias is being replaced by an appreciation for the interdependence of all living things. Still, many years will pass before the status of all the flora and fauna of Canada is as well documented as it is for the species described in this report.

This book has been written primarily for a general audience — people who are interested in the natural world around them and concerned for its well-being, but not necessarily specialists in ecology or wildlife management. Indeed, specialists may wonder at the taking of a few liberties with the ways in which material has been presented. The information on species biology and ecology is current, gathered from contemporary books, reports, and journals, and has been closely checked for accuracy by several qualified scientific reviewers. Rather than adopt a rigidly formal approach, the authors have set as their goal a style that will inform anyone who takes an interest in the environment.

It is for this reason that the accounts of endangered and threatened species are grouped not in accordance with the rules of scientific taxonomy or a sophisticated system of land classification, but in relation to seven broad "life zones" in which they occur, and which are relatively familiar to most Canadians. Thus, readers who live on the Prairies, or on the West Coast, or along the St. Lawrence waterway will find the species of their native region grouped together. While this may not adhere to scientific orthodoxy, it has the advantage of making it easier to realize that the endangerment of a single species seldom occurs in isolation. The problems of each threatened animal or plant tend to be interconnected in a broader picture of environmental damage and habitat loss in the region where it lives. It is important that the difficulties be understood in this light. Only then is it reasonable to expect support for the kind of far-reaching program of conservation, restoration, and protection that is needed to sustain a healthy global environment.

Grouping the accounts of endangered and threatened species in this informal fashion does entail certain risks of over-simplification, which are best acknowledged at the outset. What is referred to here as the Pacific/Mountain life zone, for example, includes the Pacific coast, the interior plateau and interior mountains of British Columbia, as well as parts of the Yukon and Alberta. These divisions, in turn, can be further subdivided into sharply contrasting ecological zones: alpine tundra, coastal rain forest, grassland, desert, and many more, each with its own character and its own plant and animal community. The same process of increasingly refined subdivision could quite properly be applied to each of the other major life zones that have been chosen. However, there is no shortage of detailed reference material available for any reader who wishes to pursue the subject of ecological classification at greater depth than is practical in this book.

A second potential risk of confusion stems from the fact that a number of species are not confined to a single life zone, but range across much of the country. The piping plover, for instance, occurs on the Atlantic coast and on the Prairies, and may still persist on the shores of the Great Lakes as well. One race or another of the peregrine falcon was historically found virtually everywhere in Canada, and the range of the endangered *anatum* subspecies still stretches from Alberta to Labrador. In such cases, a decision has been made, somewhat arbitrarily, to present the detailed account of the species in one zone where its presence may serve to illustrate a particular type of problem or a special chance of recovery. To minimize confusion, the range maps for such widespread species show their entire territory, and their names appear in the species list for each life zone where they are found.

A stark truth comes home to anyone who spends much time examining the plight of endangered wildlife: No place on earth is immune to the stresses placed on the environment by one species — our own. The earth, however, has remarkable recuperative powers. In Canada we have the good fortune to be addressing most of our problems of habitat deterioration and species extinction before they have advanced beyond hope of recovery. Restoring our natural environment to health and diversity will challenge our commitment and creativity to the full; but if we act now, in the knowledge that our own survival is ultimately linked to the outcome, then the goal is within our reach.

A Danger to One:
A Danger to All

◆

"And no birds sing..." A Worst-Case Scenario

The time: sometime in a possible future. The place: somewhere in Canada.

The grip of winter breaks at last, and spring advances over a reluctantly thawing land. Melting snow saturates barren, unprotected soil. Eroding trickles turn to muddy rivulets, then to silt-laden torrents that choke rivers and discolour lifeless lakes and seas. No grass greens in the warmth of the strengthening sun. No apple blossoms perfume the air. No birds sing.

The season has arrived that was foretold by Rachel Carson in Silent Spring, written in 1962 when humanity still possessed the freedom to choose between moderation and excess, between stewardship and exploitation of the environment. Generally, the human race exercised the second option with deadly effectiveness, looting and laying waste in the name of short-term advantage until the earth's ecosystems could withstand the abuse no longer and collapsed with terrifying rapidity and disastrous results. All choices gone, the survivors wait and watch the relentless advance of the Silent Spring.

It hasn't happened yet, not on a global scale at any rate, although around the world it is easy enough to find examples of environmental destruction that evoke nightmare fantasies of an ecological doomsday. The close of the twentieth century is no time for comfortable platitudes about bountiful nature. It is a time for prudently assessing all manner of human activities in terms of their short- and long-term effects on the future of life on this planet.

Less than thirty years ago, manned orbital space flight enabled the human race to see the whole earth for the first time. Those now-familiar photographs of a jewel-like sphere of blue and white and gold set in the black emptiness of space have had a profound effect on our perception of where we live. What every previous generation had conceived of as a world without limits was revealed as a finite, fragile, and beautiful speck suspended in the immensity of the universe. Along with that revelation came the further reali-

zation that this planet is the only place within our ken, or within our reach, that is capable of sustaining life. It is the only home we have. Lose it, and we lose all.

Just how finite and fragile our world is can be better appreciated if we consider how little of it is actually suited to life. Imagine a beach ball one metre in diameter with a skin one millimetre thick. That skin accounts for a single one-thousandth of the distance through the ball from side to side; yet it is the part that gives shape and meaning to the entire object. The diameter of the earth is about 12,800 kilometres. Its outer surface is covered by a skin of air and soil and water in which the processes of organic life occur. On average, that skin, which we call the *biosphere,* is only about 12 kilometres thick, a single one-thousandth of the distance through the planet; yet it is the part that gives shape and meaning to the entire living world.

"Our Common Future" – Living Together on a Small Planet

This book is about endangered species of wildlife in Canada — that is to say, about one critically important aspect of the state of the biosphere in one part of the world. Before embarking on an exploration of that topic, it may be helpful to define a term which will appear often in the following pages, and to consider how our changed view of the planet Earth has influenced the way we apply that definition. The term is *ecosystem,* and it refers to any natural unit made up of a physical location and the living species that interact with it and within it, in a stable relationship sustained by continuous exchanges of materials. Those exchanges constitute the processes of life. If the relationships which govern them lose their stability or become unbalanced, then life is threatened and the ecosystem itself is put at risk. The biosphere is the largest example of such a unit, but within it there exist thousands of other relationships between physical environments and the life forms that inhabit them, and these too are sufficiently distinct to be called ecosystems.

One of the most simple and elegant illustrations of the principle underlying every ecosystem is to be found in a spider's web. The classic structure of radiating spokes linked by a spiral of sticky thread is a marvel of unconscious engineering. No matter what part of the delicate tracery an intruder may brush against, the vibrations of its touch are transmitted to every corner of the web, alerting the spider to feast or to flee.

Everything interconnects. Even seemingly insignificant events may trigger far-reaching consequences. It is a principle to keep in mind whenever humans propose to alter the natural ecosystems of the earth. Not every action is harmful; but every action has inevitable repercussions, some of them far more profound than we might suppose.

The fundamental ways and means by which people alter the world are not new. They include virtually the whole range of human economic activities from the clearing of subsistence garden plots by peasant farmers, to the reshaping of whole landscapes by giant corporations and government agencies. What is new and alarming is the rate at which these activities have accelerated in recent years. Unprecedented growth in population and technology has increased the environmental impact of political and military struggles, industrial processes, and even the simple acts of hunting for food and gathering fuel, to the point where collectively they threaten tens of thousands of species, hundreds of ecosystems, and possibly the survival of the whole biosphere.

In 1987 the United Nations' World Commission on Environment and Development published a report entitled "Our Common Future." Motivated by an awareness that human activities around the world are placing dangerous strains on the global ecosystem, the commission had set out to chart a course for building future economic and social prosperity for mankind without exhausting or destroying the living world in the process. After nearly three years of concentrated study of global economic and environmental trends and challenges, its message to the nations of the world is a succinct and classic combination. There is good news and bad news.

The bad news is that in the forty years since the founding of the United Nations, human beings have inflicted more severe and lasting damage on the global environment than in all the previous time that we have existed as a species. If the trend continues, the planet may survive, but there is a distinct possibility that humanity will not. The report does not hesitate to characterize the global state of the environment as one of crisis.

The good news is that there is still time to make amends. Although some of the damage may be irreparable, there is still time to offset much of it. "Our Common Future" challenges the peoples and governments of the world to initiate a new era of responsible environmental stewardship in which human beings can co-exist with the other living components of the world in a sustainable fashion.

What does that mean? Until recently, until men and women were able to extend their vision beyond the biosphere, look back, and see the earth for the fragile, beautiful ecosystem that it is, one dominant assumption of contemporary industrial culture was that we humans were the superior life form on the planet, and as such had a right to dominate and exploit the world for our own economic advantage. This view deemed nonhuman members of the biosphere, such as other species of animals and plants, to be "resources" — a convenient shorthand way of claiming ownership of them and the right to exploit them whenever and however we might wish. Many people today still believe unquestioningly in man's inherent right of dominion over the earth.

Increasingly, however, the proponents of this view are being left behind. The contemporary understanding of an integrated and vulnerable biosphere requires that we abandon domination/exploitation in favour of environmental conservation. Such a shift in philosophy holds profound implications for how we deal with the natural world. The rights of ownership are replaced by the duties and privileges of stewardship, especially the duty to ensure that our privileged use of a natural resource for short-term benefits must not jeopardize the long-term viability of that resource or others that depend on it, now or in the future. It argues that since we have explored the uses of only a tiny fraction of the multitude of species and ecosystems on earth, then it is foolish, wasteful, and dangerous to eliminate them.

Beyond that essentially pragmatic position in favour of conservation, yet another insight is starting to emerge, based on the idea that all living things are participants in an integrated, global ecosystem. A wide variety of issues, such as species' rights, for example, are at the leading edge of this evolving position. The argument runs that if we ourselves are parts of a system, then we cannot set ourselves apart from it, either as exploiters or as stewards, but must assess all our interactions with other species in terms of their value for the survival of the biosphere itself. Often, in the coming pages, we shall see that a species survives and prospers in an ecosystem because it possesses traits that give it an advantage in a particular habitat. If our own species owes its success in populating and dominating the earth to the possession of self-awareness and an inventive intellect, then it may now be in our best interest to apply those attributes less exclusively to ourselves, and more broadly to the well-being of the world.

Regardless of whether we view ourselves as stewards of the natural world or as self-aware, responsible members of it, the option of un-bridled economic exploitation of the environment is no longer one that we can afford to countenance. The endangerment and extinction of plant and animal species, as a direct or indirect result of such exploitation, is one of the most pressing elements of the world crisis described in "Our Common Future."

Defining Some Useful Terms

Nowadays, so much information — some of it quite technical — is available about matters of environmental life and death that the nonscientist who wants to understand the processes that occur within ecosystems may find it useful at this point to consider the definition of a few scientific terms. The first is *ecology*. The word is derived from the Greek roots *oikos* = habitation, and *logos* = study. It is the branch of biological science that concerns itself with the study of plants and animals in relation to each other and to the environments in which they live. From this it is easy enough to see why the word *ecosystem* was coined to describe an integrated and stable association of organisms functioning within a defined physical location. As noted previously, the term ecosystem may be applied to a unit as large as the entire biosphere. More often, though, it refers to some smaller division of the world. Where climate, life forms,

and geographical features combine to form a large, regional ecosystem, an ecologist may call such a region a *biome*. Tundra, grassland, coniferous forest, and marine biomes are four which figure largely in describing the natural history of Canada. On a smaller, more local scale, a pond or woodlot which is distinguishable from the surrounding area by its particular array of plants and animals, and its particular conditions of water, soil, climate, and exposure to the elements, may also quite correctly be referred to as an ecosystem.

Collectively, all the living organisms that occupy an ecosystem are often referred to as a *community*, while all the individuals belonging to a given species within that community constitute a *population*. Population is a rather flexible term, being applied with equal validity to the total world population of a species or to the members of that species which inhabit a region or even a local area.

The environment in which a population occurs is properly called its *habitat*. The concept of habitat includes not only the place where a species is found, but also the particular characteristics of that place, such as climate or the availability of suitable food and shelter, which make it especially well-suited to meet the life-cycle needs of that species.

Although the definition of the term *species* is itself a matter of debate among some biologists, it is generally accepted as referring to a group of individuals that share certain identical physical characteristics and are capable of producing fertile offspring. A number of closely related species may be grouped together as members of the same *genus*. If a particular population of a species is isolated from others of its kind for a long time, it may develop distinctive traits which are not typical of the species as a whole. That particular population may then be classified as a separate *race* or *subspecies*. Should the influences of isolation and specialization result in changes that are sufficiently profound and permanent, a local subspecies may eventually emerge as a new species.

The characteristics that distinguish one species of organism from another are controlled by *genes*, chemical codes present in all life forms. They have been described as "life's way of re-membering how to perpetuate itself." Genes are bound up in molecules of a substance known as deoxyribonucleic acid, or DNA for short. When an organism reproduces, it is the *genetic code*, the unique combination of genes peculiar to that species, that ensures its identifying characteristics — not to mention those of the subspecies, and even the individual parent(s) — will be passed on to the next generation.

Through thousands of years of selectively cross-breeding preferred varieties of plants and animals to emphasize desirable characteristics, farmers have made practical use of a biological process that science has only succeeded in describing with any accuracy in the past thirty years. The genetic code determines virtually everything about an organism, from its colour, size, and shape, to its ability to digest a certain food or resist a certain disease. *Genetic diversity* — the infinite variation of possible genetic combinations among individuals — is what enables a species, a subspecies, or a population to adapt to changes and challenges in its environment, and ultimately to survive. When a species is extinguished, or a population is extirpated, all the past heritage and future potential of the genetic information carried in its members is lost to the world for all time.

Extinct Means Gone Forever

Extinction is an ugly word. No other conveys a more absolute sense of finality. In the simplest terms, extinction means that all populations and all individuals of a species have ceased to exist; all hope for the preservation of that plant or animal vanishes. It is gone forever. A close cousin to extinction is *extirpation*: the total disappearance of a living species from a particular area in which it was once native. It, too, has ugly connotations, less so than extinction only to the extent that the possibility remains of an extirpated species being restored to a former range.

The process of extinction can occur in many ways. It is, moreover, a process that has occurred continually ever since life emerged on this planet. Geologists, paleontologists, and paleobiologists examine the physical records of the earth's history in rocks and fossils. They interpret the rise and fall of mountains, oceans, jungles, and deserts, and with them, the appearance and disappearance of worms, ferns, fish, grasses, dinosaurs — a parade of millions of species that have

evolved, flourished, and fallen. Just as the process of evolution has constantly brought forth new species in response to new conditions and opportunities, so the process of extinction has eliminated those that can no longer adapt to a changing environment.

Genetic diversity has fuelled these processes, endlessly experimenting with new combinations of genes. Some succeed; some fail. The resulting variety of life forms is almost beyond imagining. More than 1,700,000 species of plants and animals have been described to date. Millions more are still undiscovered. The most cautious scientists estimate a total of between 5 and 10 million, but recent studies of tropical ecosystems have revealed such enormous numbers of new ones, especially among insects, that some experts now suspect the world may actually contain more than 30 million species. Many of these will never be described or known to us before they vanish in the rapid deforestation of the tropical rain forests.

This wealth of successful genetic combinations has always been the best assurance of the continued prosperity of life on earth. Even after episodes of mass extinction, such as the disappearance of the dinosaurs at the end of the Cretaceous Period some 65 million years ago, the sheer number and diversity of species has meant that although many tens of thousands of species might be lost each time, they have been replaced with a new and equally amazing variety of flora and fauna within the relatively brief span of a few million years.

Studies by present-day ecologists have revealed a great deal about the dynamic processes of extinction. There are three main factors which influence the survival or extinction of any species: its genetically determined characteristics, its ability to make effective use of available habitat, and the structure of its population.

First, the physical, physiological, and behavioural characteristics of a species determine its adaptability to change. To take a familiar example, the common loon has its legs set far back on its body. Because of this adaptation, the bird is a powerful underwater swimmer and predator, but is unable to move on dry land without great difficulty. It requires a sizeable body of water in which to feed, by which to nest, and from which to take flight. If a drastic change in climate were to dry up the myriad lakes that dot the boreal coniferous forest biome of North

America, the specialization which makes the loon admirably suited for present-day conditions would almost certainly result in its extinction.

Second, in order to thrive, a species must have access to a sufficient quantity of habitat, and that habitat must be of good quality in terms of providing appropriate food and shelter. The illustration of the common loon's vulnerability owing to specialization demonstrates equally well how the loss of suitable habitat might lead to extinction.

Third, survival depends on sufficient numbers of a species being present in good health amid suitable habitat to guarantee a rate of reproduction equal to or greater than the natural rate of mortality. An example of this can be found in the account of the *anatum* race of the peregrine falcon, which demonstrates how a population with ample food and suitable habitat could nonetheless be doomed to extirpation because of widespread reproductive failure.

Extinction can be caused by an imbalance in any one of these three factors, or by any combination of two or three of them. In some cases the cause may be direct: the removal of something essential, or the introduction of something lethal in the environment. At other times, the process may be indirect: a nonlethal event or influence may reduce a population to the point where it is suddenly much more vulnerable to pressures which it could normally withstand. Frequently, extinction takes place as the result of a combination of direct and indirect influences. For example, loss of habitat may fragment a population to the point where its members have less chance of breeding successfully and are also more exposed to external forces such as disease, predation, or a failure of food supply.

Although there is considerable debate over the causes of past extinctions, it is widely agreed that they have been caused by so-called natural phenomena such as volcanic activity, meteorite impact, or a shifting of the planet's axis. One of the reasons for concern about extinctions in the modern world is that they are most frequently caused by human activity. By deliberate mass slaughter, by destroying or degrading natural habitats, by introducing competitors, predators, toxic pollutants, or diseases to the environment, we increase the mortality of species, reduce their productivity, drive them from their ranges, and disrupt the continuity of their life-cycles. The worst irony of all is that so little is known about

the workings of the physical world and its complex ecosystems that we inflict much of this irreparable damage out of ignorance.

In the present century, we appear to be inducing the largest and fastest mass extinction of species ever experienced on earth. Most ecologists who are studying the phenomenon of contemporary extinction agree on several points. They feel that at present we are losing several species every day, as compared to an average rate of less than one a year over the entire span of life on earth. They fear that this rate may increase to several species per hour by the year 2000. They predict that before a new ecological equilibrium can be established, 50 percent or more, that is, 15 to 20 million species of life forms on earth may be lost. Apart from the costs and risks which this process entails for the human species, an event of this magnitude is likely to handicap the life-producing and life-sustaining capacity of the biosphere itself for many millions of years.

Anyone who follows environmental issues in the media is aware of the extent to which mass extinction is concentrated in the tropics. We read of the destruction of forests and endemic wildlife in far-off places like Borneo and Sri Lanka, or look at satellite pictures of the pall of smoke rising from land-clearing operations in the rain forests of the Amazon. It is true that by far the greatest number of extinctions occur in tropical regions. The reason is threefold: the tropics have far more species to be destroyed; tropical environments are often among the most highly specialized and hence the most vulnerable to the impact of human colonization and exploitation; and the global crisis of human population growth, with its attendant pressures on the environment, is most concentrated in the tropical and subtropical regions of the world.

A tropical paradise in the Indian Ocean provides a graphic example of the mass extinction process at work. Isolated by the sea from most external influences, Madagascar was a hotbed of uninterrupted evolutionary productivity for millions of years. A century ago, it has been estimated, there were about 12,000 plant species and perhaps 190,000 species of animals on the island. As many as 60 percent of them were found nowhere else on earth. Today, at least 93 percent of the forests of Madagascar have been cut down. It is estimated that half the original species of the island — 6,000 plants and 85,000 animals — have already disappeared or are on

9

the verge of extinction. And these may well be conservative estimates.

By comparison, Canada has lost little more than a dozen species and lists fewer than 100 as endangered or threatened. This is really no cause for rejoicing. Canada's original complement of species is a mere handful compared to that of almost any tropical region. Twelve thousand years ago, most of Canada was covered by the continental glaciers of the last ice age. By ecological standards, 12,000 years is a very short time for the repopulation of a region after it has been scraped bare of most forms of life. From the point of view of species diversity, Canada is an extremely young country indeed. It is in a state of biological development where the loss of genetic potential represented by the extinction of a single species may be as damaging as the loss of several hundred in a smaller, more highly specialized ecosystem elsewhere.

Another important and sobering thought is that to date Canada has begun to deal only with threats to vertebrates — i.e., species with backbones — and plants. It is estimated that invertebrates — insects, spiders, shellfish, worms, etc. — make up more than 95 percent of the life forms in Canada. There are about 1,800 known vertebrates in this country, while invertebrates are believed to number about 100,000. These, too, are participants in the biosphere; yet only one Canadian authority, the Province of Ontario, has granted protection to a single invertebrate, the West Virginia white butterfly, under its Endangered Species Act.

All the wildlife species described in detail in this book are in danger of extinction or extirpation. All are resident in Canada for at least some important stage of their life cycle. For some, the danger is terrible and immediate; for others, it is more remote, a vulnerability that may lead to annihilation if nothing is done to deter it; for several, it is receding, thanks to protective measures taken in time to be effective. For a few, the danger is gone forever. They are the extinct and extirpated: silent victims of the sublimely arrogant belief that all living things are ours to use, to abuse, and to destroy.

The **passenger pigeon** is the example, par excellence, of a wildlife species obliterated by human greed and exploitation. Once the most numerous bird in North America, it came under truly excessive pressure with the growth of industrial cities in the nineteenth century. In 1851,

close to 2 million pigeons were shipped to market by rail from a single site near Plattsburg, New York. Under such pressure throughout their range, flocks that had once darkened the sky in migration were wiped out within decades. By the 1890s they were rare. The last reliable sighting in Canada was at Penetanguishene, Ontario, in 1902, and the last passenger pigeon in the world died in captivity at the Cincinnati Zoo on September 1, 1914.

The **great auk** was a large, flightless seabird, which bred on islands in the North Atlantic from the Gulf of St. Lawrence to Iceland and Scotland. Newfoundland's Funk Island, with an estimated population of 100,000 pairs, held the world's largest great auk colony. As the Grand Banks fishery expanded in the seventeenth and eighteenth centuries, Funk Island became a regular provisioning stop for hundreds of European vessels. The crews came ashore armed with clubs to stock up on fresh meat and eggs. In 1795 one observer wrote: "It has been customary . . . for several crews of men to live all summer on the island for the purpose of killing birds for the sake of their feathers. . . . If a stop is not put to that practice, the whole breed will be diminished to almost nothing."

By 1800, the prophecy had come true. A few birds remained, scattered across their North Atlantic range for another few decades, and the last two great auks were killed near Iceland in June 1844.

Along the rocky coasts and offshore islands of New England and the Maritimes lived the **sea mink,** a member of the weasel family very much like the American mink, but up to twice as large. It was essentially a solitary animal and spent much time at sea, like the sea otter of the Pacific coast. Its size and the quality of its fur made it a trophy much sought-after by early trappers. All indications are that it was never an abundant species, and the pressure of trapping was likely sufficient to push it to extinction. The last known sea mink was killed on Campobello Island, New Brunswick, in 1894.

The **Labrador duck** was a sea duck that bred in southern Labrador and wintered along the East Coast from the Maritimes south to Chesapeake Bay. So little is known of its natural history that explanations of its extinction are only speculative. It seems to have been a highly specialized bird that never attained great numbers. If it already led a precarious existence, then persecution by man in the eighteenth and nineteenth centuries may have been sufficient to exterminate it. The last sighting of a living Labrador duck in Canada occurred at Grand Manan, New Brunswick, in 1874, and the last in the world at Elmira, New York, on December 12, 1874.

Commercial fishermen and anglers alike prized the **blue walleye** of Lake Erie and Lake Ontario. Millions of kilograms were taken annually by largely unrestricted fishing until the population crashed between 1956 and 1959. It is thought that over-exploitation, combined with a rapid decline in the water quality in the lower Great Lakes during that period, as a result of increasing agricultural and industrial pollution, pushed the subspecies out of existence during the 1960s.

Two other commercially important fish of the Great Lakes, the **deepwater cisco** and the **longjaw cisco,** have also been lost to extinction in this century. A more detailed treatment of their disappearance will be found in the section on the Great Lakes/St. Lawrence life zone.

The **Banff longnose dace,** on the other hand, was not a victim of excessive commercial or sporting pressure. This small (18–54 millimetre) minnow-like fish was exterminated inadvertently. Occurring only in a single marsh in Banff National Park, its survival was threatened by tropical fish that had been released in its habitat, and by the disposal of chlorinated water and sewage from public baths at the Cave and Basin Hot- springs in Banff. It was declared extinct in 1987.

The list of extirpated species is slightly less discouraging, if only because populations of its members still persist elsewhere, and in a few instances, re-introduction to former Canadian ranges is actually possible.

The **gray whale** is now thought of as a Pacific Ocean species where, since coming under the protection of the International Agreement for the Regulation of Whaling in 1937, its numbers have recovered well. Only a few bones and historical documents remain to indicate that gray whales were ever present in the North Atlantic. There is no evidence of their numbers, nor of how or when they were extirpated. The one certain fact is that they are gone.

Two fish species have been declared extirpated in Canada. One, the **paddlefish,** is a primitive species native to the Mississippi River system. A small, isolated population persisted in the Great Lakes up to the beginning of the twentieth century, but as no specimens have been reported in Canada for at least seventy years, it is presumed that the population simply dwindled to the point where it was no longer viable.

The **gravel chub** occurred in the Thames River drainage basin in southwestern Ontario until at least 1958. A species that inhabited areas of clear water with clean sand or gravel bottoms, its habitat became choked with silt resulting from land clearance and soil erosion.

Not even plant species are immune to the threat of extinction, although only one is known to have been extirpated from its Canadian range so far. A rare blue and white wildflower with the charmingly homespun popular name of **blue-eyed Mary** *(Collinsia verna)* appeared occasionally in rich, moist woods in southwestern Ontario. The last confirmed Canadian occurrence of the plant was a dense stand discovered in Elgin County in 1954. Since then the woodland site where it grew has been cleared.

The **Atlantic walrus** is still a viable species in Canada's eastern Arctic, but it was once numerous enough to be the object of a major industrial fishery along the east coast to the Gulf of St. Lawrence and Sable Island. During the seventeenth and eighteenth centuries, tens of thousands of barrels of walrus oil and tons of ivory tusks were shipped to Europe from stations on Sable Island and the Magdalen Islands. By 1798, a Captain Crofton of the Royal Navy reported that the walrus fishery was "totally annihilated" in the Gulf of St. Lawrence. There are no indications that it will ever return.

The **black-footed ferret** is a mink-sized, buff-coloured weasel with dark brown or black face, legs, and tip of tail. In Canada, it occurred in southern Alberta and Saskatchewan. A regular predator on grassland rodents such as ground squirrels and prairie dogs, it was extirpated in the 1930s when pest eradication programs virtually eliminated the prairie-dog towns that were its chief hunting grounds.

The **swift fox,** on the other hand, shows promising signs of making a comeback. This fleet-footed, cat-sized canine occupied much the same range as the black-footed ferret, and fed on many of the same species, although its diet also included rabbits, birds, and insects. Commercial fur trapping, incidental poisoning as a by-product of pest-control campaigns, and the conversion of native grassland to agricultural uses resulted in the extirpation of the swift fox by the 1930s. How private citizens and government agencies have collaborated to re-establish this native species to the Canadian prairie is recounted in a later section.

Extinction – A Question of Values

The fact that sufficient data have been gathered and analysed to make it possible to describe and categorize the status of extinct and extirpated species in this manner is a convincing indication of how much the thinking of individuals and governments has shifted in the past few decades. Only recently have concerns about the global effects of species loss and ecosystem destruction begun to appear as important priorities on the political and economic agendas of the world.

What we do over the next few years, collectively and individually, about the current unprecedented cycle of mass extinction will undoubtedly reveal a great deal about our values. It may also be the ultimate test of our own fitness for survival as a species. In ecological terms, ours is simply one of millions of species inhabiting the earth, consuming air, food, and water, and interacting with the rest of nature. We are every bit as dependent on the finite resources of the global ecosystem as any other species, and if our behaviour undermines the integrity of our habitat beyond our ability to adapt to the changes we have initiated, we too can become extinct, as surely as any other species.

For the past two hundred years, western thought has held that value is a uniquely human concept, and that nothing can have value except as defined by man. The knowledge that we have acquired in this century, and the concurrent sense of the enormity of our ignorance about the natural world, are causing a number of people to question that presumption of human superiority and to reconsider whether value may not be inherent in functioning natural systems. For those who are open to this line of argument, it is not hard to accept the idea that environmental responsibility is a requirement that goes along with our role as the currently dominant species on earth. However, it is not necessary to delve this deeply into philosophy in order to be seriously concerned about environmental protec-

tion and species preservation. A wide array of human-centred values also support the basic premise that man must stop doing wanton damage to the biosphere, and instead initiate measures to preserve biological diversity.

Some of these values are wholly utilitarian and practical. The growing human population needs food. At least 80,000 species of plants around the world are known to be edible, yet only 150 have ever been widely cultivated as food crops. Of those, fewer than 20 produce 90 percent of the world's food supply. We have good reason to preserve wild species if only because the agricultural potential of more than 99.8 percent of them has never been tested. Many untried species may have capabilities, under cultivation, to produce food in deserts, or under other severe climatic limitations, or in soils that are too acid, too saline, or too depleted of nutrients for conventional crops. If we lose potential food species — be they plant or animal — we reduce our own chances of long-term survival.

Still in the realm of agriculture, crop scientists tell us that specialized strains of crops are often vulnerable to disease. Without the capacity to develop new, resistant types, the incidence of famine could increase. Wheat, for example, so long a mainstay of western Canadian agriculture, is descended from wild grains that have now all but disappeared from their original ranges in the Mediterranean basin. If we lose the genetic diversity inherent in wild strains of the plants we use, we risk losing the means, by selective breeding, of developing strains of plants and animals that will be resistant to blights and diseases yet unknown.

The argument that species should be preserved for their future value to mankind applies to the pharmaceutical and medical fields as well. A wide range of important drugs, from painkillers to cancer inhibitors, has already been derived from plants; yet only a fraction of the existing species have been tested for the presence of compounds with medicinal potential. Studies of various animals have also provided keys to a tremendous variety of medical discoveries, but here, too, the research has barely begun.

The human population also needs clothing, shelter, and a wide variety of other goods and services which can only be provided on a global scale through organized economic activity. As we learn more about biology and genetics, we are just beginning to appreciate the economic possibilities of bio-engineering, not only in agriculture, but also in fields as disparate as energy production, manufacturing, and communications.

To summarize, if we reduce genetic diversity by allowing preventable extinctions to occur, we may unknowingly lose important resources for combating world poverty, hunger, and disease. Conversely, by preserving endangered species and ecosystems from thoughtless and unrestricted human exploitation, we protect a treasury of natural properties, as yet undiscovered, which may someday prove to be of inestimable value.

Society attaches values to the natural world at the cultural level as well. Once people have secured the basic necessities of life, such as food, clothing, and shelter, then a secondary set of needs assumes great importance. For example, the recreational and aesthetic values of the natural world, as antidotes to the stresses of the manmade environment, are undeniable. A survey by Statistics Canada of outdoor recreational activities indicated that at least 20 percent of Canadians make special trips for the purpose of observing or studying wildlife. Still higher proportions enjoy participation in outdoor sports such as hiking, skiing, boating, and swimming, all of which require access to an undamaged environment. Furthermore, many people simply like to know that a large part of the world is still wilderness. Whether we prefer to appreciate nature as observers, or to interact with it more directly through the physical challenges of outdoor adventure, it is in our interest to protect it from abuse and to consume only that which can be replenished by natural means.

Throughout history, another important human value, the intellectual satisfaction of pure scientific inquiry — the study of how things are, how they came to be, and what they may yet become — has depended largely on the continued healthy functioning of the object of our study, namely, the natural world and all its wonders. With each extinction of a species or each disintegration of an ecosystem, we lose forever the chance to gain knowledge that may be intrinsic to our understanding of the whole earth and our place in it.

The last of the pragmatic arguments in favour of species and ecosystem protection, and the most telling of all, is that ecological responsibility may be the only strategy for survival that remains open to mankind. As stated earlier, the science of ecology studies the web of interconnecting links between all living things and their living and nonliving surroundings. The stability of those relationships is a characteristic of any functioning ecosystem, as is the ability to adjust to changes. But there are limits to the degree of stress that a species or an ecosystem can tolerate before its inherent stability is jeopardized. Frequently we discover those limits only after pollution, habitat loss, or unrestrained resource exploitation have done irreparable harm.

The disappearance of a species from the earth marks not the beginning but the end of a process of deterioration. It is a sign that the ecosystem in which the species played its integral role has also been damaged. At some point, the ecosystem itself may be so destabilized by the loss of interactive species that it will lose its integrity and collapse. Should the actions of man place that sort of stress upon the biosphere, then the human species, for all its inventiveness, could well be the author of its own extinction.

At present, the options are still open. We have the freedom to choose between moderation and excess, between short-term exploitation and long-term co-existence with the rest of nature. The choice we make will be crucial for the whole world.

The Marine Coastal Life Zone

◆

*The rhythm of life in marine
coastal ecosystems is established by
the ceaseless movement of tides
and currents . . . Although the marine
environment might seem impervious
to change, it is as vulnerable to
the impact of external factors as
any terrestrial life zone.*

The Marine Coastal Life Zone

The Canadian marine ecosystem includes the Pacific coastal waters off British Columbia, the Arctic waters, and the waters of the Atlantic coastal shelf encompassing the Bay of Fundy, the Gulf of St. Lawrence, and the St. Lawrence River as far inland as the mouth of the Saguenay.

The featureless surface of the water hides seabeds as varied as any earthly landscape. Off the east coast, the extensive submarine plains of the continental shelf slope gradually away from the shore for nearly 200 kilometres, reaching a depth of 100 to 200 metres or more before dropping into the abyss of the North Atlantic. On the west coast, by contrast, the continental shelf is narrow, typically less than 45 and seldom more than 95 kilometres in width. The inshore waters are a maze of inlets and straits, defined by hundreds of headlands and islands. In such enclosed waters the outflow of large rivers — the Fraser, for example — has a significant effect on currents and the movements of marine wildlife. In the Arctic, the most distinctive features of the marine ecosystem are vast expanses covered by ice year round — as much as 7.5 metres thick in some places — and areas within them known as polynyas which remain virtually ice-free all year.

The rhythm of life in marine coastal ecosystems is established by the ceaseless movement of tides and currents. Where currents meet, the collision of masses of water results in an upwelling of nutrients from the bottom, and the growth of profuse blooms of phytoplankton — single-celled, microscopic plants. This attracts swarms of zooplankton — minute animal life such as copepods, shrimp, and crab larvae — and small fishes to feed upon it. These, in turn, draw the attention of larger predators. In certain areas, conditions of tide, current, and nutrient supply combine to produce concentrations of plankton rich enough to satisfy the energy requirements of the world's largest animals — the baleen whales. Several locations within Canada's marine ecosystem, notably the Bay of Fundy and parts of the Gulf of St. Lawrence, the Fraser estuary and Strait of Georgia, and a number of the Arctic estuaries, are especially productive feeding grounds for these enormous creatures.

The marine life zone is the home of a rich and diverse array of wildlife. Some of its fish species number in the billions; some of its sea birds, in the millions. At the other extreme, many marine species have been pushed to the brink of extirpation in Canadian waters. The gray whale and the Atlantic walrus disappeared from the east coast long before the idea of wildlife conservation became a social concern. Other marine species have fared somewhat better. The blue whale, thought to be on the verge of extinction in the late 1960s, has recovered since the cessation of whaling to the point where an estimated 1,700 individuals occupy the North Pacific range and an-

HABITAT REGIONS
1) MARINE COASTAL
2) PACIFIC / MOUNTAIN
3) ARCTIC
4) BOREAL
5) PRAIRIE
6) GREAT LAKES / ST. LAWRENCE
7) ATLANTIC MARITIME

Mammals

Gray Whale:	
Atlantic	Extirpated
Walrus	Extirpated
Sea Otter	Endangered
Bowhead Whale	Endangered
Right Whale	Endangered
Beluga Whale:	
St. Lawrence River	Endangered
Ungava Bay	Endangered
Eastmain	Threatened
Humpback Whale:	
North Pacific	Threatened
Blue Whale	Rare
Fin Whale	Rare
Sowerby's Beaked Whale	Vulnerable

Fish

Pacific Sardine	Extirpated
Bering Wolffish	Vulnerable
Blackline Prickle-back	Vulnerable
Fourhorned Sculpin	Vulnerable

Reptiles

Leatherback Turtle	Endangered

Species listed as Endangered or Threatened in the above table are covered in detail in the accounts that follow; those classified as Extirpated, Rare, or Vulnerable are not.

As of 1989 the classification Rare is being replaced by Vulnerable. See Introduction, page 2, for a detailed explanation.

other 500 are found in the northwest Atlantic, some of them ascending the St. Lawrence River as far as the mouth of the Saguenay.

Although the marine environment might seem impervious to change, it is as vulnerable to the impact of external factors as any terrestrial life zone. The first element is the pressure of harvesting. Because the marine ecosystem, especially on the Atlantic and Pacific coasts, is enormously productive, it has long attracted an active and intense commercial fishery. Historically, over-harvesting of several valued fish species has been documented. Physical restructuring of the ecosystem for human purposes may also influence local conditions. Hydroelectric dams, for example, can cause profound changes in the biological productivity of estuaries, where rivers flow into the sea, because they alter the seasonal flow of fresh water.

Yet another major external influence on the marine ecosystem is pollution. Its sources are many and varied. Partly by accident and partly by design, the oceans have become a dumping ground for all manner of toxic materials. Oil, domestic sewage, industrial and agricultural wastes, and non-biodegradable plastics find their way into Canada's coastal waters at a rate of thousands of tonnes every day, constituting a multifaceted threat to many wildlife species. Controlling this abuse of the marine coastal life zone is one of the most urgent and difficult conservation challenges.

Sea Otter
(Enhydra lutris)

The story of the sea otter in Canada is a chronicle of shame and hope: shame because, by 1929, relentless hunting and trapping had wholly extirpated this remarkable marine mammal throughout its Canadian range; hope because, in 1969, a plan for re-introduction was begun that now appears destined to succeed.

Along the rocky west coast of Vancouver Island between the Brooks Peninsula and Nootka Sound, the kelp beds sway rhythmically with the rise and fall of the long Pacific swells. Kelp plants are giant brown algae that grow at depths of up to 30 metres, forming graceful underwater forests that support a complex ecological community. On the bottom, sea urchins graze on the holdfasts which anchor the kelp to the seabed, cutting the ribbon-like plants adrift and threatening the stability of the marine forest. At the surface, sea otters bask among the kelp fronds and dive from time to time to hunt for sea urchins, their favourite prey. By keeping the urchins in check, they preserve the kelp, which shelters a host of aquatic life forms.

The sea otter was once a common resident of the entire coastal arc that curves from Japan to California. The largest of the mustelids, or weasel family, it attains a length of close to 2 metres and a weight of 40 kilograms. With feet that are more like flippers, it is agile in the water but awkward on land, preferring to spend its days and nights afloat, and actually wrapping itself in strands of kelp to keep from drifting away with the current while it sleeps. It shares with the chimpanzee and with man the distinction of being a tool-user. A sea otter will often retrieve a flat stone from the seabed, and then, floating on its back and balancing the stone on its chest, crack open urchins, mussels, crabs, and clams by pounding their shells on this makeshift anvil.

Sea otters are gregarious, sedentary, and sociable, living in loosely structured "pods" that sometimes include several dozen animals. Otters of both sexes and varied ages are present in these groups, feeding, resting, preening and grooming their fur, and playing together. Because an aquatic life style in cold water consumes a lot of energy, they must eat at least 20 percent of their body weight daily in order to meet their protein requirements.

With a life expectancy of 15 to 20 years, sea otters reach sexual maturity at three or four. Females ordinarily bear a single cub every two years. A nonmigratory species, they seldom travel far from their home range at any time of the year unless population growth forces them into new areas in search of additional food. Unique among marine mammals, the sea otter has no thick coat of blubber to retain body heat; rather, it is insulated by a lustrous fur pelt so soft, so fine, and so dense as to be impenetrable by water.

Its fur was nearly the otter's undoing. For centuries, sea otters had been killed in modest numbers by Japanese, Chinese, and Amerindian hunters. It was not until Vitus Bering and James Cook ventured into the North Pacific in the mid-1700s, on behalf of the Russian and British governments respectively, that Europe discovered a seemingly limitless source for the luxurious fur. At once, a rush for wealth began. Prices rose to as much as $4,000 per skin, and the hunt, at its peak in the mid-1800s, saw as many as 120,000 of the animals taken from Russian territories alone in a single season. It took little more than a century to extirpate the species from the entire west coast of North America, with the exception of a few locations in Alaska and a small remnant population in northern California. In 1911, an international treaty between Canada, the United States, Russia, and Japan granted them full protection, but it seemed to have come too late. The last sea otter taken in British Columbia was killed illegally near Kyuquot in 1929.

Forty years were to pass before wild sea otters swam again in Canadian waters. In 1969 the first of three groups of otters, 28 adults and 1 immature, was transplanted from Amchitka Island, Alaska, to Checleset Bay, Vancouver Island, in the hope of re-establishing a breeding population. The next year 14 more were brought in, and in 1972 the third and largest group, consisting of 8 adult males, 22 adult females, and 16 immature otters, was released at the same location.

For the next few years, little was heard of the transplanted sea otters. Occasional sightings were

Sea Otter

VANCOUVER

PACIFIC   ISLAND

OCEAN

reported, scattered widely from Barkley Sound, 220 kilometres southeast of the release site, to the Queen Charlotte Islands and the northern mainland of British Columbia, as much as 320 kilometres to the northwest. Then, in 1977, the Pacific Biological Station at Nanaimo, British Columbia, conducted aerial surveys which revealed a minimum of 55 animals at Checleset Bay and another 15 at Bajo Reef, about 75 kilometres to the southeast.

The number of otters and their wide distribution seemed to indicate the establishment of two colonies. COSEWIC responded in 1978 by assigning Endangered status to the sea otter. For once, the classification was not an indication of decline, but one of tentative recovery from extirpation. In 1981 British Columbia designated Checleset Bay as an ecological reserve, assuring a degree of protection for this critical location.

For some time thereafter, the Canadian population of sea otters increased at a healthy annual rate of 12 percent. A census in 1984 found a total of 345 animals: 196 at the original release site at

Checleset Bay and 149 at Bajo Reef. It is worth noting that the growth of the sea otter population in these locations was accompanied by a corresponding increase in the extent of the kelp beds, and a decrease in the number of sea urchins.

A large part of the British Columbia coastline is suitable for otters in terms of food and terrain. It seems likely, if the established areas fill to their natural carrying capacity, that some individuals will re-colonize other parts of the former range. This pattern has been observed in Alaska, where the population has recovered from a low of about 2,000 in 1911 to around 120,000 in the early 1980s.

For the time being, the Endangered status of the species in Canada is fully justified. Recent surveys indicate that the initial 12 percent rate of recruitment — i.e., the replenishment of the population with new adults — may have levelled off since 1984, although there appears to be ample habitat to support a larger population. Since the otters do not seem to extend their range widely except when overcrowded, consideration is being given to the establishment of addi-

Sea Otter – Endangered

tional colonies elsewhere along the British Columbia coast. This would not only accelerate the process of recovery, but would also contribute to the probability of long-term success. As long as the breeding population of sea otters in Canada remains limited to two locations, they will be extremely vulnerable to environmental hazards.

Fortunately, such hazards are few. Natural predation appears not to be a serious problem, although killer whales and sea lions probably eat some of the aquatic mammals. The main competition for food and habitat comes from humans, but the otters seem to be fairly tolerant of recreational and shellfishing activities. In the absence of trapping, the greatest threat at present seems to be the risk of oil contamination. Lacking blubber, the otters depend on the insulating properties of a meticulously clean, dry coat to maintain their body temperature. Even small amounts of oil can penetrate their fur and allow frigid sea water to reach the skin, bringing death by hypothermia. It is too soon to claim victory yet, but barring a major oil spill in the vicinity of the colonies, the prospects for sea otter recovery look promising.

Bowhead Whale

(Balaena mysticetus)

Bowhead Whale

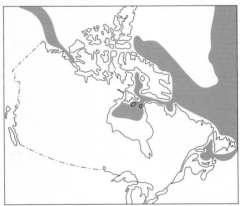

It is ironic that William Scoresby should be acknowledged as the author of the best general account yet written on the habits of the bowhead whale. His book, *An Account of the Arctic Regions*, though published in 1820, is still cited by cetologists as an important primary source of information. The irony is that Scoresby was a whaling captain, who recognized the importance of knowing his quarry if he wished to excel at his trade. Thus, he not only recorded his observations concerning the natural history of this endangered baleen whale, he also did his part in pushing it close to the brink of extinction.

In the 1600s, the bowhead whale was so abundant in the waters of its main breeding ground off eastern Greenland and in the Barents Sea that it was often simply called *the whale*, or in French, *la baleine*. Whalers anchored at Spitzbergen for the summer and slaughtered the large black cetaceans with the white chin markings till the holds of their ships were overflowing. By Scoresby's day, however, the original herd was already seriously depleted, and the attention of many whalers had shifted to the smaller but still plentiful stocks of the eastern (Davis Strait and Hudson Bay) and western (Bering and Beaufort seas) Arctic.

To understand the phenomenon of the Arctic whale fishery, one must realize that whale oil and baleen occupied much the same niche in the economy of the seventeenth, eighteenth, and nineteenth centuries as petroleum and plastics do today. Whale oil comes from the layer of fat or blubber lying beneath a whale's skin. It was burned in lamps or made into soaps and high-quality lubricants. Baleen is the name given to the fringed plates (made of a light, flexible, horny substance called keratin) used by bowheads, right whales, and other so-called baleen whales to filter their diet of zooplankton from the surrounding water. It was manufactured into a host of consumer products, not the least among them being the whalebone corset stays dictated by fashion.

Of all the species in the world's oceans, none were more attractive to the early whalers than the bowhead, and the closely related right whale. Slow swimmers, they were easy to catch and kill; naturally buoyant, they floated after death. An 18-metre adult bowhead weighing 70 tonnes might carry a layer of blubber 60 centimetres

Right: Bowhead Whale

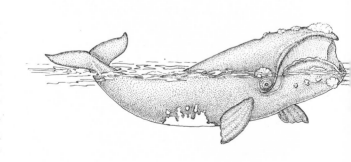

thick and as much as a tonne of baleen. At a time when baleen sold for $5 a pound, sea captains had a strong economic incentive to go whaling.

By definition, the traditional whale fishery was unregulated. Market-driven, the kill simply continued in a given area until local breeding stocks were unable to sustain themselves. It took nearly 200 years, from 1719 to 1915, to slash the eastern Arctic herd of bowheads from an initial stock estimated to have numbered about 6,000, down to the point of commercial extinction — that is, to the point where it was no longer profitable to hunt them. It is calculated that during that time approximately 30,000 bowhead whales were taken in the waters of Davis Strait, Baffin Bay, and Hudson Bay. As demand for the precious commodities increased, so did the pressure on the whales, however, and little more than a century was needed for the bowhead herd of 20,000 or more that ranged the Bering and Beaufort seas to be reduced to the same unprofitable remnant.

Today, the International Whaling Commission estimates the world population of the bowhead whale at about 19,600. The largest group of these moves in time with the seasonal movements of the arctic pack ice — southward to the Bering Sea where they calve in winter, and northward to the Beaufort Sea where they feed in summer. They range as far east as Banks Island, but are separated from the eastern herd by the islands of the arctic archipelago. The eastern stock is smaller, being comprised, at most, of 600 individuals. Some cetologists speculate that this population may in turn be subdivided, with one group in the Baffin Bay/Davis Strait area, and a remnant group of a few dozen, perhaps too small to be viable, in Hudson Bay.

Bowheads are generally found near the edge of the pack ice, where they feed on krill (euphausiid shrimp), copepods, and other zooplankton in productive areas of their range. Observers surmise that they may be more varied in their feeding habits than the closely related, top-skimming right whale, both in the range of preferred prey and in their readiness to forage at any depth in the water column, from surface to sea bottom.

The bowhead whale has been listed as a protected species by the International Whaling Commission (IWC) since 1946, and is also protected under the Convention on International Trade in Endangered Species of Wild Fauna and Flora (CITES). It was classified as Endangered by COSEWIC in 1980. The only exception to total protection from hunting throughout North America is a small, officially sanctioned, carefully limited harvest by natives of coastal areas in Alaska.

It would appear from field observations over the past several years that, despite a small annual kill, the Bering/Beaufort stock of the bowhead whale may be making some progress. With human predation being the main threat to the species for many generations, the end of the commercial whale fishery brought respite and a chance for recovery. The reproductive status of the eastern population is less certain, and it may be, given the continuing pressure of occasional aboriginal kills, that their numbers are just too small to allow for any significant increase. This risk may be greatest for the bowheads in Hudson

Bowhead Whale – Endangered

Bay, where, if they are indeed separate from the rest of the eastern Arctic stock, it seems likely that very few individuals remain.

One other factor could threaten the future of the bowhead whale, and especially that of the larger, more viable, western population. That is the possibility of oil spills resulting from development of petroleum resources along Alaska's North Slope, and in the shallow waters of the Beaufort Sea. When foraging or travelling beneath the pack ice, the whales must be able to reach open leads in order to breathe. If these were blocked by a thick layer of crude oil, drowning or suffocation would be equally fatal alternatives for any bowhead trapped below.

Right Whale
(*Eubalaena glacialis*)

The right whale is one of a group of cetaceans known as baleen whales, the name being adopted from the baleen, or whalebone filters, with which they strain their food from the water. They prey most commonly on copepods of the genus *Calanus*, tiny zooplankton that swarm in dense masses in certain areas of the oceans.

The right whale was a target for Basque whalers in the Bay of Biscay as early as the twelfth century. Thereafter, until the species came under the protection of the International Whaling Commission in 1946, it was hunted relentlessly around the world by ships of every whaling nation. There is no doubt as to why it was a preferred quarry for the early commercial hunters. Its enormous head and the bulk of a body 15 to 18 metres long slowed its passage through the water so much that it was easily overtaken by oar-driven boats. Whale oil constituted such a high proportion of its total body weight that it floated on the surface even after death, unlike many other cetacean species, which had to be quickly secured with floats in order to prevent them from sinking. Understandably, it earned its common English name by virtue of being the "right" whale to pursue.

Today, even after nearly half a century of virtually total protection around the world, the right whale remains one of the rarest of the great whales. Because of its widespread distribution, it is impossible to determine exactly how many individuals still roam the world's oceans, but estimates range from 2,000 to 3,000, of which the majority inhabit the southern hemisphere. A northeast Pacific stock estimated at about 120 individuals passes the summer in the Bering Sea and spends some time off the coast of British Columbia. Another regional population, thought to number between 150 and 200, follows a more or less regular migratory circuit in the northwest Atlantic. From widely dispersed wintering grounds between the southeastern seaboard of the United States and the islands of Bermuda, these right whales travel to the Grand Banks in

the spring, and may extend their range as far north as Davis Strait during the summer months. Several dozen gather annually around the mouth of the Bay of Fundy, presumably to feed on the copepods that swarm there in the late summer and fall.

Since the late 1970s, these seasonal concentrations of right whales in the Bay of Fundy and the Gulf of Maine have been the subject of close observation by scientists, and also by vacationers taking part in popular whale-watching excursions. As a result, a body of information about the biology and behaviour of the species is beginning to accumulate. The gathering of information has been aided by a physical peculiarity of right whales: namely, the presence of thickened patches of horny skin, called callosities, on the head and jaw. These patches, usually encrusted with barnacles, are distinctive enough to permit identification of specific whales within a group. By comparing whale photographs taken at different locations, observers have been able to trace the seasonal movements of some individuals.

Until recently, almost nothing was known about the reproductive biology of the right whale. Since observation became more regular, however, courtship behaviour has frequently been observed in the Bay of Fundy, and cows accompanied by calves have been sighted there. Thus, although the location of calving grounds remains unknown, as does the rate of recruitment of young to the population, it would appear that

some potential exists for the recovery of the northwest Atlantic stock.

Unfortunately, knowledge of the general natural history of the species is still so scanty that most statements concerning its survival must be largely speculative. It appears, for instance, that females do not bear young before 11 years of age,

Right Whale

Right: Right Whale

and then only once every three to four years. It has been suggested that the annual birthrate for the northwest Atlantic right whales is only about 4 or 5 percent, and that, allowing for a natural mortality rate of about 4 percent, this small remnant group may be able to do little more than sustain its present numbers. If these estimates are at all accurate, it could take 15 to 20 years of regular observation to determine whether there is any significant growth in the right whale population. On the other hand, hopes for growth could readily be dashed by a combination of limiting factors, or even by a single catastrophic event.

A critically small stock of any species may lack the genetic diversity to offset the loss of vigour resulting from repeated inbreeding, and so dwindle away. Competition for preferred prey from other whales, sea birds, and fish may also limit reproductive potential. Problems re-lated to human activity, such as collisions with boats, harassment by shipping, entanglement in nets, or the loss of habitat through pollution by toxic wastes, all pose real threats to recovery when the total numbers are so low. Because right whales feed by skimming through swarms of plankton at or near the surface of the water, an oil spill from a tanker en route to the refineries at Saint John, New Brunswick, could be disastrous.

At present, the right whale remains extremely vulnerable to almost any threat to its survival. For this reason, COSEWIC assigned the species to the Endangered category in 1980 and reaf-firmed it in 1985, indicating the immediate dan-ger of its being extirpated in Canadian waters. Beyond this recognition, and the practice of sound measures for environmental protection in areas frequented by the right whale, there is dis-tressingly little of a concrete nature that can be done to assure its preservation.

Beluga Whale
(*Delphinapterus leucas*)

Canadian waters are home to three populations of beluga whales that have been designated as either Threatened or Endangered. One group is in the St. Lawrence River; the other two live in the Arctic. The Eastmain group inhabits eastern Hudson Bay, while the third group, a very small population indeed, can be found further east in Ungava Bay.

Thirty years ago, passengers on the ferry crossing the Saguenay River at Tadoussac would often find the boat surrounded by a throng of small, robust, blunt-headed cetaceans. They were beluga — toothed whales native to the world's arctic seas. The creamy-white adults, 4–6 metres in length, stood out in sharp contrast to the dark blue water of the river. The brown-to-blue-gray coloration of the young made them much harder to spot.

The St. Lawrence beluga population is the southernmost concentration of this species in the world, a relic of the Ice Age that has survived in a habitat profoundly influenced by the counter-current of extremely cold water that moves up the Laurentian Channel from the North Atlantic and surfaces near the mouth of the Saguenay.

From the arrival of Jacques Cartier onward, sailors and fishermen noted the abundance of beluga in the river and the Gulf of St. Lawrence and harvested them at will. The population is thought to have numbered about 5,000 a century ago, and nineteenth-century records tell of as many as 1,800 being taken in a single season. As recently as the 1930s, Québec's provincial fisheries department was paying out bounty money on an average of 323 kills per year. Even in the 1960s, an estimated 1,200 to 1,500 beluga ranged the river between Québec City and Les Escoumins. Yet by 1977, extensive surveys of known beluga habitat in the St. Lawrence indicated that the population had dropped to approximately 550 individuals. It has remained at about this level ever since.

Why this geographically distinct population of white whales should have declined so markedly leads inevitably to questions about cause. It seems almost certain that over-hunting was the principal problem. More recently, however, since the virtual elimination of the hunt, no corresponding recovery in numbers has been noted. The population has remained low but stable. It would seem that other limiting factors are at work, influencing those conditions that are critical for the beluga's success.

One element may be the reproductive potential of the remaining population. Historically, the natural rate of recruitment among the beluga of the St. Lawrence was only about half that which was observed among the more numerous populations found in Arctic waters. Since falling below a certain critical density in the St. Lawrence range, the remaining population may be too small in number to offset normal losses by attrition and hence, unable to produce true recruitment.

Loss of habitat is another possible factor. Beluga feed on a mixed diet of crustaceans and schooling fish such as sand lance, capelin, herring, and smelts. Female beluga with young are known to favour relatively shallow areas which support ample supplies of these species. Traditionally, the estuaries of large fresh-water rivers have attracted concentrations of beluga, for purposes of calving and feeding. But when major hydroelectric projects upstream significantly altered estuarine temperatures and biological productivity at the mouths of the Bersimis, Manicouagan, and Outardes rivers in the 1960s, whales ceased to congregate in those locations. Historically, these three major estuaries once constituted as much as one-third to one-half of the

Beluga Whale

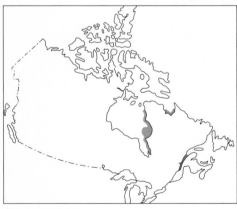

EASTMAIN
UNGAVA BAY
ST. LAWRENCE

Right: Beluga Whale

Beluga Whale :
St. Lawrence and
Ungava Bay –
Endangered;
Eastmain –
Threatened

critical summer habitat for beluga in the St. Lawrence.

Competition for available food stocks has been suggested as another potentially limiting factor. Capelin, herring, and smelt are important prey not only for beluga, but also for fin and minke whales, and for commercial fishermen as well. The fact that the greatest losses of white whales seem to be occurring among newly weaned juveniles suggests that the young may be unable to compete effectively with adult members of their own or other species for the available food resources.

Besides a possible limitation of food supplies and the actual loss of a number of crucial habitat sites, another important consideration is the environmental quality of the lower St. Lawrence, which has deteriorated in recent years as a result of increased disturbance by commercial and pleasure craft, extensive channel and harbour dredging, and increased thermal and chemical pollution from municipal sewage and industrial wastes. Since 1982, autopsies performed on the carcasses of 15 stranded individuals have indicated concentrations of 15 different toxic chemicals and 9 heavy metals in beluga tissue samples. Among the substances found were manmade industrial chemicals and chemical by-products, such as PCBs and PAHs, DDT and other pesticides, and metals including mercury, cadmium, cobalt, and lead. Several of the compounds were present in sufficient quantity to have a high impact on animal health. Whatever the actual cause of death may have been, these beluga specimens were found to be suffering from unusual types and quantities of tumours, ulcers, lesions, and other health problems.

Since 1979 the white whales of the St. Lawrence have been protected under the Beluga Protection Regulations of the Fisheries Act. In 1983 they were designated as Endangered by COSEWIC. Currently, federal and provincial authorities are moving to protect critical habitat areas and to minimize disturbance to the remaining animals.

The herculean task of removing toxic contaminants from the Great Lakes/St. Lawrence system is somewhat more daunting. In 1988 the federal and Québec governments announced a series of measures directed to a cleanup of the St. Lawrence River and its tributaries, and the development of a research facility to determine the effects of pollution on the aquatic ecosystem. Over-exploitation, reduction of habitat and population, diminished food supplies, harassment, and pollution have all combined to limit the beluga's ability to survive and multiply in the St. Lawrence. It remains to be seen whether well-informed management can succeed in bringing about its recovery.

As noted above, the beluga is a circumpolar species. Apart from the geographically isolated St. Lawrence population, its range in Canada is confined to Arctic waters. Throughout its northern ranges, it gathers in leads and polynyas where currents keep the surface ice-free in winter, and moves to shallow bays and the estuaries of northern rivers during the summer months.

In the North American Arctic, a western population in the Beaufort Sea is separated from eastern populations by a longitudinal barrier of ice-covered water which lies roughly between 100° and 120° west. Protected in Canada under the Beluga Protection Regulations, these northern beluga may only be killed by Inuit, and only for use as food. An annual kill of 300 whales in Canadian and Alaskan waters is clearly well below the sustainable yield, as the Beaufort population has apparently increased from a level of 4,000–6,000 animals in the early 1970s to at least 11,500 today.

Beluga in the eastern Arctic are subdivided into five distinct populations, of which two are in no apparent danger. One of these, in Lancaster Sound, is only lightly hunted by native subsistence hunters and is probably stable at about 10,00 animals. A second population, in western Hudson Bay, also numbers close to 20,000, having increased from about 7,000 over the past 30 years.

Of more doubtful status is a population in Cumberland Sound, which consisted of at least 5,000 whales in the 1920s. Heavy commercial harvests reduced this group to 800 by the 1960s, and despite the termination of the commercial hunt and the imposition of a quota of 40 animals per year for native people, the slide has continued. The Cumberland Sound herd is now estimated at less than 400, and although no formal designation has yet been assigned to it, it may be in serious jeopardy.

The population in eastern Hudson Bay, known as the Eastmain group, was granted Threatened status by COSEWIC in 1988. This population had declined from pre-exploitation levels of about 6,600 to present-day numbers of 1,100–1,200, with an additional 700–2,000 animals in James Bay. Although native hunting pressures are thought to surpass the sustainable yield, another factor also weighed heavily in arriving at the COSEWIC decision. Hydroelectric dams have already seriously disrupted estuarine habitats where some northern Québec rivers flow into Hudson Bay. If current long-range plans for further development are carried out, virtually every river in the eastern Hudson Bay/James Bay watershed could be affected, eliminating most of the preferred calving sites used by this group of whales.

Finally, a population of over 1,000 animals in Ungava Bay in the 1800s was reduced by commercial hunting to a few hundred by the 1970s. Despite protection, the decline has continued, and since 1985 fewer than 100 beluga have been sighted in Ungava Bay. In 1988 COSEWIC assigned Endangered status to this population. It is disturbing that, like the St. Lawrence population, the beluga in Cumberland Sound and Ungava Bay have shown no sign of recovery. It lends credibility to the argument that in these areas the species may have declined to a level so low that the rate of recruitment is less than the rate of mortality, and that regardless of protective measures, recovery is therefore mathematically and biologically impossible.

Humpback Whale
(Megaptera novaeangliae)

During the 1970s, the humpback whale became one of the best-known cetaceans to range through North American waters. Two factors contributed to this unusual degree of celebrity. The first was the discovery, and subsequent popularization on long-playing recordings, of the fact that adult male humpbacks sing lengthy, elaborate, and melodious "songs." The second was a sudden, and at first inexplicable, increase in the number of humpbacks becoming entangled in fishnets off the coast of Newfoundland. Both factors evoked a sympathetic response from the North American public — a response that conferred symbolic status on the humpback whale as the focus of a specific campaign to "Save the Whales," and of a more general concern for environmental conservation.

The concern was not inappropriate, considering that the species had been reduced by whaling from an original population estimated at more than 100,000 world-wide, to a remnant that may have sunk as low as 3–4 thousand by the time the International Whaling Commission extended its protection — 1955 in the North Atlantic, and 1966 in the North Pacific. In Canadian waters, it was once abundant off the Atlantic and Pacific coasts,

and exploitation by whalers in Newfoundland and on Vancouver Island continued to be heavy until well into the twentieth century. At the time when COSEWIC classified the humpback as Threatened, in 1982, there were fears that the northeast Pacific stock might have fallen to as few as 650 animals, although the northwest Atlantic population appeared to have recovered from a presumed low of a few hundred to a healthy level of more than 2,000. Taken together, these two stocks probably contained a majority of the world's humpback whales.

Humpback Whale

Recently, knowledge about the humpback has been greatly increased by several years of collaborative research by Canadian and American scientists working in Hawaii, Bermuda, and the Caribbean. There is likely more known now about the natural history of the humpback than about any other of the great whales.

Humpbacks are large baleen whales, attaining lengths of 14–19 metres and an average weight of 34,000 to 45,000 kilograms. Black-backed, and white on the underside, they have distinctive black-and-white patterns on their tails and on the oversized, deeply scalloped flippers which may measure up to one-third as long as the body. Like those of the blue, the fin, and other members of the *Balaenopterid* family, their throats are deeply grooved, enabling them to take in vast gulps of prey when feeding, separating nutritious euphausiid shrimps and fish from the seawater by straining it through 300 or more plates of relatively short (65 centimetres), coarse baleen that line the upper jaw.

The humpback has some unusual physical features, even among whales. The head and jaws, for instance, are studded with fleshy bumps, from which grow long, coarse hairs. The skeletons of some individuals include bones of vestigial hind limbs, providing intriguing evidence that cetaceans evolved from a land-based ancestor. Indeed, one humpback which was taken off Vancouver Island in 1919 is reported to have had external hind legs that were 1.2 metres long.

Humpback whales generally frequent coastal areas, and prior to the research efforts of the last decade, it had been supposed that separate groups occupied geographically discrete territories. Since then, however, photographic identification of

Left: Humpback Whale

Humpback Whale :
North Pacific –
Threatened

the unique tail patterns of hundreds of individual whales has shown that large populations regularly traverse thousands of kilometres of open ocean in annual migrations. During the winter, the northeast Pacific herd occupies warm shallows around the Hawaiian Islands and off Baja, California. The northwest Atlantic herd gathers on or near two or three banks in the West Indies to calve and mate. With the coming of spring, the whales move to cold northern waters where they feed on krill and schooling species of fish, such as herring, sand lance, and capelin, for the summer months. The Pacific stock moves to British Columbia and Alaska; the Atlantic stock to Newfoundland and Labrador, the Gulf of St. Lawrence, and the Maritimes.

Perhaps it is simply because humpback whales have been studied more extensively than other species of large cetaceans that their behaviour seems to reveal a distinctive character. At times, singly or in groups, they perform gargantuan leaps, propelling their huge bodies wholly out of the water in acrobatic displays of play or courtship. A single male may rest immobile, suspended between seabed and surface, for fifteen minutes or more, emitting an elaborate, far-reaching, cyclical sequence of sounds which can only be adequately described as singing. Comparing recordings of the same singers over several seasons indicates not only that the songs of different whales and of different areas have recognizable characteristics, but that the songs of the individual whales change, subtly but unmistakably, over the years.

Although humpbacks have always been assumed to be peaceful creatures, it has been discovered that this is not always so. During courtship, a female may be closely accompanied by a dominant escort while one or more rivals follow in close pursuit of the couple, vying to exchange body slams and violent flipper blows with the favoured male in the usually vain hope of winning his place.

Co-operative fishing techniques have been observed in which two humpbacks swim round and round a school of fish or shrimp in an upward spiral, creating a dense net of bubbles from their blowholes to concentrate the prey and increase the nutritional pay-off realized from each mouthful. In time, it may be found that other species engage in similar activities; for now, these exceptional behaviours continue to make the long-flippered humpbacks especially fascinating to human researchers.

Like most of the world's large cetaceans, the humpback whale remains vulnerable to a number of risks, most of them related to human activity. Critical habitat areas such as the specialized calving and mating grounds in Hawaii and the Caribbean could be destroyed by mineral exploration. The growing popularity of whale watching, though well intentioned, could stress the whales or drive them from preferred feeding areas.

Competition from commercial fishermen for key food stocks can be a threat to such voracious feeders, and starvation is not the only risk. When offshore stocks of capelin decreased off Newfoundland in the late 1970s, hungry whales moved closer to land in pursuit of inshore schools of the little fish, and many humpbacks became entangled in fishermen's nets. At least 17 died in this way in 1980; in addition, the damage to costly fishing gear motivated some fishermen to shoot at whales or to call for a resumption of whaling. As capelin stocks recovered, the whales withdrew from the inshore areas, but a similar sequence could occur again, in Newfoundland or elsewhere.

In recent years, the humpback has demonstrated an excellent potential for recovery. Apart from small-scale aboriginal hunts by Greenlanders and by natives of Bequia, a tiny island in the West Indies, it has enjoyed virtually complete protection from whaling. In the northwest Atlantic its numbers have increased to an estimated 4,000 or more, and a review by COSEWIC in 1985 reclassified this population as no longer Threatened, but Rare. The northeast Pacific group has also increased, to about 2,000 individuals, though not yet enough to justify downgrading its status as a Threatened species.

Leatherback Turtle
(*Dermochelys coriacea*)

Strictly speaking, the world's largest turtle is an international, rather than a Canadian, species. The leatherback is most frequently found in tropical or subtropical waters, and until recently, there seemed to be little reason to include it as a

Canadian species. Once in a while, Maritime fishermen would catch one in their nets, and a few had also been reported from the Pacific coast — on the west side of Vancouver Island and off the southern tip of the Queen Charlotte Islands. One, caught near Nootka Island in 1934, weighed 545 kilograms.

As the Nootka Island record indicates, the leatherback turtle is huge; it is, in fact, the largest living reptile in the world, attaining a weight of up to 900 kilograms. The longitudinally ridged upper shell, or carapace, measures up to 2.5 metres in length. Unlike the hard bony shell of other species, the carapace of the leatherback, as the name suggests, is covered with a leathery, black or gray-brown skin highlighted with yellowish or white markings.

Leatherbacks are widely distributed around the globe, breeding in Florida, the Caribbean,

Leatherback Turtle

Left: Leatherback Turtle – Endangered

and on the Pacific coast of Mexico and Costa Rica, as well as in West Africa, Australia, Malaya, and India. Except when the females come ashore to bury their clutches of 50–170 eggs in the sand of secluded beaches, the turtles are pelagic in their habits. That is, they prefer to remain at sea, sculling themselves through the open ocean with their enormous flippers.

For many years it was assumed by scientists that the occasional appearances of leatherback turtles along the coast of Atlantic Canada were purely accidental. However, when J. Sherman Bleakney of the Biology Department at Acadia University began a reappraisal of this opinion in the early 1960s, he found that Nova Scotia fishermen spoke of "the turtle season" as a regular occurrence extending from June to October each year. Further research revealed records of some 29 specimens of Atlantic leatherback turtles having been taken in eastern Canadian waters as far back as 1889. The fact that seven captures were reported in 1964 suggested that the interest of a researcher may have been all that was required to elicit evidence that Canadian specimens of this species were not strays, but seasonal visitors at the northern edge of their range. While the greatest number of sightings in Atlantic Canada were recorded off Halifax, others came from Cape Breton Island, the Northumberland Strait, the Bay of Fundy, and Newfoundland. In 1973 one leatherback turtle was even taken some forty-five kilometres northeast of Nain, Labrador, at 56°45' north latitude.

In 1979, the establishment in Newfoundland of a toll-free service for reporting unusual occurrences, such as the entrapment of whales in fishing gear, brought still more reports of leatherbacks in Atlantic Canada. Fishermen reported 17 encounters with the giant reptiles between 1981 and 1985. On 2 occasions, a turtle was found dead; 4 others were observed swimming free in the ocean; the remaining 11 were caught in fishing nets or lines. Of these, 2 were killed and 2 died before they could be released, but 7 were released alive. The reports imply that the species is a much more regular visitor to Canadian waters than had previously been supposed.

Even with the recent increase in sightings and captures, records are too scant, and distribution too widespread, to establish authoritative population data for the leatherback turtle in Canada. Their ability, as a tropical species, to survive in apparent good health in the cold waters of the North Atlantic has intrigued researchers. Reptiles are generally assumed to be cold-blooded — i.e., unable to generate body heat and therefore dependent on the ambient temperature of their surroundings for the warmth needed to sustain life. It has now been determined that the leatherback's chances for survival in cold waters are enhanced by mechanisms that enable it to produce and maintain a body temperature as much as 18° C above that of the surrounding water.

The reason why leatherback turtles venture as far north as Canadian waters remains unclear. The seasonal movements of a preferred prey

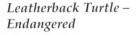

Leatherback Turtle –
Endangered

species may hold the answer. Sea turtles feed on jellyfish. In the North Atlantic, jellyfish of the genus *Cyanea* — giant, red-orange medusae popularly known as "lions' manes" — attain a body diameter of two metres or more, quite big enough to make a square meal even for a predator as large as a leatherback. The turtles Bleakney examined contained pieces of the bodies and tentacles of *Cyanea capillata* in their digestive tracts, suggesting that the annual northward-drifting migration of the jellyfish may well be the lure that leads the leatherbacks into Maritime coastal waters.

Although in some countries the leatherback is killed for its oil, and eggs are taken from its nests, it is not under such stresses in Canada. The principal risk in Canadian waters has been entanglement in fishing nets. Recently, however, another more sinister threat has become apparent. Over the past few years, several dead leatherbacks have washed ashore along the east coast of the United States, their intestines clogged with plastic debris. Conceivably, they mistook plastic bags or containers for jellyfish and attempted to eat them. Because the turtles' throats are lined with spines to aid in the swallowing of their soft, slippery diet, it appears that the plastic, once ingested, could not be regurgitated.

In view of this macabre discovery, the classification of the leatherback turtle as an endangered species may serve two purposes. It will focus public attention on the need to protect sea turtles world-wide, and also sound an alarm regarding the threat of pollution by nonbiodegradable plastics as a bizarre and fatal hazard to marine wildlife in general.

The Pacific/ Mountain Life Zone

◆

From misty coastal rain
forests and steaming hot springs
to deserts and high alpine tundra,
this zone encompasses
many ecosystems.

The Pacific/Mountain Life Zone

The Pacific/Mountain life zone consists of a complex of ecozones occupying most of the province of British Columbia and the southwestern fringe of Alberta. This is a region of dramatic contrasts. From misty coastal rain forests and steaming hot springs to deserts and high alpine tundra, it encompasses many ecosystems, some extensive, others limited to particular valleys or mountainsides. Near the coast, up to four metres of annual rainfall produce stands of Sitka spruce, western red cedar, western hemlock, as well as Canada's largest tree, the Douglas fir, towering as high as 90 metres above the ground. A significant remnant of this remarkable temperate rain-forest habitat will be preserved in the Queen Charlotte Islands with the creation of South Moresby National Park. A different forest type occurs in the Gulf Islands, where Garry oak and arbutus are typical trees. In the inland valleys, ponderosa pine may appear on the upper slopes, overlooking expanses of dry grassland and sagebrush.

The ecosystems of this region vary not only with distance from the sea, but also with elevation. A mountain situated within sight of the Pacific may exhibit the characteristics of several distinct zones at different levels. Such variety and isolation have resulted in a remarkably varied flora and fauna within the relatively limited area of this life zone. In the Queen Charlotte Islands, for example, there evolved the Charlotte unarmoured stickleback and the giant stickleback, two fish found nowhere else in the world, as well as the pealei subspecies of the peregrine falcon, and the now-extinct dawsoni subspecies of the woodland caribou. The temperate rain forest of the Gulf Islands is the only Canadian habitat of the sharptail snake, while another reptile, the night snake, occurs within Canada, but only in the arid southern Okanagan Valley. The presence of such biological rarities is one very important reason for creating parks and reserves, such as the proposed South Moresby National Park in the Queen Charlottes, to protect generous portions of all the distinctive ecosystems in this fascinating life zone.

The great variety of climate and topography in this large combined zone also results in a wide variety of human activity. It includes large urban centres where growth, development, and industrialization impose stresses of pollution and habitat loss on surrounding areas. It includes mining operations that may damage waterways with silt and toxic chemicals. A destructive oil spill in January 1989 underlined the vulnerability of the coast to the hazards of heavy marine traffic. In short, the human influences on the region are as varied as the natural ecosystems themselves.

It should come as no surprise, then, to discover that there are several endangered and threatened species in the Pacific/Mountain life zone, or that the prescriptions for preserv-

HABITAT REGIONS
1) MARINE COASTAL
2) PACIFIC / MOUNTAIN
3) ARCTIC
4) BOREAL
5) PRAIRIE
6) GREAT LAKES / ST. LAWRENCE
7) ATLANTIC MARITIME

Mammals

Vancouver Island Marmot	Endangered
Fringed Myotis	Rare
Keen's Long-eared Myotis	Rare
Pallid Bat	Rare
Queen Charlotte Islands Ermine	Rare
Spotted Bat	Rare
Wolverine	Rare

Birds

Spotted Owl	Endangered
Common Barn-owl	Rare
Cooper's Hawk	Rare
Flammulated Owl	Rare
Great Gray Owl	Rare
Peregrine Falcon	Rare

Fish

Salish Sucker	Endangered
Enos Lake Sticklebacks	Threatened
Shorthead Sculpin	Threatened
Charlotte Unarmoured Stickleback	Rare
Giant Stickleback	Rare
Green Sturgeon	Rare
Lake Lamprey	Rare
Speckled Dace	Rare
Squanga Whitefish	Rare
Umatilla Dace	Rare

Reptiles and Amphibians

Pacific Giant Salamander	Vulnerable

Plants

Southern Maidenhair Fern	Endangered
Giant Helleborine	Threatened
Mosquito Fern	Threatened

Species listed as Endangered or Threatened in the above table are covered in detail in the accounts that follow; those classified as Rare or Vulnerable are not.

As of 1989 the classification Rare is being replaced by Vulnerable. See Introduction, page 2, for a detailed explanation.

ing them differ greatly. Here, in a region of dramatic contrasts, are found some of the most dramatic challenges to environmental protection and the preservation of biological diversity.

Vancouver Island Marmot

(Marmota vancouverensis)

Vancouver Island Marmot

Time and again, isolation has been a key factor in both the emergence and the loss of biological diversity. Geographic isolation over a long period of time can promote specialization by enforcing the repetition of a limited selection of genetic traits in successive generations. The isolated population eventually may become so distinctive as to justify its classification as a subspecies or even a separate species. On the other hand, isolated species often occur in such extremely limited ranges that any substantial change in habitat conditions may constitute a threat to their survival. The Vancouver Island marmot provides a striking illustration of this ecological dilemma.

As its name suggests, this mammal is endemic to Vancouver Island, where it occurs on the upper slopes of a few of the higher mountains in the interior. Closely related to the hoary marmot of the mainland, it is thought to have descended from a population that became physically isolated during the last ice age, about 12,000 years ago. The process of specialization produced a new species, a rather stout-bodied rodent, somewhat larger than a woodchuck but smaller than a hoary marmot, with a glossy coat of chocolate-brown fur and a whitish muzzle.

The species is herbivorous, or plant-eating, and lives in burrows among the rocks on lush, steeply sloping subalpine meadows. Heavy snowfall and avalanches tend to keep these areas free of trees, encouraging the luxuriant growth of a wide variety of palatable herbs and grasses. The same factors necessitate a long annual hibernation of up to seven months, and a highly efficient conversion of food during the short growing season.

In the immediate postglacial period, alpine habitat was widespread on Vancouver Island, and the marmot may have been quite common throughout its range. As the climate grew warmer, forests invaded the lower elevations, and areas of alpine ecosystem shifted up the mountainsides to higher levels. It is likely that the marmot population then contracted and retreated along with the habitat, until colonies persisted on only a small number of isolated mountain meadows.

Even had it been left to its own devices, the Vancouver Island marmot might have faced serious survival problems because of its mountain-top isolation. Suitable habitat is not only scarce but widely scattered, affording little opportunity for populations to expand or to recolonize abandoned sites. Furthermore, because of the distance between sites, there is some risk that inbreeding could have diminished the genetic vigour of colonies, and hence the diversity of the species. In view of the small number of marmots, predators such as cougars, eagles, wolves, or bears could also have a serious impact on local colonies.

By 1978, however, when a status report on the species was submitted to COSEWIC, these biological risks had been superceded by a more immediate danger. Encroachments by human activities such as logging and recreational traffic threatened to disrupt the delicate alpine ecosystem. It was not clear what effect logging adjacent to subalpine meadows might have on the Vancouver Island marmot. If it caused erosion and destabilization of the mountain slopes, loss of critically important habitat could have a disastrous effect on resident colonies. On the other hand, the fact that young marmots had been observed in logged-over areas invited speculation that, to some extent, the clearing of trees might help restore overgrown habitat or provide avenues for migration to other sites.

Steadily increasing recreational pressures in the interior mountains posed another risk of unknown proportions. Some activities, such as the development of ski resorts, might, by delaying the spring melt and the early growth of vegetation, destroy occupied habitat, or render vacant sites uninhabitable. Pursuits like hiking, mountaineering, and sight-seeing could also be harmful. Observers had noted the Vancouver Island marmot to be an extremely wary species. Frequent disturbance of a colony by inconsiderate or uninformed visitors could disturb crucial breeding and feeding cycles, or even lead to eventual abandonment of the site.

*Vancouver
Island Marmot –
Endangered*

When the Vancouver Island marmot was designated as Endangered, only four colonies were known to be active. Interest in the plight of the species stimulated further research on populations and habitats. A survey by the Vancouver Island Marmot Preservation Committee in the summer of 1979 examined 92 potential sites, recording 45 marmots at 11 locations. Active burrows were found at 2 others, and it was felt that further intensive searching might uncover additional colonies.

The researchers identified several unoccupied sites that appeared to offer suitable habitat, and British Columbia wildlife officials began considering the feasibility of re-introducing breeding stock to such locations. Studies of habitat and diet were conducted at established colonies in 1981 and 1982 in an attempt to gain a better understanding of which elements in the alpine ecosystem provide optimal conditions for the marmots. Specific protective measures were also recommended: the creation of habitat reserves and protective buffer zones; the prohibition of access to marmot colonies by all terrain vehicles and motorcycles; close control of access by all visitors; and stiff penalties under the provincial

Wildlife Act for harming or harassing the species.

Since then, regular field surveys have confirmed the existence of more than 25 active Vancouver Island marmot colonies, comprising an estimated population of close to 300 animals. The main colonies are distributed into at least 4 distinct groupings or subpopulations, while a few isolated colonies may also represent the nuclei of distinct subpopulations in the making. An encouraging discovery about marmot distribution is that new colonies have sprung up in areas cleared by logging, apparently confirming the hypothesis that cutting might create temporary extensions of habitat. There are similarly encouraging indications that the species can be productive and successful in ski areas. Shooting, vandalism, and harassment by dogs appear to be more serious threats associated with human presence.

With regard to the implementation of protective measures, one prime marmot site has been designated as an ecological reserve, and a second is under the management of the provincial wildlife branch. To date, there have been no attempts to re-introduce marmots to vacant sites, but in anticipation that such a project might be undertaken in the future, testing is under way to determine the genetic variability of the four population groups. If all the marmots are genetically identical, it will not matter which groups supply breeding stock for transplanted colonies. On the other hand, if the geographic isolation of each subgroup has led to the emergence of distinctive bloodlines, it may be desirable to mix stock from different groups in order to maintain diversity and guard against inbreeding.

While it is too early to claim that the future of the Vancouver Island marmot is secure, there is hope that the next COSEWIC report on the species may be able to recommend a downgrading of its status from Endangered to Threatened. In the global war against extinction, such events are precious victories.

Spotted Owl
(*Strix occidentalis caurina*)

For countless years towering Douglas fir, western hemlock, and red cedar clad the steep slopes of British Columbia's Pacific and Cascade ranges. The twilight corridors of the ancient climax forests provided a specialized ecosystem inhabited by a variety of wildlife species, among them the spotted owl. A century ago, when European entrepreneurs began in earnest to pursue their self-appointed task of subduing the stately mountain wilderness, the large, dark-eyed raptor (bird of prey) occurred in the vicinity of Vancouver itself. As the giant trees were converted to lumber and sawdust, the retiring owl withdrew before the onslaught until it was rarely found outside the confines of the steepest remote ravines and gorges, places where the cost of logging outweighed the profit to be gained.

Spotted Owl

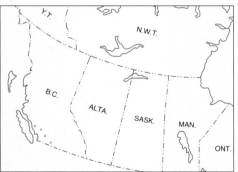

In the 25 years from 1922 to 1947, the species was reported in British Columbia on 17 occasions; from 1948 to 1973, only 9 times; and from then until 1985, not once. To the south, in Washington and Oregon, a parallel decline was less severe, but in Canada, on the northern edge of its range, the spotted owl appeared to be near the point of extirpation and was listed by COSEWIC in 1984 as Endangered.

The spotted owl is an attractive, round-headed bird, similar in size and appearance to a more abundant and widespread relative, the barred owl. The plumage of the spotted owl is predominantly dark brown, with white spots on the head and transverse bars on the breast and abdomen. Prominent facial discs surround its large black eyes. A nocturnal hunter, it preys on forest rodents such as wood rats, white-footed mice, and chipmunks. It is a year-round resident of dense, old-growth coniferous forests in mountainous country from southwestern British Columbia to central Mexico. Throughout this range it chooses a cavity in a large tree, or occasionally a cave, as a nest site, and there lays two or three plain white eggs in March. Because of the rarity and reclusiveness of the species, little else is known about its life history in Canada.

Even when no spotted owls were reported in British Columbia for years at a time, the reputation of the species for reclusiveness led observers to suppose that a few pairs persisted. In 1985 an all-out effort was undertaken to confirm the supposition. Between April and September, personnel of the British Columbia Ministry of Environment and members of the Federation of British Columbia Naturalists spent a total of 212 person-hours searching accessible areas of the bird's Canadian range for proof of its existence. Concentrating the search in forests more than 200 years old, they travelled the back roads and trails at night, playing tape recordings of spotted owl calls in the hope of luring the birds close enough to be identified.

The effort was repaid with the highest count of spotted owls on record (in a single survey) in Canada: a total of seven birds, at six different sites within a triangle bounded by Lillooet Lake to the north, Howe Sound to the west, and Manning Provincial Park to the east. They included a pair at Lillooet Lake, as well as three males and two females at five other locations. It was impossible to determine whether the latter birds were single or paired. All the owls were found in old-growth forests in very rugged terrain.

The intensive search confirmed that the spotted owl is still a fairly widespread, albeit very rare, local resident in much of its historic Canadian range. Based on a general estimate of available habitat, its population in British Columbia is thought to consist of more than 25 but fewer than 100 birds. The number is perilously low, especially considering the vulnerability to logging of the scattered remnants of old-growth coniferous forest which are apparently the only acceptable habitat for this species. Two of the sites where the searchers located owls were slated for cutting within five years of the 1985 survey.

If the spotted owl is to survive in Canada, corrective measures will have to be implemented soon. A plan already in operation in the state of Oregon has been recommended for use in British Columbia as well. It involves establishing protective management zones around the nesting and roosting areas of each resident pair of owls. An obvious precondition to be met before this practice can be instituted in Canada will be to locate these pairs and define their territories. The task can be accomplished, but it will require time and resources. Meanwhile, the Endangered status of the spotted owl provides one more urgent reason to cease the relentless exploitation of a once-great forest ecosystem.

Spotted Owl –
Endangered

Salish Sucker

(*Catostomus* sp.)

Sometimes the mechanics of extinction are obvious. Historically, the marketplace has offered strong economic incentives to exploiters of wildlife. Moderation is a virtue seldom recognized by such commerce, and species after species has disappeared, or been pushed perilously close to oblivion, by relentless harvesting.

On the other hand, some species are endangered without ever becoming the chosen prey of man. Often these are the small, or obscure, incidental victims of human activity. A few mammals, more birds, many fish, and most of the plants that appear on the COSEWIC list fall into this category. Their decline results from degra-

dation or loss of habitat caused by human alteration of the environment. A good example of this process can be seen in the plight of the Salish sucker, a small, inconspicuous fresh-water fish that occurs in the headwaters of a handful of streams in the southwest corner of mainland British Columbia and across the border in the Puget Sound region of Washington State.

The Salish sucker is a little-known member of the sucker family of the genus *Catostomus* — one, indeed, that has yet to be formally described as a species, although it appears to be very closely related to the widely distributed longnose sucker. What makes it intriguing to zoogeographers is the fact that it occurs in only a few locations between the Chehalis River, in Washington's Olympic Peninsula, and the Fraser Delta. The Chehalis watershed remained ice-free during the Pleistocene Era and is thought to have formed a

refuge where remnants of a number of fish species avoided extinction during the Ice Age. Having remained effectively isolated from the suckers in the Fraser and Columbia watersheds for about 200,000 years, the Salish sucker has an unusual evolutionary history, and whether it is a unique species or an isolated variant of an existing one, it represents a special opportunity for comparative study.

The Salish sucker is a bottom-feeding fish, about 140–200 millimetres in length, which frequents the cooler, upper reaches of slow-moving streams within its limited range. It spawns on fine gravel beds in March and April, and the newly hatched young may fall prey to juvenile coho salmon, cutthroat trout, and prickly sculpin, all of which inhabit the same waters.

Up to the mid-1950s, the Salish sucker was relatively common in two Canadian rivers — the Salmon and the Campbell — which lie just south of Vancouver. Unfortunately, from that time to the present, rapid urbanization of the area drained by these streams has resulted in profound changes of habitat. Alder thickets that shaded and protected the banks of the streams have disappeared, and much of the adjacent land has been converted to residential or industrial uses. As a result, once-stable water courses became subject to extreme fluctuations, ranging from flash floods during spring spawning, to mere trickles of warm water in the summer months.

In spite of intensive searches, not a single Salish sucker specimen has been taken from the Campbell River since the mid-1960s, and by 1983 the breeding stock of the Salmon River had fallen to fewer than 100 adult fish. Prospects for the survival of this fish in Canadian waters were not good. Hope was somewhat revived in the early 1980s, however, with the discovery of additional populations in Bertrand and Pepin creeks, near the headwaters of the Salmon River, and in Salwein Creek, some 40 kilometres to the east. Bertrand Creek, unfortunately, is badly polluted, but Pepin Creek is largely unspoiled and flows, for much of its length in Canada, through designated parkland.

There seems to be no doubt that the decline of the Salish sucker can be attributed directly to habitat changes in its native streams as a result of urban growth. At present, it appears that further urbanization of the suburbs south of Vancouver is inevitable. Therefore, unless additional populations are discovered, and sufficient unspoiled habitat is preserved to maintain their viability, it would seem that this fish is destined for extirpation.

Salish Sucker

Enos Lake Sticklebacks

(*Gasterosteus* spp.)

Enos Lake is little more than a large pond, just 17.6 hectares in area and averaging less than 10 metres in depth. It lies roughly midway between the city of Nanaimo and the village of Parksville, on the east coast of Vancouver Island. Because it supplies water for the settlement of Nanoose Bay and for a nearby Canadian Forces Base, vehicle access to the tiny lake is restricted, offering some protection of water quality. On the other hand, urban expansion in the area is proceeding at such a rate that it could one day conceivably result in depletion of the water supply. None of these

details would seem especially significant, were it not that the only fish known to breed in Enos Lake are two species of stickleback, and that these two species are not known to breed anywhere else in the world.

Sticklebacks are a widely distributed family of small fish found in shallow inshore areas of marine and fresh waters throughout the northern hemisphere. Their name refers to the array of 2–9 spines that stand erect on their backs, just ahead of the dorsal fin. They are voracious feeders and aggressively territorial. In most species, the male stickleback builds a barrel-shaped nest of vegetation, in which he entices one or more females to deposit a store of eggs. He then guards the eggs until they hatch, and the fry until they are able to fend for themselves.

One common member of this widespread family is the threespine stickleback (*Gasterosteus*

41

aculeatus). A small fish, it averages about 50 millimetres in length. It occurs in fresh and marine waters and appears in such a confusing variety of forms and geographically distinct locations that taxonomists have come to believe that the fish referred to by this name belong not to one, but to a complex of many, species. The two Enos Lake sticklebacks belong to this group of *Gasterosteus* species.

In general appearance, both fishes are similar, their most noticeable difference being that the body of one is slightly deeper than that of the other. Genetically, however, they are distinct, and although they live in the same lake, they occupy different zones. One prefers deeper, open water, while the other lurks in the aquatic vegetation near the shore. They also employ different feeding strategies. The former pursues free-floating plankton, while the latter browses on the lake bottom. They do not appear to interbreed. Interestingly, it is thought that similar species or species pairs of these sticklebacks may occur in other, similarly isolated lakes of Vancouver Island, Texada Island, the Queen Charlottes, and other islands off the West Coast.

Understanding the mechanisms that produce biological diversity is a fundamental goal of biology. One such mechanism is speciation: the process whereby a single species becomes two or more new species. Because the process is usually assumed to require tens, if not hundreds, of thousands of years, and to occur at least in part as a result of geographic separation, it is exceedingly rare to discover it actually taking place. Nonetheless, that is what appears to be happening (or to have happened within the last 12,500

Enos Lake Sticklebacks – Threatened

years) with the Enos Lake sticklebacks. The speed of the apparent split, and the fact that it has happened in the confines of such a small body of water, make this species pair a rare scientific treasure.

For the moment, the Enos Lake sticklebacks are in no danger. Each of the species pair is estimated to be sustaining itself adequately with a population of about 100,000 individuals. Nonetheless, it has been deemed advisable to classify them as Threatened. There are two grounds for this decision. First, there is the long-term risk already alluded to — i.e., that urban expansion may eventually increase the demand for water supplies to such an extent that the lake level will be seriously reduced, with a resulting loss of breeding habitat. The establishment of limits on the amount of water that may be drawn from Enos Lake would be one way of avoiding this danger.

The second threat may be more difficult to ward off. Two exotic species, the brown bullhead *(Ictalurus nebulosus)* and the pumpkinseed sun-fish *(Lepomis gibbosus)*, are spreading gradually through lakes along the east coast of Vancouver Island. In large lakes they seem to have little impact on native species, but in small bodies of water like Enos Lake they have been known to wipe out sticklebacks in as little as two years, apparently by predation on the eggs and young. Both these predators are being spread by a means that is virtually impossible to foresee or prevent. Specimens taken alive by young children, either by hook and line or in dip-nets, are sometimes kept for a time as pets and later released into the waters of a different drainage system. Against such an inadvertent and unpredictable method of dispersal, even the most stringent regulations may be powerless.

Enos Lake Sticklebacks

Shorthead Sculpin
(Cottus confusus)

The process of assigning Threatened or Endangered status to a species is by no means infallible. Although the best available data are gathered and assessed in order to arrive at a decision, it is a fundamental principle of science that a theory is always subject to revision in the light of new and more definitive data. The case of the shorthead sculpin illustrates the point.

The shorthead sculpin is not a well-known fish. It was not even described as a distinct species before 1963, and is so hard to distinguish from other related sculpins that the Latin label *confusus* (confused) seems well chosen. Broad at the head, its tapering body reaches a length of little more than 100 millimetres. Its colour is a dull, mottled, yellowish brown. Its most noticeable features are a wide mouth and fan-like pectoral fins.

Prior to 1987 it was known to occur in Canada only in the watershed of the Flathead River, which rises in southeastern British Columbia and flows southward into the Columbia river system. The mountains of the border ranges separate it from Waterton Lakes National Park to the east, and from the Kootenay watershed to the west. Scientists had supposed that this physical isolation from other drainage basins explained why the shorthead sculpin, a not uncommon fish in the northwestern United States, occurred in Canada only in the Flathead River and some of its tributary creeks. The species was designated by COSEWIC as Threatened on the grounds that suitable habitat within its Canadian range would be damaged if plans for a major coal-mining operation in the Flathead area were to be implemented.

It came as no small surprise, then, when field researchers collecting for the Royal British Columbia Museum in the Kettle, Slocan, and Columbia rivers found not only the mottled sculpin *(Cottus bairdi)*, which they had expected, but also specimens that corresponded closely to the scientific description of the shorthead sculpin. Another complication arose when it was observed that some of the specimens appeared to be intermediate forms that displayed character-

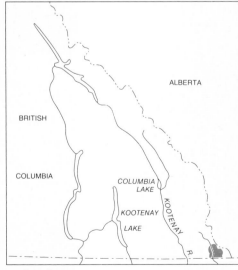

Shorthead Sculpin

istics of both species; the presence of such individuals could be evidence of hybridizing between the two. Further comparisons also revealed a marked similarity between shorthead sculpins from the Flathead River and mottled sculpins found in the Milk River drainage system in Alberta and Montana. Such similarities and distinctions, while mystifying to the nonspecialist, are visible evidence of that genetic diversity that forms the basis on which species and subspecies are described and defined. In time to come, further study and analysis will determine the relationships among all these spiny and confusing little fishes. Therefore, although the latest discoveries may diminish the precision and certainty with which the shorthead sculpin is deemed to be — or not to be — a threatened species, they also represent a small but significant advancement of scientific knowledge.

Shorthead Sculpin –
Threatened

Southern Maidenhair Fern
(*Adiantum capillus-veneris*)

The Fairmont Hot Springs lie in a valley between the continental divide and the Purcell Mountains. Here, water warmed by volcanic activity deep in the earth emerges, bathing the rocks and saturating the soil, creating permanent greenhouse conditions where a number of plants and animals requiring warm, temperate, or even subtropical ecosystems can thrive.

Canada has only two species of maidenhair ferns — the maidenhair, widespread in cool, shaded forests with limestone-based soil, and the southern maidenhair, found in Canada only at Fairmont Hot Springs. Outside Canada, the closest colony of the southern maidenhair is at another hot spring in the Black Hills of South Dakota. It is common, however, across the southern United States and into the tropics.

The fern is a calciphile, meaning that it loves to grow in soils rich in calcium. The Fairmont Hot

Southern Maidenhair Fern – Endangered

Springs offer just such an environment, with the large accumulating deposits of porous limestone that precipitate out of the water providing numerous sheltered crevices and slopes where this delightful fern can thrive.

The fern was first seen at the hot springs in 1888. Despite the development of a resort at the springs, it remained abundant up to and throughout the 1940s and 1950s. The beginning of the end for these colonies came in the 1960s when the owner of the land made major alterations that destroyed the natural outflows of the spring. Installing a series of pipes, the aim was to direct all spring sources into the bath pools.

The alterations of the 1960s were believed to have caused the extirpation of all plants. A small colony was discovered in 1974, however, on a vertical rock trench that had been cut during the construction of the original bathhouse in 1911. The last spore-bearing specimens were collected here in 1978. By 1982, all that remained of this species in Canada was a colony less than half a metre long. The plants did not set spores that year, suggesting that even the remaining colony was under ecological stress.

Despite this, there is still hope for the survival of the southern maidenhair in Canada. In a natural hot-spring environment, with exposed hot water sources running over the calcium-rich limestone rocks, the species reproduces quickly and abundantly. This means that it may be entirely possible and practicable to bring this species back — perhaps not to its former abundance, but at least to a secure population.

Southern Maidenhair Fern

Giant Helleborine
(Epipactis gigantea)

The giant helleborine is a native orchid with elongate wands of greenish to red-tinged flowers. Its range extends from central Mexico to southern British Columbia. In Canada, it has been found at only 15 widely scattered sites, half of which may no longer exist because of hydro dam flooding and other developments. Several of its native colonies grow or used to grow on the warmer, calcium-rich soils around hot springs. As these habitats are wiped out, however, the orchids vanish. Old records show that it was present at Radium Hot Springs, and, until recently, was abundant at Fairmont Hot Springs, where it grew intermixed with maidenhair fern. At this location, it is now restricted to a number of colonies at a single site.

Not all colonies, however, are dependent upon hot-spring habitat. Some of the places where it was previously collected are today more or less unmodified. Several colonies have been found around Kootenay Lake, Lake Okanagan, and at Cultis Lake, where it occurs in wet creek meadows and nearly always at the very edge of water. There are about 50 hot-spring sites in southern British Columbia, and it is possible that some of these may harbour native colonies of this beautiful threatened plant.

Mosquito Fern
(*Azolla mexicana*)

People expect to find ferns growing in deep shaded woods, rocky outcrops, canyon walls, seepage areas, and the like. But that is not the kind of habitat where one finds the mosquito fern. This peculiar fern floats freely on open water. When conditions are just right, a population explodes, multiplying so rapidly that it covers the sheltered waters in oxbows or other sheltered pools with solid mats in a short period of time. This life form is yet another example of the seemingly never-ending ability of earth's living things to evolve in surprising and beautiful ways and adopt most unusual and unexpected strategies for survival.

The mosquito fern is widespread in the tropics, Mexico, parts of the American Midwest, and along the west coast of the United States. In Canada there are four small but thriving populations in British Columbia, south of Shuswap Lake.

A single plant of the mosquito fern is only one to three centimetres in diameter. Close examination reveals that unlike the leaves of water-lily, pondweed, or duckweed, the plants of this fern are intricately branched with numerous tiny overlapping fleshy upper leaves and short hanging roots. Although the plants are pale green in summer, they turn into solid red carpets in the fall. A peculiar characteristic of the mosquito fern is the necessary presence of tiny blue-green nitrogen-fixing algae growing symbiotically in cavities within the tiny leaf lobes.

The mosquito fern uses two strategies for reproduction, which is accomplished partly by spores. In the fall, when plants are mature, clouds of spores descend through the water to the bottom of the pond. One or more years later, when conditions are just right, some float to the surface to produce new plants. Thereafter, further reproduction is by vegetative means.

Drainage, filling-in of ponds, or pollution are all threats to the survival of the remaining populations of this species. Thus, while it is estimated that in a recent year the astounding number of 13,500,000 plants were present in three pools in Shuswap Lake, any of these pools can readily be destroyed. Some in the area, in fact, have already been filled in for housing developments. Because of this, COSEWIC designated the mosquito fern as Threatened in 1984.

Mosquito Fern

Facing page:
Giant Helleborine –
Threatened

The Arctic
Life Zone

◆

*Bare rock, erratic boulders, and
gravel eskers and moraines are prominent
surface features of a landscape where heaths,
herbs, and lichens are the typical plants,
and where tree species such as willows
grow only a few centimetres high.*

The Arctic Life Zone

With a surface area of about 2.4 million square kilometres, the Arctic life zone is the second largest in Canada. It is also the least hospitable to most varieties of flora and fauna, the most remote, and the least well known. It is a region of climatic extremes, from polar cold in the dark of winter to intense heat during the brief summer season. Because much of it emerged from beneath the ice cap only a few thousand years ago, it has very little soil capable of supporting large or deeply rooted vegetation. Even in summer, what soil there is remains firmly frozen, often to within a few centimetres of the surface, a condition commonly referred to as permafrost. Bare rock, erratic boulders, and gravel eskers and moraines are prominent surface features of a landscape where heaths, herbs, and lichens are the typical plants, and where tree species such as willows grow only a few centimetres high.

HABITAT REGIONS

1) MARINE COASTAL
2) PACIFIC / MOUNTAIN
3) ARCTIC
4) BOREAL
5) PRAIRIE
6) GREAT LAKES / ST. LAWRENCE
7) ATLANTIC MARITIME

Despite its wasteland appearance, however, the Arctic is rich in wildlife. Herds of caribou and musk ox have grazed on its plains for thousands of years, occupying an ecological niche similar to that of the bison and antelope on the prairies to the south. Smaller herbivorous mammals, such as lemmings, are common on land, while predators include polar bears and barren-ground grizzlies, wolves, foxes, ermine, the rare wolverine, snowy owls, and gyrfalcons. During the summer months, immense numbers of waterfowl, shore birds, and sea birds (including rare Ross' gulls and ivory gulls) congregate to nest and raise their young.

Only in the years since the Second World War has the human presence begun to have a serious impact on the Arctic. Now, however, petroleum and mineral exploration, road building, and scientific and military testing and research have introduced a wide variety of pressures and materials into an ecosystem that is perhaps the most delicately balanced and the least capable of absorbing such impacts of any natural zone in Canada. Vehicle tracks may remain sunken in the permafrost for decades after a trip across the tundra, reminding all who follow that in this environment, any damage can be long-lasting.

So far, wildlife in this zone appears to have suffered little harm from these recent human incursions. As can be observed on the chart, there is only one endangered species in the Arctic, although five others are classified as either Threatened or Rare. There is a sinister note, however, in the fact that residues of pesticides and other toxic chemicals are now being found in the tissues of Arctic flora and fauna. Remote, austere, and especially vulnerable to the effects of on-the-spot human activities and long-distance airborne substances, environmental conditions in Canada's Arctic life zone will need careful monitoring in the years to come if threats to its well-being are to be identified and neutralized in time to prevent irreparable damage.

Mammals	
Beluga:*	
Ungava	Endangered
Eastmain	Threatened
Peary Caribou	Threatened
Wolverine	Rare

Birds	
Eskimo Curlew	Endangered
Peregrine Falcon:	
tundrius	Threatened
Ivory Gull	Rare
Ross' Gull	Rare

Fish	
Bering Wolffish	Vulnerable
Blackline Prickle-back	Vulnerable
Fourhorned Sculpin	Vulnerable

Species listed as Endangered or Threatened in the above table are covered in detail in the accounts that follow; those classified as Rare or Vulnerable are not.

*The Beluga is discussed in the Marine Coastal section of this book.

As of 1989 the classification Rare is being replaced by Vulnerable. See Introduction, page 2, for a detailed explanation.

Peary Caribou
(*Rangifer tarandus pearyi*)

If Santa Claus collected his eight tiny reindeer in Canadian territory, it is almost certain that what he really got were Peary caribou. These delicate-looking deer with proportionately large hooves and heavy-beamed, upright antlers are the smallest of all North American subspecies of caribou, and the ones whose range extends closest to the North Pole.

Contrary to their dainty appearance, they are also tough. They need to be. The islands of Canada's Arctic archipelago are among the harshest desert environments in the world. The term desert may seem novel in a northern context, but it is nonetheless accurate. Arid conditions, a short summer, and extreme winter cold combine to make this a habitat suitable only for specialized life-forms that have evolved to meet its challenges. One of these is the Peary caribou.

The emergence of this caribou as a subspecies is thought to result from the isolation of a particular population during and after the last ice age. Its current range is restricted to islands of the Canadian Arctic, and viable populations of the pure form now occur only on the Queen Elizabeth Islands. Caribou on Banks, Victoria, Prince of Wales, and Somerset islands, the Boothia Pen-

insula, and even, occasionally, on other parts of the mainland, are sometimes mistakenly referred to as Peary caribou. In these regions it appears that interbreeding with overlapping populations of the barren-ground caribou (*R. t. groenlandicus*) has significantly diluted the pure Peary caribou strain.

Throughout most of the Arctic archipelago, bare rock and ice severely restrict the available range, even for such a well-adapted mammal. In summer, Peary caribou herds graze widely on sedges, willows, grasses, and other plants. Winter resources consist largely of dry sedges, mosses of unknown food value, and lesser amounts of other plants and lichens. Winter foraging often takes place on or near the crest of hills or ridges, or on raised beaches — areas which are snow-free, or where snow cover is shallow and soft. In areas where the snow is shallow but hard-packed, or where loose snow is over 30 centimetres deep, they use their hooves and muzzles to uncover hidden vegetation. Though the food supply is sparse, there is little risk of overgrazing. The caribou occur in low numbers, in small, widely scattered herds that put little stress on the fragile ecosystem.

In recent years, in fact, their numbers have declined to dangerously low levels. A compre-

Peary Caribou

Peary Caribou –
Threatened

hensive estimate of the total number of Peary caribou is not available, largely because of the high cost of surveying such a large and isolated territory. In 1961 the population in the Queen Elizabeth Islands was estimated at about 26,000 animals, about 94 percent of which were on the western islands, with the remaining 6 percent on the three major eastern islands. Today, the best estimate is that only 3,300 to 3,600 of them remain.

A population drop of 90 percent in less than 30 years can best be described not as a decline, but as a crash — a disturbing reminder that once a trend is established in an ecosystem, the best efforts of human science and environmental management are sometimes powerless to do anything but document the results.

Initially, the status of the Peary caribou became a matter of concern to wildlife biologists in the late 1960s and early 1970s. Extensive oil and gas exploration projects were being undertaken in the high Arctic. The introduction of new technologies and increased human traffic to a complex and delicately balanced ecosystem inevitably brings significant environmental risks. It would therefore be important to monitor the impact of preliminary resource development

activities on the physical environment and on indigenous wildlife species.

Field studies revealed that the Peary caribou were in serious trouble, but the evidence did not establish human activity as the critical factor in their situation. It was true that the herds were susceptible to disturbance by the operation of seismic machinery and aircraft; true, too, that the explorations were generating an influx of people, snowmobiles, and firearms which could result in increased hunting pressures by Inuit and by visitors from the south. However, the most serious negative influence on the Peary caribou during the period of precipitous decline would have occurred regardless of human activity. It was the weather.

Peary caribou have a life expectancy of about 15 years. Females from 2–13 years of age are theoretically capable of producing one calf per year. In fact, though, reproduction is directly related to the presence of adequate body fat. A year when nutritious plants are scarce or inaccessible because of severe weather conditions can result in a lowering of fat reserves and a consequent reproductive failure for one or more years following. Food shortages can also lead to increased mortality among calves in their first year, and to an increased risk of death by malnutrition among weakened adults.

In the early 1970s, a series of particularly harsh winters inflicted severe stress on the Peary caribou. Calving occurred in 1970 and 1971, but researchers found that few, if any, calves born in these years survived to maturity. In 1972 there was little or no calving, a reflection of the severe conditions of the preceding two years. Ironically, the winter of 1972–73 was a mild one when a high calf survival rate might otherwise have been expected. An abundant calf crop in 1973 was largely wiped out in the winter of 1973–74, and that season was so severe that few young were produced in 1974 either. Most of those that were born perished within days of their birth. Thus, for five consecutive years, very few calves were added to the population. At the same time, adult caribou appear to have suffered high mortality in four of those five years. High mortality

and low replacement combined to cause a radical reduction in the number of caribou. It was estimated that it would take 20 years of normal reproduction for the herds of this threatened species to recover to their pre-1970 numbers.

Unfortunately, several of the subsequent winters have been severe as well, and the number of Peary caribou has continued to fall. At present, it must be questioned whether the populations on some of the smaller islands are still viable or even extant. Since the animals became so scarce, they are no longer hunted to a significant degree, but the pressure of wolf predation may now be sufficient to keep them suppressed, or even extirpate them in some areas. Meanwhile, although the potential threat of human activity has not yet materialized to the degree that had been feared, the fact remains that harassment or disturbance of such a small population of caribou could have disastrous effects.

Eskimo Curlew
(*Numenius borealis*)

There is no safety in numbers. The more man comforts himself with the fiction that a species of wildlife is inexhaustible, the more grave is the peril of that species. The story of the Eskimo curlew illustrates the point.

One hundred and fifty years ago, the Eskimo curlew was among the most numerous birds in Canada. Today, it may be the rarest. In the mid-1800s it was known on the Great Plains as the prairie pigeon; it seemed to contemporary observers to rival the passenger pigeon in its numbers. Eyewitness accounts indicate that flocks of many thousands of birds were commonplace; yet by 1900, the Eskimo curlew, like the passenger pigeon, was hovering on the brink of extinction. Unlike the passenger pigeon, however, it has survived, if barely. A recent estimate suggests that there may be a world population of 40–50 birds: perilously few, but enough to sustain a faint glimmer of hope for the future of the curlew as a viable species.

The odds of seeing an Eskimo curlew are extremely remote. Between 1945 and 1985, about 25 probable sightings were reported, most involving single birds or groups of two to four. The

most encouraging exception to this pattern was a flock of 23 curlews seen on May 7, 1981, on an island in Galveston Bay, Texas, by two experienced observers, D. R. Blankinship of the National Audubon Society, and K. A. King of the United States Fish and Wildlife Service. Their report, published in *American Birds* (38:6, pp. 1066–77), underlines the difficulty of identifying this species reliably in the field:

"Our initial reaction was that the birds were too small a nd short-billed t o be Long-billed Curlews (N. americanus), *and that they must be Whimbrels* (N. phaeopus). *We then checked for the distinctive Whimbrel head pattern, but the only pattern visible was a faint light stripe above the eye. The slightly decurved bills did not appear any longer than those of the Long-billed Dowitchers* (Limnodromus scolopaceus) *that were feeding on nearby mudflats. . . . The birds appeared slightly larger than the dowitchers.*

"When the birds flushed . . . [we had] an excellent view of the colour of the belly and underwing. . . . We concluded that the birds could only have been Whimbrels or Eskimo Curlews. Bill length can be deceiving, but the lack of head striping and the presence of cinnamon wing linings would seem to eliminate the Whimbrel. We feel it is probable that the

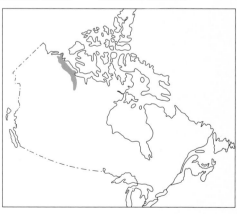

Eskimo Curlew

Eskimo Curlew –
Endangered

TERRY GREGORASCHUK

23 birds observed were Eskimo Curlews."

Fortunately, the yearly cycle of the Eskimo curlew was documented by observers in the eighteenth and nineteenth centuries. Nests of the brown, pigeon-sized shore bird with the down-curved bill were widely dispersed in the tundra and woodland transition zones of the Mackenzie District in the Northwest Territories, and possibly as far west as Alaska or even Siberia. A clutch of four eggs was laid in June in a shallow depression in the ground. The young hatched in July, and toward the end of that month, Eskimo curlew flocks began to gather on the barren grounds in preparation for the fall migration.

For most of the population, the migratory path led east to the Ungava Peninsula, then down the Labrador coast to Newfoundland and the Gulf of St. Lawrence. Feeding heavily on berries and snails, the birds built up their energy reserves; then, barring occasional storm-related stopovers in the Maritime Provinces and Cape Cod, they flew 4–5,000 kilometres nonstop to northeastern South America en route to wintering grounds in Uruguay and Argentina. Smaller numbers of

curlews followed an alternate route via Hudson Bay, Ontario, and Québec, reaching the coast of New York and Pennsylvania before embarking on the transoceanic leg of the journey. In spring, the return trip probably followed the Central American isthmus to the Yucatan Peninsula before crossing the Gulf of Mexico to Texas. Moving north over the Great Plains at a fairly leisurely pace, the birds fed on earthworms and insects in the grasslands before returning again to their Arctic breeding grounds.

Except during the June-July nesting period when it was dispersed over vast areas of barren-ground terrain, the Eskimo curlew was an easy year-round target for hunters. Many observers noted that members of a flock showed great attachment to one another; when one of their number was killed, the remainder would circle the site at close range, offering an easy target to the gunners below. The bird was a favoured fall quarry in Labrador and a delicacy on the menus of the best restaurants of Buenos Aires in winter. Pressure on the species in the midwestern United States intensified steadily as market hunters sought alternatives to the hordes of passenger pigeons which they had already consigned to oblivion. During spring migration, curlews were shipped by rail to markets in the east, packed 300 to a barrel!

And then, quite suddenly, the curlews disappeared. The last big spring hunts in Texas took place in 1875; in Kansas the year was 1878; in Nebraska the hunt continued into the 1880s. In Labrador and Newfoundland the number of fall migrants remained undiminished until 1891 or 1892, when they abruptly declined. Since about 1900, the Eskimo curlew has been extremely rare throughout its range.

Whether hunting can be blamed as the sole cause of the Eskimo curlew's near extinction is a question that may never be resolved. The suddenness of the species' decline introduces an element of mystery to an otherwise straightforward case of extermination at the hands of man. Although vast numbers were killed, the size of the flocks that continued to be reported right into the 1880s suggests to some researchers that the total population was large enough to have withstood that much hunting pressure for far longer, under normal circumstances, before reaching a point of crisis.

Other factors coinciding with the years of heaviest hunting may have contributed to a rapid downward spiral of the curlew population. It was a time when the natural grasslands, both on the wintering grounds in Argentina and along the spring migratory path across the Great Plains, were being ploughed under and replaced by cultivated crops. Radical change of so much traditional habitat may have severely reduced the number of birds returning to breed each year.

Climatic influences could also jeopardize the survival of a severely stressed species. Changes in the direction and severity of autumn storms might drive large flocks off-course during fall migration; rather than making a safe landing in South America, such unfortunates would drown in the South Atlantic Ocean. Drought on the prairies could reduce the spring supply of insects, grubs, and worms, leaving the curlews deficient in vital energy as they approached the breeding season. Cold wet weather on the tundra might cause severe mortality among nestlings. Such speculations, though inconclusive, illustrate an important truth: extinction may follow as readily from a combination of negative factors as from a single, disastrous event.

When Canadian author Fred Bodsworth published his classic novel, *Last of the Curlews*, in 1954, there was every reason to suppose that its moving account of the extinction of the Eskimo curlew might be not merely prophetic, but descriptive of a process that was actually occurring at that time. Sightings in 20 of the subsequent 30 years (including the flock of 23 birds noted above) argue strongly that despite predation, inclement weather, and habitat disturbance by man, a handful of Eskimo curlews still make the yearly circuit from Arctic tundra to Argentinian pampas and back again. And while they do, the hope that this endangered species may recover remains alive.

Arctic Peregrine Falcon
(Falco peregrinus tundrius)

In the summer of 1982, a male Arctic peregrine falcon was found dead at Rankin Inlet on the northwest shore of Hudson Bay. Tissue samples were tested for the presence of toxic chemicals, and researchers found that the bird's brain contained 2 ppm (parts per million) of the pesticide dieldrin, 14 ppm of DDE, 1.1 ppm of oxychlordane, and 60 ppm of PCBs. The verdict of the inquest was that the bird had died of chemical poisoning in an area hundreds, if not thousands, of kilometres from the nearest location where most of these manmade chemical compounds should normally be in use.

One of the more disheartening lessons of the past few decades has been the discovery that there is now virtually nowhere in the world that has not been fouled with the by-products of human activity. Up to midcentury, a person confronted with obvious instances of pollution and urban sprawl might take comfort from the belief that these occurrences were isolated and containable. That naive illusion can no longer be sustained. The acceleration of global economic development in the years since World War II has spread contaminants literally to the ends of the earth, threatening a wide variety of wildlife species with extinction.

The Arctic peregrine offers a striking example of this process of what might reasonably be called long-distance endangerment. The northernmost subspecies of the peregrine falcon is distinguished by its small size and pale coloration in comparison to the *anatum,* or continental, subspecies native to most of Canada and the United States. The Arctic variety occurs in tundra regions of Canada, Alaska, and western Greenland, possibly breeding as far north as Axel Heiberg Island. It also migrates the greatest distance southward, banded individuals having been recovered in southern Brazil, Argentina, and Chile.

The availability of nest sites and of prey species appear to be the critical characteristics in determining habitat acceptability for peregrine falcons. In common with other forms of the species, Arctic peregrines usually nest on ledges or in shallow caves on the face of cliffs close to open areas that abound in the waterfowl, shore birds, ptarmigan, and small rodents that make up their summer food supply. There is no lack of such habitat in the Arctic tundra ecosystem, but the vastness of the region and the ruggedness of its terrain have made it very difficult to arrive at an accurate assessment of the bird's population and distribution.

In the 1960s it became apparent that both the *anatum* and the *tundrius* races of the peregrine falcon were declining in much of their ranges. Field studies initiated in Canada and the United States, including extensive population surveys every five years, indicated that agricultural pesticides such as DDT had played a major role in the extirpation of the *anatum* subspecies from most of its historic range.

By preying on species that had ingested traces of these poisons, peregrines and other raptors received concentrated dosages. While the intake was not always enough to be lethal, it inhibited eggshell development in the oviducts of female birds, so that eggs tended to be thin-shelled and easily broken by the normal movements of the brooding adults on the nest. Rates of reproduction dropped to zero. After the use of DDT was banned in Canada and the United States, levels of the chemical and its by-products in the eggs and tissues of surviving raptor populations declined markedly. In fact, this trend contributed significantly to the decision to re-introduce *anatum* peregrines to areas from which they had been extirpated (see Atlantic Maritime life zone, later in this book).

One might wonder, though, how Arctic peregrines, nesting so far from agricultural or industrial activities, could be threatened by exposure to toxic chemicals. Although they have been less afflicted than their southerly counterparts, eggs collected from various sites throughout their farflung Arctic range between 1967 and 1984 have shown varying amounts of pesticides and other contaminants, such as mercury and PCBs (polychlorinated biphenyls). It is probable that the birds are exposed to some of these substances when they prey on birds native to the wintering grounds in South and Central America where DDT and other pesticides are still in use. In addition, the shore birds and other species on which the peregrines habitually feed in the Arctic, also winter in and migrate through areas where they would be likely to ingest traces of persistent toxic materials.

How serious a problem this may be in relation to the Arctic peregrine falcon is difficult to assess at the present time. Initial survey results in the 1970s were not promising; it looked as if the Arctic birds were going the way of their southern cousins. More recently, however, surveys indicate that subpopulations are reproducing normally throughout most of the species's historic range, and especially around Ungava Bay. In addition, field surveys have led to the discovery of previously unknown active nesting sites in the areas of Wager Bay, Melville Island, and Somerset Island.

Although the Arctic peregrine falcon is rare, it appears to be more widely and abundantly distributed across the immensity of Arctic Canada than had previously been supposed. Its presence re-affirms the integrity of the Arctic tundra ecosystem. Its sensitivity to toxic pollutants may serve as a valuable indicator of global environmental quality, and a compelling argument for better handling of chemicals around the world.

Arctic Peregrine Falcon

Facing page: Arctic Peregrine Falcon – Threatened

The Boreal Life Zone

◆

It is by far the largest ecological region in Canada, accounting for fully half the land in the country, and supporting its own distinctive wildlife community.

The Boreal Life Zone

The Boreal life zone stretches in a broad arc from Newfoundland northwestward to the southern Yukon and northern British Columbia. It actually encompasses five ecozones: Boreal Shield, Boreal Plain, Taiga Shield, Hudson Bay Plain, and Taiga Plain. It is by far the largest ecological region in Canada, accounting for fully half the land in the country. The climate is generally cool and moist, with a short growing season and long cold winters.

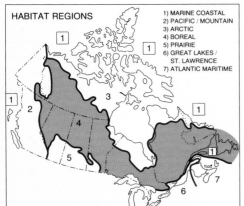

The typical boreal forest cover is dominated by coniferous trees — notably spruces, pines, and firs — interspersed with stands of white birch, trembling aspen, and a few other broad-leafed species. Soil types vary greatly, and water is an important feature throughout the zone, in lakes, rivers, and a wide variety of wetlands such as sloughs, swamps, and muskegs.

In terms of human settlement, this vast region is sparsely populated. Economic activities have been largely related to the resource extraction industries. Mining and forestry are of particular importance, although agriculture assumes some significance in the Boreal Plain. Trapping has been an important economic activity since the earliest days of European exploration, and tourism and recreation have become increasingly significant in the latter part of this century.

The Boreal zone has its own distinctive wildlife community. In addition to the tree species mentioned, plant life includes a wide variety of wild orchids, heaths, grasses, sedges, and mosses, nearly all of them tolerant of boggy, acidic conditions. Since the Boreal zone is a preferred breeding ground for large numbers of finches, warblers, and waterfowl, bird life is rich and varied during the summer months. Few species other than grouse, owls, ravens, and woodpeckers, however, remain as year-round residents. In contrast, the mammal population is largely nonmigratory. Moose, wood bison, and woodland caribou are the region's largest mammals, with beaver, hares, and a wide variety of small rodents making up the rest of the herbivorous population. Predators include wolves, foxes, lynx, and members of the weasel family, from the wolverine to least weasel.

Compared with the situation in other, more densely populated regions of Canada, few boreal wildlife species appear on the COSEWIC lists. In part this reflects the fact that much of this enormous area is still relatively unspoiled by human exploitation. The principal threats to wildlife here stem from the logging of large areas of forest habitat, the pollution of watersheds by poorly contained mine wastes, and in some cases, from excessive exploitation of fur-bearing or game species by trappers, hunters, and anglers. As global awareness of airborne pollution increases, however, there would seem to be valid grounds for concern that this huge ecological region of Canada will face more urgent problems in the future.

Mammals	
Eastern Cougar*	Endangered
Eastern Wolverine	Endangered
Newfoundland Pine Marten	Threatened
Wood Bison	Threatened
Western Woodland Caribou	Rare

Birds	
Peregrine Falcon: *anatum**	Endangered
Whooping Crane	Endangered
Caspian Tern	Rare
Cooper's Hawk	Rare
Great Grey Owl	Rare
Trumpeter Swan	Rare

Fish	
Aurora Trout	Endangered
Shortjaw Cisco**	Threatened

Plants	
Athabasca Thrift	Threatened
Tyrrell's Willow	Threatened

*The Eastern Cougar and Peregrine Falcon: *anatum* are discussed in the Atlantic Maritime section of this book.

**The Shortjaw Cisco is discussed in the Great Lakes/St. Lawrence section of this book.

Species listed as Endangered or Threatened in the above table are covered in detail in the accounts that follow; those classified as Rare are not.

As of 1989 the classification Rare is being replaced by Vulnerable. See Introduction, page 2, for a detailed explanation.

Eastern Wolverine
(Gulo gulo)

According to certain traditions of native folklore, the wolverine is the personification of evil. Trappers and woodsmen have long known it as an insatiable robber of traps and destroyer of food caches, and have called it, unflatteringly, glutton, devil-bear, and skunk bear to express their feelings. Few mammals on earth have a worse reputation. Tales abound of how wolverines attack and kill adult deer and caribou, carry off whole quarters of moose or elk, and drive wolves, cougars, or even bears from their prey.

Indeed, even allowing for flagrant exaggeration, this largest member of the weasel family is not a creature to be taken lightly. An adult male wolverine measures somewhat more than a metre in length from pointed nose to bushy tail, stands about 30–40 centimetres at the shoulder, may weigh as much as 15–25 kilograms, and strongly resembles a powerful miniature bear. Females are smaller, but share their mates' notoriety as muscular, aggressive carnivores, ready to tackle predators or prey much larger than themselves. Strong jaws and teeth are fully capable of ripping frozen meat and crushing all but the heaviest bones. Sharp, semiretractable claws on all four feet enable the animal to climb trees, rip open logs, or disembowel an adversary with ease. In all fairness, however, it should also be mentioned that in a number of cases where wolverines were raised from infancy by humans, they are reported to have been friendly, responsive, and gentle companions.

As befits a species with a name for ferocity, the wolverine is a solitary animal. One may occupy a home range of several hundred square kilometres, travelling tens and sometimes hundreds of kilometres daily in a ceaseless search for food. Only during the summer mating season do adult wolverines temporarily abandon their reclusive habits and travel in pairs. Early the following spring, the female seeks shelter in a cave, a snow tunnel, a burrow, or a den under an uprooted tree. Here she bears a litter of two or three, or occasionally as many as five. The kits are weaned at about eight weeks of age, but remain with their mother for their first year before dispersing to territories of their own. Many females do not produce a litter every year. The result is that the rate of reproduction for the species is low, perhaps averaging less than one young per female per year.

Although they are capable of hunting and

Eastern Wolverine

Eastern Wolverine –
Endangered

killing sizeable prey, wolverines are primarily scavengers, performing a role similar to that of the hyena in the ecosystem of the African plains. They are usually found close to abundant populations of grazing mammals: deer, caribou, elk, moose, or mountain sheep. Preying on weak and sickly individuals from these herds, or perhaps more often appropriating the kills of other predators, a wolverine will gorge on a carcass, then bury the remainder or cache it in the branches of a tree, and return to feed again over a number of days until everything is consumed. Deer and sheep do not die every day for the convenience of wolverines, however, and when large mammals are unavailable, rabbits, hares, grouse and ptarmigan, and even mice become acceptable. The wolverine displays considerable skill as a hunter in catching enough of such small prey to satisfy its voracious appetite.

Nevertheless, a species that depends on an abundance of carrion as its principal source of food cannot normally afford heavy population densities. The solitary, wide-ranging behaviour and large territorial requirements of the wolverine reflect the central reality of its existence. It was never a common animal, even in former times when it ranged across the mountain, tundra, prairie, and boreal life zones from Alaska to Labrador.

Today wolverines are sparsely distributed in the boreal forests of northwestern Ontario and the Prairie Provinces. They occur in relative abundance in the mountain and alpine zone of British Columbia, Alberta, and the Yukon, and are widely but thinly spread across the western tundra of the Northwest Territories and as far north as Ellesmere Island. They were extirpated from western New Brunswick and southern

Québec over a century ago, and their survival anywhere south and east of Hudson Bay is now in serious doubt. Only five wolverine sightings have been reported from Québec since 1977, all of them in the remote northeastern area toward Ungava Bay. The trapping of wolverines has now been completely banned in both Québec and Newfoundland for about ten years.

Strangely, most threats to the survival of the wolverine are indirect. It has virtually no natural enemies, although there is at least one record of an individual being killed by a pack of wolves. Although its fur brings a high price, it has never been an important quarry for trappers, perhaps because of its scarcity in any given area. A fairly steady commercial harvest, averaging about 700 pelts per year, has been recorded since the 1920s, and some skins are retained for personal use by trappers, who prize them because of an unusual characteristic: since frost does not adhere to wolverine fur, it is the ideal trim for parka hoods in a cold climate.

Such consistent trapping of wolverines in western Canada over so many years does not suggest serious overexploitation, but rather a sustainable harvest from a small but stable population. If any human activity has endangered the species in northern and western Canada, it is more likely to have been poisoning as a side effect of campaigns to eradicate wolves. In the East, however, where the species seems always to have been more scarce, trapping, habitat destruction, and the near disappearance of caribou herds as a result of heavy hunting, may have gradually reduced and isolated the surviving wolverines until they dropped below a viable level.

COSEWIC designated the wolverine as Endangered in eastern Canada in 1989. The first and most appropriate remedial action might be to establish how many individuals actually remain in central Ontario, Québec, and Labrador. Then, transplanting programs coupled with strict protective measures might be considered, with the hope of re-establishing the species in its former eastern range.

Newfoundland Pine Marten

(Martes americana atrata)

Lithe, alert, inquisitive, fiercely aggressive, the pine marten is a typical member of the weasel family. It is about twice as big as a large squirrel, and like its close relative the mink, has been much sought-after by the fur trade for its thick, lustrous pelt. Its colour varies from dark brown or near black to pale buff, with irregular markings of cream or orange on the throat and/or underside.

Across Canada, pine martens live in dense, mature or over-mature coniferous forests—typically of fir, cedar, and hemlock in the West, or black spruce and white cedar in the East. Throughout their range they spend much of their time in the treetops, and generally avoid logged or burned-over areas except when travelling from one stand of heavy forest to another. Like many carnivores, or meat-eaters, they are essentially solitary animals, spread thinly over the territories they inhabit. Becoming sexually mature at three years of age, males and females associate with each other only during the summer breeding season. The resulting litters of one to four young, born the following spring, are reared solely by the females.

Marten food preferences vary quite widely, depending upon the availability of prey. Red squirrels are a preferred quarry, and in keeping with this, the marten's classic hunting strategy consists of a high-speed chase through the upper storey of the forest. On the ground, hare, voles, and mice are highly favoured prey, but martens will also take ruffed grouse and other birds, wild berries, insects, and even carrion from deer carcasses when necessity or opportunity dictates a change of diet.

Despite its solitary ways, the marten's innate curiosity has made it notoriously easy to trap. A biologist who was live-trapping martens in a Newfoundland study reported that one individual was attracted by a bait of strawberry jam! During some years in the nineteenth century, as many as 180,000 marten pelts were traded by the Hudson's

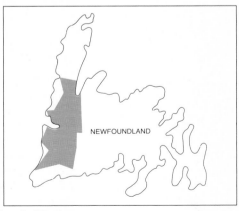

Newfoundland Pine Marten

Bay Company, a harvest which attests to the ease with which the mammal could be captured. Trapping on such a scale reduced the species greatly throughout its range, and by the 1950s the annual kill had fallen to an average of just over 17,000 pelts per year.

The impact of trapping was especially devastating to the pine marten population in Newfoundland. Because islands are physically separate from continental land masses, the diversity of their native flora and fauna tends to be much more limited than that of neighbouring mainland areas. The island of Newfoundland is no exception, with only 14 species of mammals in its array of native wildlife. Of these, the pine marten is one of the rarest. Martens were probably never very abundant in Newfoundland. Few of their favourite prey species are found there, and the extensive stands of large, mature trees that make up their preferred habitat are not common on the island. Still, references to martens date back to at least 1795 in provincial historical sources, and trappers took them regularly until declining numbers resulted in the permanent closure of the trapping season in 1934. In spite of protection, the population decline continued, and the pine marten is presently restricted to the western portion of the island. The greatest concentrations occur in the general vicinity of Grand Lake and Corner Brook. In the early 1980s it was estimated that the entire marten population was between 630 and 875 animals. Subsequent research has not provided any grounds to suppose that this number is increasing.

In 1973 the Newfoundland Wildlife Division designated a tract of land south of Grand Lake as a Marten Study Area. Within this territory, the trapping or snaring of all mammals was prohibited in order to protect the capture-prone martens from being caught accidentally in traps set for other fur-bearers. While the population in this protected zone has remained fairly stable, there is no indication that it has served as a pool from which surplus animals might disperse to repopulate areas where the species had previously been extirpated. One possible explanation is that martens setting out for new territories are accidentally trapped once they leave the reserve area. Another possibility is that the supply of quality habitat for martens has become so seriously depleted that the conditions that would favour a significant recovery of the population simply no longer exist.

If trapping caused the initial decline of the

Newfoundland Pine Marten – Threatened

pine marten in Newfoundland, it is highly probable that current forest resource management methods are largely responsible for keeping its numbers low. The preference of the species for large tracts of undisturbed, mature forest has been well established. Unfortunately, this is a habitat type already in short supply, even in the southwestern part of the island where the animals persist. Although the marten is protected, marten habitat is not. Forest harvesting in this area of Newfoundland consumes about 4,000 hectares of trees per year, and there are strong economic pressures in favour of continuing and even accelerating this rate of exploitation.

For many years, the standard method of timber harvesting in Newfoundland has been to clear-cut readily accessible, merchantable stands of black spruce and balsam fir. Less desirable, or less accessible, residual stands have often been left untouched. In recent years, however, increasing demands for wood fibre and the development of new forest harvesting machinery have made the intensive exploitation of even the more remote stands of timber economically feasible. This is bad news for the pine marten. Research in the state of Maine has shown that clear-cutting of forests reduces the population of pine martens in the affected areas by 60 percent — a severe, if not terminal, cutback for a threatened species to endure. Further, it has been found that areas in Newfoundland's designated study area that were clear-cut 25 years ago have shown no indication

of renewed use and occupancy by martens, despite a quarter century of forest regeneration.

On the positive side, it has been shown elsewhere that martens can be successfully restocked in certain areas. In the early 1980s, for example, an attempt was made by the Canadian Wildlife Service to re-establish pine martens in Terra Nova National Park. Although it is too early to judge the results of the experiment, wildlife managers are optimistic. Also, in order to make well-informed assessments of management options, the Newfoundland Wildlife Division, with the co-operation of Corner Brook Pulp and Paper Limited, is sponsoring further research into the impact of timber harvesting on marten habitat use, movements, feeding habits, and prey populations.

At present, the Newfoundland race of the pine marten is not in immediate danger of extinction. The COSEWIC designation of Threatened reflects its current status as a population that could either recover or disappear, depending on which management priorities are adopted. If timber harvesting continues in western Newfoundland as planned, further declines in the marten population seem inevitable. On the other hand, if accidental trapping can be minimized, if forest harvesting methods can be altered to reduce habitat damage, and if large areas of undisturbed, mature forest can be reserved specifically as marten refuges, there is still hope that the species can be saved in Newfoundland.

Wood Bison
(Bison bison athabascae)

To anyone raised on lore of how the West was won, the words bison and buffalo conjure up a montage of vivid images: vast herds of bison thundering across the prairie grasslands in their annual migrations; native hunters testing their prowess with bow or lance, harvesting the shaggy mammals for food, clothing, and shelter; the railroad, transporting parties of commercial marksmen to the buffalo hunt, and trainloads of meat and hides back to eastern markets; bones, bleaching under the western sky. In less than a century, a seemingly inexhaustible population of

plains bison, estimated to have numbered 50–60 million animals, was reduced to ragged remnants by a campaign of organized carnage that must rank among the most appalling and wasteful of man's atrocities against nature.

Protected since 1893 and actively managed since the 1920s, the plains bison made a modest comeback. Several thousand remain in captive herds at various locations in Canada and the United States.

Far less well known than the plains bison is the wood bison, a taller, darker-coloured subspecies that also came close to extinction. Whereas the plains bison migrated several hundred kilometres annually over the Great Plains, the wood bison

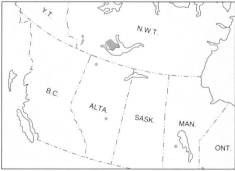

Wood Bison

Wood Bison –
Threatened

was nonmigratory. Although herds were widely distributed over a range that stretched from the aspen parkland of central Saskatchewan and Alberta to the eastern slopes of the Rocky Mountains and the coniferous forests of the Mackenzie Valley, their annual movements were strictly localized.

Historical information is too scanty to permit an accurate estimate of its original population, but the wood bison was never as abundant as its grassland counterpart — perhaps numbering in the hundreds of thousands. For this reason, although hunting pressure on these animals came later, it was all the more devastating. By 1891 it was estimated that no more than 300 survived. It was in part to preserve this remnant herd that Wood Buffalo National Park was established, and by 1922 the herd had grown to 1,500–2,000 animals. In the mid-1920s, however, a well-intentioned wildlife management initiative came close to wiping out the race entirely. A herd of 6,673 plains bison was moved from Wainright, Alberta, to the park. The two races interbred freely, and though the total population increased, the wood bison genetic strain was severely diluted. By the 1940s the subspecies was believed to be extinct.

Then, in 1957, an isolated group of 200 animals

that displayed the characteristics of the true wood bison were discovered in the Nyarling River area near the northern boundary of the park. A number of these animals were transferred to an area northwest of Great Slave Lake, now known as the Mackenzie Bison Sanctuary, where they were allowed to range at will. Another group was moved to an enclosure in Elk Island National Park, where a captive breeding and selection program was undertaken to ensure the survival of a disease-free, pure strain from which stock might eventually be taken to re-introduce the subspecies in other parts of its original range.

Conditions for re-introduction were close to ideal at the Mackenzie Bison Sanctuary. Indeed, the original nucleus of 18 animals has grown at a phenomenal rate to a present-day herd of about 2,000. Their summer range consists largely of upland prairie and open forest where grasses are abundant. In winter they graze on sedges that protrude above the ice at the margin of frozen lakes. Adequate food, protection from hunting, a low incidence of disease, and the absence of predation by wolves have combined to permit the bison to expand rapidly in this highly suitable habitat. In recent years they have begun to expand their range to the northwest, beyond the limits of the sanctuary, a development that has led to the drafting of a management plan by the government of the Northwest Territories, and discussion of the potential for a regulated hunt.

Suitable habitat for wood bison is quite widely distributed in northern Saskatchewan, Alberta, and northeastern British Columbia, as well as adjacent parts of the Northwest Territories and the Yukon. In these areas, mineral extraction and cattle ranching represent the only competing uses of the land. Plans are under way to repeat the experience of the Mackenzie Bison Sanctuary through the introduction of breeding stock into a number of protected habitat reserves. As indicated in the chapter on recovery programs, the preliminary success of this program justified the downlisting of the subspecies from Endangered to Threatened in 1988. Further, there are grounds for hope that the wood bison will one day re-occupy a significant part of its former range and merit removal from the list of endangered and threatened wildlife in Canada.

Whooping Crane
(Grus americana)

If there is a single species that has come to symbolize the struggle to preserve North American wildlife, it is the whooping crane. The plight of this elegant bird has captured and held the imagination and sympathy of the public to an unprecedented degree. Each step in the slow, tenuous retreat from the brink of extinction has been hailed as a small victory for environmental sanity.

Standing more than 1.5 metres tall, the adult cranes are pure white, except for black wing tips, black legs, and a red crown. Legs and necks outstretched, gliding majestically on wings that span two metres, they touch down on marshes in the Northwest Territories at the end of April or in early May, having migrated in the course of three to four weeks from wintering grounds on the gulf coast of Texas at the Aransas National Wildlife Refuge. Each pair stakes out a territory of

Whooping Crane –
Endangered

Whooping Crane

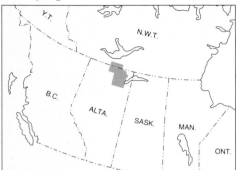

about five square kilometres and selects a secluded site for a metre-wide nest of bulrush stalks and other marsh vegetation. Here the female lays her eggs, ordinarily two, occasionally one or three. For about 30 days both birds take turns incubating them. The downy, reddish-brown young emerge about the beginning of June. As a rule, only one survives. For the next few months, each family forages in the wetlands, the adults keeping their chick supplied with a diet of marsh invertebrates, and later with larger prey — a frog, a mouse, or possibly a small snake or duckling.

In the nineteenth century the whooping crane wintered on coastal marshes from northern Mexico to Louisiana, and nested on marshes, lakes, and prairie sloughs from central Illinois and Iowa to the Northwest Territories. It was not a common bird; as long ago as 1850 it is estimated that the population was below 1,300. Requiring solitude and specialized, undisturbed habitat, the cranes disappeared with the spread of agriculture and the pressure of unrestricted hunting. The last nesting record in a settled area came from southwestern Saskatchewan in 1922. The number of birds appearing on the wintering grounds each year continued to decline until, by 1941, the known population had sunk to 23 birds, including 2 in captivity. Clearly, the whooping crane was perilously close to extinction. Government and voluntary agencies in Canada and the United States agreed to collaborate to prevent its loss. Since that time it is possible that more resources have been dedicated to the preservation and restoration of the whooping crane than to any other endangered species.

For several years the wild population hovered at about two dozen birds. Then, in 1954, there came a breakthrough with the discovery of a pair of adult cranes and their unfledged chick in the northeastern sector of Wood Buffalo National Park. It was the first conclusive identification of a breeding area in more than 30 years. Several nests were found the following year, and it became possible to monitor the rare birds throughout their breeding cycle.

Closer attention to the birds, and public awareness of their plight resulted in a gradual reversal of the trend toward oblivion. From 1955 to 1966 the wild flock increased in size from 28 to 43

birds, but the rate was painfully slow. Direct interventions, such as artificial incubation of eggs at Patuxent, Maryland, to establish a captive flock, and the fostering of eggs in the nests of greater sandhill cranes at Grays Lake, Idaho, were initiated to speed the process. Best of all, despite this regular removal of eggs from the nests of wild cranes, the flock in Wood Buffalo National Park expanded at an accelerating rate.

By 1988 the world population of whooping cranes had increased to about 200 birds as follows: 136 in the wild flock at Wood Buffalo National Park; 45 captive birds at Patuxent; and 16 fostered birds in Idaho. While a population increase of that magnitude is encouraging, the species still faces an uphill battle for survival in the face of hazards traditional and new. Some risks, such as adverse weather conditions, are largely uncontrollable. A hurricane striking the Aransas Refuge in Texas after the arrival of the fall migrants could conceivably disperse or destroy the entire wintering flock at a single blow. If drought were to become a regular climatic feature in northern Alberta and the Northwest Territories, chick mortality could rise, as the cranes would be more vulnerable to terrestrial predators. In August 1979 field researchers documented a case in which an immature bird, well grown but flightless, was killed and eaten by a wolf in Wood Buffalo National Park.

Human technological developments may also pose serious hazards. The migration corridor followed by the wild birds each spring and fall passes through areas where industrial density increases every year. No previous generation of cranes ever had to pick its course through a maze of power lines and microwave towers. In recent years, several have died following collisions with overhead wires. Along the Texas coast, tankers and barges ply the Intracoastal Waterway laden with petroleum products and chemicals that could fatally pollute the birds' wintering grounds at Aransas.

In the face of this array of dangers, the slow but steady recovery of the whooping crane is a testimonial to the vitality of the species, and to nearly 40 years of concerted conservation efforts. Clearly, it will be some time before the birds are numerous enough to constitute a secure, viable, self-sustaining population. Should that day come, then Canada and the United States will have accomplished a joint wildlife conservation goal of which they can be justly proud.

Aurora Trout
(Salvelinus fontinalis timagamiensis)

After many years of public inquiry and debate, the idea that acid rain is a serious environmental hazard is now well established in the public mind. Still, to many people the risk seems abstract and distant; they need concrete examples. There are few more graphic illustrations of the destructive power of acid precipitation than the history of the aurora trout.

The aurora trout, sometimes referred to as the aurora char, has been variously described as a distinct species, as a subspecies, or simply as a geographically distinct stock, of the brook trout. Certainly the similarities — in body shape, in habits, and in colour — are striking. The only visible difference is the absence, in the aurora trout, of the red and yellow speckles, typical of the brook trout, on its sides.

The brook trout, renowned and valued as a game fish, is widely distributed throughout northeastern North America. So far as is known, however, the aurora variety has never occurred naturally other than in four small lakes — White Pine, Whirligig, Aurora, and Wilderness — situated in northeastern Ontario about 100 kilometres north of the city of Sudbury. Within this re-

stricted area, the fish were common until the 1950s. Thereafter, the population declined rapidly, and by 1971 it would appear that the aurora trout had been extirpated from its original range. Only because specimens had previously been procured for an Ontario Ministry of Natural Resources fish hatchery did the original genetic stock remain in existence.

When an isolated population of some species of wildlife is threatened by externally induced changes to its environment, there is an element of double jeopardy. Until a threat is identified, authorities may perceive no valid reason for the special monitoring of factors such as water quality in a few, small, isolated lakes. By the time the need has been established, the damage to the species in question may already be irreversible. In the case of the aurora trout, the threat to its survival in its natural habitat went unrecognized until it had been virtually extirpated.

Acidity and alkalinity are measured on a pH scale that runs from 0, the most acid, to 14, the most alkaline or basic. The midpoint on this scale, or pH 7.0, represents a neutral balance between the two extremes. Generally speaking, life forms do well in the presence of pH values near

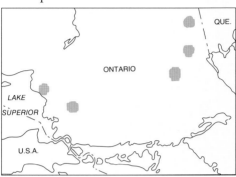

Aurora Trout

Aurora Trout – Endangered

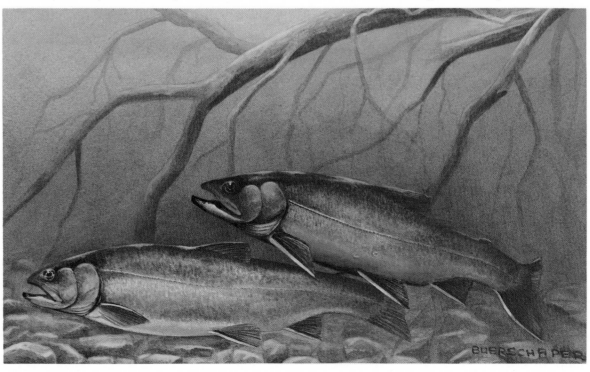

that neutral point, and function less successfully as conditions change toward either end of the scale. Trout, for example, thrive in water with a pH reading between 7.0 and 6.0. At pH 5.5, adverse effects, such as impaired reproduction, start to show up. Below pH 5.0, trout populations ordinarily cannot survive.

When sulphur dioxide (SO_2) and nitrogen oxides (NOx) are released into the atmosphere by industrial and energy-generating processes, they react with atmospheric moisture to form a dilute solution of acid popularly known, when it falls to earth, as acid rain. In some areas, alkaline soils and rock can neutralize the effects of acidic precipitation, and the pH of lakes and streams may remain relatively unchanged for a long time. Where this buffering capacity is low, however, as in the Precambrian Shield, the acidifying effect can be rapid and disastrous.

Historically, the normal pH level for the lakes inhabited by the aurora trout was about 6.8, or very near neutral. Investigations of these lakes in the late 1970s and early 1980s, however, indicated a sharp decrease in pH, to around 4.8–4.5, and a significant increase in the presence of heavy metals in the water. This degradation of water quality can be correlated to a drop in the pH level of rainfall in the area, from about 5.0 in the 1950s to 4.2 or lower by the late 1970s.

The INCO mining and smelting complex at Sudbury has long been the largest single producer of SO_2 emissions in North America. In 1975, for instance, it accounted for 3.9 percent of the continental total. Although the company has acted to reduce pollution in recent years, the acidification of Whitepine and other nearby lakes in the Sudbury-Temagami region of northeastern Ontario took place before such abatement measures were in place.

Since the native population of the aurora trout was eliminated, the Ontario Ministry of Natural Resources has attempted to introduce the variety into other lakes by releasing hatchery-raised fish into waters that seem to offer appropriate habitat conditions. Unfortunately, studies indicate that the trout have had no significant spawning success in these lakes. Efforts to re-establish breeding populations continue, but for the time being, the survival of the aurora trout remains dependent on hatchery stock.

Athabasca Thrift
(*Armeria maritima interior*)

Tyrrell's Willow
(*Salix planifolia tyrrellii*)

In the heart of the Boreal zone, along the south shore of Lake Athabasca in northern Saskatchewan, there is a unique desert-like ecosystem of rare and threatened plants. The area is characterized by large, active sand dunes separated by shallow blowouts. All is not sand, however, for at the edges of blowouts and occasionally extending up the faces of the dunes, a most peculiar kind of willow provides pockets of greenery against the hills of yellow sand. Between the dunes and stony areas are oases of low greenery — shrubs, sedges, grasses, and wildflowers. Ten unique kinds of plants are found here and nowhere else in the world. These include Tyrrell's willow, Athabasca thrift, a grass, three other willows, a yarrow, a rock cress, a sedge, and a tansy.

Tyrrell's willow and Athabasca thrift have been the subject of special studies for COSEWIC and are now officially designated as Threatened. Some of the other rarities might also be so designated but studies of them have not yet been made.

Athabasca thrift is closely related to, and thought to have been derived from, the widely distributed arctic thrift, the most northern member of the everlasting family. A small, herbaceous, perennial wildflower, Athabasca thrift has a short branching stem about 20 centimetres high bearing spherical heads of straw-coloured to pinkish flowers. It occurs in small groups in areas of cobblestone and on drier sand plains among the dunes where it has the ability to survive burial by small amounts of wind-blown sand. Today it occurs in three separated dune areas along the lake.

Tyrrell's willow was named for an early geologist explorer of this region, Joseph Burr Tyrrell.

Athabasca Thrift

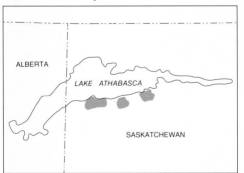

It is a good-sized shrub, its seedlings taking root in the moist depressions among the dunes. As the sand moves, the plants survive by growing rapidly through the encroaching slope of the dune. As years become decades, the migrating dune passes through the colony, exposing the woody stems and roots, leaving the willows to die. The spot where the former dune stood now becomes a depression, and for Tyrrell's willow the cycle begins anew.

Adapted to life in a world of drifting sand, and found only on the Lake Athabasca sand dunes, this willow otherwise shares many characteristics with willows in southern parts of Canada. Points of similarity include the fact that some plants are female while others are male, flowering takes place in spring before the leaves are produced, and cross-pollination is thought to be by both insects and wind. Copious silky seed is set in the female "pussy willows" and readily dispersed by wind.

All the rare plants of the Athabasca dunes have close relatives that are widely distributed across the northern portion of the continent, and sometimes in northern Eurasia. The Athabasca dunes are believed to have provided, in the short time since the retreat of the last glaciers, an environment where specially adapted species have evolved from their more widespread ancestors.

The most serious potential threat to the rare species of the dunes comes from all terrain vehicles. The Saskatchewan government has built a winter road into Lake Athabasca from the south; should a summer road penetrate this region, the fragile dunes would need to be placed off-limits to ATV machines. Otherwise, major destruction of this sand-based ecosystem would result and extinctions of rare species could be expected.

As the dunes contain so many rare plant species (and possibly insects as well), and because they form such an unusual landscape in the boreal world, they have attracted the attention of naturalists and ecologists, who recognize this special area as one of Canada's truly unique and fragile ecosystems.

Tyrrell's Willow

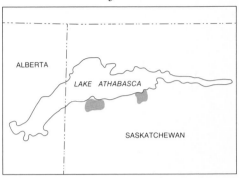

Left: Athabasca Thrift – Threatened

Tyrrell's Willow – Threatened

The Prairie Life Zone

◆

Relative to its area and population,
the Prairie ecozone is the native habitat
of a disproportionate number
of threatened and endangered species
of Canadian wildlife.

The Prairie Life Zone

Extending northward from the Great Plains of the central United States, the Prairie life zone of Canada consists of nearly half a million square kilometres of open, flat to gently rolling country, covering most of southern Alberta, Saskatchewan, and Manitoba. This zone can be divided into three principal subzones characterized by their vegetation: the shortgrass prairie, typified by extremely low rainfall and a vegetative cover of short prairie grasses; the tallgrass prairie, where slightly less arid conditions support taller, lusher plant species; and the aspen parkland, a transition zone where a moister climate supports a light forest cover of aspen.

The indigenous wildlife community of the Prairie ecozone is one of the most distinctive in Canada. Like grassland regions around the world, the Prairie grasslands were traditionally the habitat of huge herds of grazing herbivores, in this case the plains bison and the pronghorn antelope. In the absence of forest cover, the region was favoured by bird and mammal species such as the burrowing owl, the black-tailed prairie dog and the plains pocket gopher, both now categorized as Rare,

and the now-extirpated black-footed ferret, all well adapted to the use of subterranean burrows for shelter. Prairie sloughs served not only as reservoirs for precious water, but also as breeding spots for vast quantities of waterfowl.

The settlement and development of western Canada as one of the world's great agricultural regions changed all that. The following accounts document species that disappeared because of direct pressures imposed by hunting and trapping; species that vanished unexpectedly as their habitat was destroyed, or that were deliberately exterminated because they were perceived to compete with man for the bounty of the land; and species that momentarily flourished with the coming of man, only to be diminished again as modern agricultural methods removed the habitat niches created by earlier farming styles.

Millions of bison and antelope once roamed the plains; today their place is taken by herds of cattle. Whole communities of complementary species used to occupy prairie-dog towns and the oases surrounding prairie sloughs; today intensive cultivation and drainage schemes have created a landscape of continuous golden grainfields. Relative to its area and population, the Prairie ecozone is the native habitat of a disproportionate number of threatened and endangered species of Canadian wildlife.

HABITAT REGIONS

1) MARINE COASTAL
2) PACIFIC / MOUNTAIN
3) ARCTIC
4) BOREAL
5) PRAIRIE
6) GREAT LAKES / ST. LAWRENCE
7) ATLANTIC MARITIME

Mammals

Black-footed Ferret	Extirpated
Swift Fox	Extirpated
Prairie Long-tailed Weasel	Threatened
Wood Bison*	Threatened
Black-tailed Prairie Dog	Rare
Plains Pocket Gopher	Rare

Birds

Greater Prairie-chicken	Endangered
Mountain Plover	Endangered
Piping Plover**	Endangered
Baird's Sparrow	Threatened
Burrowing Owl	Threatened
Ferruginous Hawk	Threatened
Loggerhead Shrike	Threatened

Plants

Small White Lady's Slipper***	Endangered
Prairie White-fringed Orchid	Rare
Soapweed	Rare
Western Silver-leaf Aster	Rare

Fish

Bigmouth Shiner	Rare

Reptiles and Amphibians

Northern Prairie Skink	Vulnerable

*The Wood Bison is discussed in the Boreal section of this book.

**The Piping Plover is discussed in the Atlantic Maritime section of this book.

***The Small White Lady's Slipper is discussed in the Great Lakes/St. Lawrence section of this book.

Species listed as Endangered or Threatened in the above table are covered in detail in the accounts that follow; those classified as Extirpated, Rare, or Vulnerable are not.

As of 1989 the classification Rare is being replaced by Vulnerable. See Introduction, page 2, for a detailed explanation.

Prairie Long-tailed Weasel
(Mustela frenata longicauda)

In the 1930s, the prairie long-tailed weasel was a significant, if involuntary, contributor to the income of western trappers. Hudson's Bay Company records from the period indicate that in Saskatchewan alone the catch of this mammal and its close relative, the short-tailed weasel, amounted to 60–70,000 pelts per year. Forty years later, the yearly harvest in Saskatchewan had fallen to less than 1,400 — a dramatic decline of over 95 percent!

When the population of a valued fur-bearing mammal drops so markedly in the course of a few decades, it might seem logical to presume that the decline has a single, straightforward cause: excessive trapping. Studies of the distribution and habitat preferences of the long-tailed weasel in the Prairie Provinces since the 1960s, however, suggest that in this instance the presumption would be incorrect.

The long-tailed weasel occurs throughout southern Canada from New Brunswick to British Columbia. Within this range, the prairie subspecies is found in Alberta, Saskatchewan, and Manitoba, north to the boundary between prairie and boreal ecosystems. The prairie race is quite large, reaching a maximum length of about 500 millimetres. In summer its coat is pale brown with lighter underparts, but like most northern races of the species, it turns pure white except for its black-tipped tail during the winter months. It is an opportunistic predator on a wide variety of small- to medium-sized prey, including ground-nesting birds, small ducks, mice, rats, ground squirrels, hares, and even other weasels.

Although it is not a prolific breeder, population levels are at least self-sustaining in favourable habitat. In other words, it seems unlikely that under stable conditions the level of trapping reported in the 1930s would threaten the survival

Prairie Long-tailed Weasel

Prairie Long-tailed Weasel – Threatened

of the race unless some other factor were introduced. The real threat to the prairie long-tailed weasel stems from a progressive loss of favourable habitat and a resulting destabilization of the conditions required to sustain healthy populations.

Energetic predators such as the weasels need steady and plentiful supplies of prey if they are to thrive. For this reason they frequently inhabit transition areas between ecological zones, where they have access to a wider diversity of prey species than would be available nearer the centre of a single, more uniform ecosystem. For the prairie long-tailed weasel, the fertile aspen parkland lying between the open grasslands of the Great Plains and the dense, coniferous forests of the boreal zone traditionally offered just such a location. Although it lay at the northern edge of the weasel's range, it provided many prey species, and another essential feature of favourable habitat as well: water. The long-tailed weasel will not establish in an area if there is no water nearby. In contrast to the arid grasslands to the south, an abundance of sloughs in the parkland belt satisfied this requirement.

Unfortunately for the weasel, the aspen parkland, with its fertile soil and dependable moisture, was also a magnet for agricultural settlement. It took time for the full impact of clearing, draining, and cultivating to become apparent, but in this century, farm mechanization and the increased practice of monoculture (single-crop farming) steadily accelerated the process. Understandably, the farmers chose the best land,

leaving the marginal and the unproductive. It has been estimated that 95 percent of the original aspen parkland biome has disappeared since 1930, to be replaced by improved pasture or by grainfields stretching from horizon to horizon.

It is no mere coincidence that the population of the prairie long-tailed weasel has declined by approximately the same percentage over the same time. Most of the mammal's preferred habitat has been transformed, and that which remains is severely fragmented. Modern agricultural practices have removed cover, drained standing water, destroyed burrows, reduced prey species, and introduced pesticides into the food chain. The continuation of trapping under these circumstances could only have one outcome: to push the species close to the point of extirpation.

Vigorous protective measures may still succeed in preserving the prairie long-tailed weasel in Canada. These would include the creation of habitat reserves protected from development; the closure of fur-bearer trapping in parks and reserves; and public education to advise farmers of the value of the species as a predator on rodents. Ironically, one popular conservation initiative on the prairies — the improvement of wetlands for waterfowl production — has the potential to impair weasel recovery by flooding den sites. Where two valid wildlife enhancement goals conflict in this way, the sensible management choice must be the one that favours the endangered species and the ecosystem in which it survives.

Greater Prairie-chicken

(Tympanuchus cupido pinnatus)

The greater prairie-chicken is a grouse of the western grasslands. Similar in size to the sharp-tailed grouse for which it is often mistaken, it has a heavily barred brown body and wings, and a dark tail. Males in breeding plumage display erectile neck feathers and inflatable yellow neck sacs during elaborate courtship dances in April and May. After mating, the females lay 11–14 eggs in a shallow nest hidden in grass or bushes. The downy, mottled, brown and yellow chicks leave the nest within a day of hatching, but are tended by the female until they attain independence at about six to eight weeks of age.

In the early 1800s, the greater prairie-chicken ranged as far east as extreme southwestern Ontario, where a few remnants of tallgrass prairie still persisted. As farming replaced Ontario's deciduous forests with fields and pastures, the prairie-chicken moved into this artificially created grassland, and by 1875 had spread eastward to Burlington, Toronto, and the Holland Marsh. Requiring dense cover, it could not tolerate intensive farming, and as agriculture expanded, the bird withdrew from its acquired range almost as quickly as it had occupied it.

The last prairie-chickens in southern Ontario were reported from Walpole Island in 1924.

The rise and fall of the greater prairie-chicken in southern Ontario foreshadowed, on a small scale, what was to happen to the species in western Canada, where the bird did not appear until about 1881. Because it required broad expanses of undisturbed grassland, the species did not co-exist well with the vast herds of bison that grazed the northern plains. Between 1840 and 1880, however, professional hunters virtually extirpated the bison from the grasslands of western Canada. Elk and pronghorn antelope populations were severely reduced as well. In the absence of the major ungulate (hoofed) species, the prairie grasslands were no longer subjected to constant heavy grazing. At the same time, rainfall during the late 1870s and early 1880s was much more abundant than usual. The ungrazed prairie grasses grew with unprecedented lushness, providing the greater prairie-chicken with an extension of ideal habitat conditions for both nest protection and winter cover. Under the newly favourable conditions, the species migrated from North Dakota and Minnesota into Manitoba in the 1880s and spread rapidly westward into Saskatchewan and Alberta. It is estimated that by 1900 there were a million or more of the birds in the Prairie Provinces. In later years, similar movements saw birds colonizing

Greater Prairie-chicken

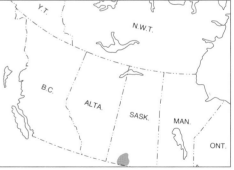

*Greater
Prairie-chicken –
Endangered*

the Kenora/Rainy River district, the Sault Ste. Marie area, and Manitoulin Island.

For a time the prairie-chickens and the farmers who were colonizing the West at about the same time provided mutual benefits for each other. Early farming in western Canada was conducted on a fairly small scale and did not greatly disturb the grassland habitat. Grain crops provided a rich food supply for the birds, while they in turn became a welcome source of meat to the farmers. With the introduction to the prairies of heavy agricultural technology, however, more and more of the lush grassland was ploughed under, relentlessly diminishing breeding habitat.

As prairie-chicken habitat decreased, pressures from the human population grew. Sportsmen and market hunters, assuming that wildlife supplies were inexhaustible, hunted the tasty birds without restriction. The first bag and possession regulations, introduced in the early 1900s, stipulated a limit of 20 prairie-chickens per day,

or 200 over a three-month season from 16 September to 14 December. By 1920 the number of birds had declined to the point that the prairie-chicken season in Alberta was limited to two weeks.

It was not hunting, however, but the ongoing conversion of natural grasslands to agriculture that spelled the end for the greater prairie-chicken. The first generation of settlers on the plains had created an opportunity for the species to expand northward into the Prairie Provinces. However, breeding populations of the birds required vast areas of tallgrass prairie to be self-sustaining. If more than 60 percent of the grassland in a district were converted to cultivation, they would quit the area. By the 1930s, the heroic sodbusting efforts of the second generation of prairie farmers and the introduction of cattle ranching to the drier, less arable areas of grassland had nearly eliminated the greater prairie-chicken from the Canadian West.

There is now no hard evidence that the species persists as a breeding bird in Canada, although sightings are reported often enough to sustain the hope that it has not been wholly extirpated. It is possible that some of these reports actually referred to sharp-tailed grouse or hybrids of the two species. The fact that this latter species is known to interbreed with the greater prairie-chicken is a further obstacle to wide-spread re-introduction of the bird as a resident breeding species. The long-awaited creation of Grasslands National Park — some 900 square kilometres of land in southern Saskatchewan — may protect enough unbroken habitat to permit the re-establishment of a permanent flock of greater prairie-chickens — a living memorial to the birds that briefly dominated the grasslands a century ago.

Mountain Plover
(Charadrius montanus)

The mountain plover was probably never a common bird in Canada. Although fairly plentiful in Montana, Colorado, and Wyoming, it appears to have reached the extreme northern limit of its range in southeast Alberta and southwest Saskatchewan where the dry shortgrass prairie extends northward to the Cypress Hills. The American observer Elliott Coues, travelling in northern Montana in 1874, found the species "breeding in considerable numbers" along the Milk River, within 50 kilometres of the international boundary. Around the same time, following a more or less parallel route about 100 kilometres north of the border, the eminent Canadian naturalist John Macoun made no mention of it.

Not until 1939 was there documented proof of the mountain plover in Canada — a single bird near Bracken, Saskatchewan. Occasional sightings thereafter, including a flock of eight near Val Marie, Saskatchewan, in September 1977 led observers to suspect the possibility of nesting, but confirmation of its presence as a breeding species came only in 1979. That year at least three broods of young were hatched in the Lost River area of Alberta; each year since, one to six nests have been found in the same district. Despite severe drought conditions, at least one pair nested there in 1988.

Even if the mountain plover were more common, an experienced observer might easily miss it in the field. It is a medium-sized bird, between a horned lark and a killdeer in size. Its grey-brown back and wings, grey-buff breast, and dull white underparts blend with the background colours of bare earth, prairie grass, and sage-brush almost to the point of invisibility. Black punctuates this restrained pattern in only three places: a patch on the crown, a stripe running from eye to bill, and a dark band near the end of the tail. The first two of these identifying marks are typical only of breeding plumage and are absent from immatures and from the adult birds in autumn.

The reproductive cycle of the mountain plover begins with the arrival of spring migrants on the breeding grounds in mid-April. Three small eggs (occasionally two or four) are laid in mid- to late May. They hatch in about a month; some 33 days later the young are fledged. After nesting, the birds migrate to wintering grounds in south-ern and central California, southern Texas, and northern Mexico. The specific wintering area for birds breeding in Canada is not known.

Within the vastness of the Great Plains, the mountain plover is highly specialized in its choice of breeding habitat. Acceptable nest-ing sites are patches of bare earth in areas of shortgrass prairie where the native grass species, blue gra-ma and buffalo grass, have been recently burned over or moderately to heavily grazed. This selectivity offers a clue as to why the species is endangered in Canada, and why its numbers have declined markedly throughout much of its range in the United States.

Before the days of European settlement in the Great Plains, the mountain plover belonged to a grassland ecological community that was domi-nated by a single species — the American bison. The migratory ebb and flow of the grazing herds kept the shortgrass prairie vegetation cropped to the optimum height for a ground-nesting species to keep a lookout for approaching predators. The passage of the bison, as well as the dry climate

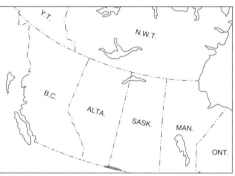

Mountain Plover

and the occasional lightning-initiated wildfire, ensured the presence of a certain proportion of bare earth for nest sites between the hummocks of grass. Where those habitat conditions coincided with an adequate food supply of grasshoppers, ants, and beetles, the mountain plover prospered.

With the nineteenth century came colonization; with the twentieth, European man's redefinition of the prairie grasslands not as an ecological community, but as an economic resource. The virtual extermination of a keystone species, the bison, broke the long-established cycle of growth and grazing on the plains, and in doing so, indirectly diminished the quality of habitat for smaller,

associated species of wildlife such as the mountain plover. At the same time, hunting had a more direct impact as well. Thousands of plovers were shot by market hunters, especially on the California wintering grounds.

A still more serious threat to the species was the cultivation of grassland for agricultural purposes. Today, close to half the original acreage of native grassland favoured by the mountain plover has been ploughed under and replaced by cereal grains and non-native forage crops. Most of its former habitat in northern Montana and a significant proportion of similar terrain in southwest Saskatchewan are now intensively cultivated. Once destroyed, the native grassland

Mountain Plover – Endangered

80

habitat type is virtually irreplaceable. Even if cultivation ceases in such areas, the replacement vegetation includes grasses, both native and introduced, that are taller than the mountain plover will tolerate in nesting habitat.

To be fair, not all agricultural practices have had negative effects. The use of natural grasslands as cattle range in southeastern Alberta and southwestern Saskatchewan has undoubtedly helped to preserve some plover habitat by providing a replacement for the grazing function of the bison. Unfortunately, the benefit tends to be only partial. Heavy grazing by the migratory bison herds served to maintain a steady rotation of suitable nesting sites that shifted somewhat from year to year. Modern range management practices, on the other hand, tend to produce a uniform, moderately grazed grassland throughout the range, one which may not offer the areas of bare ground preferred by the birds.

The other major factor which may jeopardize prospects for the recovery and/or expansion of the mountain plover population in Canada is the simple fact of human intrusion. During the courtship, egg-laying, incubation, and early rearing phases of the breeding season (roughly from mid-April to late July), the birds are reported to be very sensitive to disturbances and may abandon their eggs or young if subjected to too much

stress. An increase of unregulated motor traffic through the area, whether by visitors attracted to a unique natural area, or by ranchers doing their range-checking from trucks rather than on horseback, might be sufficient disturbance to drive the birds away.

At present, the mountain plover is protected under the federal Migratory Birds Convention Act and the Alberta Wildlife Act. In addition, the Lost River area has been proposed for special status under the Natural Areas Program of the Province of Alberta. The location, which includes all the documented mountain plover breeding habitat in Canada, is held by the province and leased to Agriculture Canada for use as experimental rangeland. A coordinated federal/provincial management scheme for the area might encompass diversified grazing patterns and occasional controlled burns to enhance habitat, as well as regulate the recreational use of the land and vehicle access to the site. Perhaps the mountain plover will never be more than a rare, occasional breeder in Canada, at the northern limit of its natural range. Yet efforts on its behalf have the potential to achieve an additional benefit: preserving not just a single endangered species, but valuable remnants of the complex shortgrass prairie ecological community.

Baird's Sparrow
(*Ammodramus bairdii*)

No less an authority than John James Audubon discovered the Baird's sparrow. The great wildlife artist named the inconspicuous little native of the prairie grasslands in honour of Spencer Fullerton Baird, one of the foremost American ornithologists of the nineteenth century. Audubon's painting of this species completed the amazing series of 500 plates with which he illustrated his celebrated work, *Birds of America.*

Accounts of Baird's sparrow up to the 1930s indicate that it was an abundant breeding resident of the mixed-grass prairie throughout southern Manitoba and Saskatchewan and southeastern Alberta, and in adjacent areas of Minnesota, the Dakotas, and Montana — much the same range where the ferruginous hawk and

the burrowing owl were traditionally most numerous. Like those species, its numbers have declined steadily as modern agriculture has advanced across the plains.

The natural history of the Baird's sparrow reflects the annual cycle of the grassland biome in which it lives. After wintering in the southwestern United States — especially Texas — the adult birds arrive on the breeding grounds about the end of April or early May. Males arrive up to a week ahead of the females and at once stake out territories of 0.4–0.8 hectares. Territories often overlap; under ideal conditions on undisturbed grassland, breeding densities as great as 22.5 pairs per hectare have been observed.

Preferred nest sites tend to be located in or beneath tufts of grass, or in depressions on the ground. Here, in June, the female lays a clutch of four to five eggs. Incubation lasts 11–13 days, and the young leave the nest within 8–10 days of hatching. Although the fledglings continue to be

Baird's Sparrow

fed by their parents for another week or more, they generally depart from the nesting territory by the 19th day, leaving plenty of time for their parents to hatch and raise a second brood in favourable years. Autumn departure is spread out over several weeks, from the end of August to as late as October.

During migration and on its winter range, Baird's sparrow feeds primarily on weed seeds. During the breeding season, however, it turns to a diet of insects and spiders, with grasshoppers accounting for up to 64 percent of the prey items. Presumably the high protein content of this fare contributes to the energy levels required for successful reproduction, but it is also true that the availability of seeds is at its lowest during the early summer.

As with many prairie species, the decline of the Baird's sparrow is linked directly to loss of its grassland habitat. The species is extremely specific in its breeding requirements. During the 1940s, 1950s, and 1960s, as more and more of the mixed-grass prairie was converted to agriculture, fewer and fewer prime nesting areas were left undisturbed. Virtually every land management technique developed for large-scale prairie farming operated against this little brown bird of the grasslands. One ornithologist wrote:

"Environmental disturbance caused by plowing, burning, brushing or mowing and raking always results in Baird's Sparrow quietly abandoning an area. Nor can it prosper on closely-cropped pastureland, and the introduction of grazing animals into a field usually causes the species to desert it."

> J. Lane in A. C. Bent, *Life Histories of North American cardinals, grosbeaks, buntings, towhees, sparrows and their allies, 1968.*

Today, it is estimated that less than 5 percent of Canada's native grasslands remain more or less intact. It is neither surprising nor coincidental, then, that the sparrow's population has also declined to less than 5 percent of its former abundance.

Although direct loss of habitat appears to be the primary cause of the population decline, agricultural practices may have contributed in other ways as well. The application of herbicides and insecticides in areas where the birds are nesting could have a negative impact either by direct poisoning, by diminishing breeding suc-

Right: Baird's Sparrow – Threatened

cess, or by reducing the availability of prey during the season when the sparrow depends largely on a diet of live invertebrates. Predation by mice, weasels, skunks, or birds of prey, while possible, is not known to be a significant threat to this species.

Whatever the combination of causes, there appears to be no doubt that the Baird's sparrow has withdrawn from significant areas of its range, and that the breeding population has continued to drop in recent years. Breeding bird survey reports indicate that a total of 126 Baird's sparrows were recorded on 13 survey routes in 1975. Ten years later, 35 birds were recorded on 7 routes. Even allowing for some natural fluctuation of the population from year to year, the downward spiral is evident. Considered to be endangered in Manitoba, rare in Saskatchewan, and threatened in Alberta, Baird's sparrow was assigned national status as a Threatened species on the 1989 COSEWIC list.

To preserve and restore this bird across much of its former habitat will require dedicated effort. Acquisition and preservation of large tracts of natural grassland are two immediate and practi-

cal steps that could be taken. Tax breaks and other incentives could promote conservation efforts by landowners who are prepared to preserve and protect uncultivated acreage as natural habitat. Beyond this, however, is a fundamental need for more field research on the species to determine its ecological requirements, its actual numbers, and its potential for recovery. If significant areas of grassland can be saved, there is good reason to believe that the Baird's sparrow can be saved as well.

Burrowing Owl
(*Athene cunicularia*)

"Their figure is peculiar, with their long legs and short tail; the element of the grotesque is never wanting . . . bolt upright . . . they gaze about with a bland and self-satisfied, but earnest air, as if about to address an audience . . . they suddenly bow low, with profound gravity, and rising as abruptly, they begin to twitch . . . and roll their eyes about in the most mysterious manner, gesticulating wildly, every now and then bending forward till the breast almost touches the ground." Thus did nineteenth-century American ornithologist Dr. Elliott Coues describe the burrowing owl in his *Birds of the Northwest,* published in 1874. The amused affection evident in his words typifies the human response to this most endearing of North American owls. It would be hard for anyone to feel otherwise who has ever watched a family of these alert and solemnly comical birds as they bob and peer atop a badger burrow, ready to duck underground at the first hint of danger, yet insatiably curious about everything that moves on the western grasslands where they live.

Burrowing owls are closely associated with the rural civilization of western Canada. They were originally native to the wild shortgrass prairie, a vast region of dry rolling grassland grazed by the plains bison. Here they nested in close association with burrowing mammals such as prairie dogs, ground squirrels, and badgers, as well as the rattlesnakes and ferrets that frequented the same subterranean sites in search of shelter and prey. At first, the owls adapted readily to the incursions of European settlers, tolerating the presence of livestock and machinery, colonizing pastures and even road and railway embankments on the outskirts of villages. Indeed, it is thought that agriculture, by increasing the acreage of grazing land, may initially have helped to increase the range, available habitat, and breeding population of the species in Manitoba, Saskatchewan, Alberta, and southern British Columbia.

Arriving in mid-April or early May from wintering grounds presumed to be in Texas or Mexico, the pigeon-sized ground owls, as they are commonly called, seek out the burrows of ground-dwelling mammals and commence the rites of reproduction. Pairs may nest singly, in loose associations within an area, or in tightly knit colonies of a dozen or more pairs in a single field. Having selected their burrow, a pair may dig to enlarge it before lining the interior with grass, roots, and fragments of dried cow or horse dung. The female usually lays four to seven eggs, though occasionally ten or more, in a subterranean nest chamber. In due course the fledgling owlets join the adults on the surface, snapping up grasshoppers, beetles, and small rodents, standing upright on their long bare legs, and staring wide-eyed at the world around them.

The presence of burrows, or occasionally culverts or other holes in the ground, is a prerequisite of burrowing owls, not only for breeding, but also to provide shelter from wind and sun, and protection against predatory hawks. If left undisturbed, a burrow complex may be used for many years. Unfortunately, disturbance and destruction of burrowing owl habitat have increased markedly in recent years, as modern agriculture has aimed to achieve maximum productivity. Cultivation of pastures and rodent extermination are two techniques that have incidentally reduced the supply of suitable burrows.

An extensive survey in 1978 indicated a broad downward trend in the burrowing owl population, a decrease even larger than what could be reasonably accounted for by the loss of habitat. In the southern British Columbia interior, for

Burrowing Owl

example, it was determined that the small breeding population had disappeared entirely. The number of burrowing owls remaining in the three Prairie Provinces was estimated to total about 2,000 pairs as follows: Alberta, 610; Saskatchewan, 1,280; and Manitoba, 110. In consequence, COSEWIC declared that the species was threatened in Canada.

Follow-up studies through the mid-1980s confirmed that the numbers were continuing to diminish — most alarmingly in Manitoba, where the reported number of pairs dropped from 76 in 1982, and 60 in 1983, to 35 in 1984, and 18 in 1987.

Many factors besides habitat loss exert negative pressures on the burrowing owl. The use of chemical pesticides to control grasshoppers, for instance, not only reduces an important food source for the owls, but can poison birds that ingest large enough quantities of contaminated insects. Climatic factors can also be damaging. Cold damp weather during incubation reduces nesting success, and instances have been noted where torrential rainfall has drowned birds in their burrows.

Burrowing owls, particularly the eggs and young, are preyed upon by snakes, skunks, foxes, badgers, feral cats, and other marauders. Sad to say, human predation is also a serious threat to this species. Some owls are shot unintentionally when they are mistaken at a distance for prairie dogs; on other occasions, whole colonies have fallen victim to deliberate vandalism.

Collisions with motor vehicles, accidental, but no less damaging to the species for that reason, are another serious cause of mortality. This appears to be a particularly severe hazard during late summer when the young are fledged and migration begins. One observer recovered close to 60 road-killed burrowing owls on a single round trip along a 25-kilometre stretch of highway outside Boise, Idaho.

To summarize, the survival of the burrowing owl is endangered in Manitoba and threatened in Saskatchewan and Alberta. Records of sightings

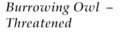

Burrowing Owl – Threatened

from Ontario and Québec, and even one from New Brunswick, fall entirely into the accidental category. In British Columbia, a recovery scheme involving the release of breeding pairs at artificial nest sites is re-introducing the burrowing owl as a breeding resident of that province.

From a wildlife management standpoint, the primary objectives for the burrowing owl ar the stabilization of present population levels and the prevention of future losses. It is important to continue accurate monitoring of numbers, and to gather information on migration in order to gain a better knowledge of threats faced by the birds while they are absent from breeding territories.

More active intervention, through capture and relocation of burrowing owl colonies, may eventually be necessary in the Prairie Provinces if major engineering projects should threaten to wipe out established nesting sites. This technique has had some success in the United States.

Perhaps the most essential protective measure, however, is the pursuit of an active public education program about the burrowing owl. For generations, the alert little ground owl has been a familiar figure in the prairie landscape. If it is to remain so, then farmers, ranchers, and the public at large need to be made aware of how precarious its survival really is. Shooting, poisoning, trapping, and cultivation in the immediate vicinity of nest sites must be stopped.

In Saskatchewan, Operation Burrowing Owl (OBO), a project of the World Wildlife Fund and several local conservation organizations, was launched in June 1987 by Prince Philip. Through this voluntary habitat protection program, landowners on whose property burrowing owls are known to nest, and who agree to protect the owls, receive gate signs acknowledging their participation. Although other hazards will remain, if the threats posed by human activity can be substantially reduced by such means, then the burrowing owl population may do more than merely stop declining; there is still hope that it may rise again.

Ferruginous Hawk
(*Buteo regalis*)

All is quiet in the prairie morning. Nothing stirs but the wind, ceaselessly bending the grass in rhythmic waves before its insistent caress. Lulled by the silence, a Richardson's ground squirrel peers from its burrow, sniffs the air for danger, and emerges to browse on the tender green shoots of early summer. An instant later, a shadow blots out the sky. There is a scuffle, a squeak of panic, a scream of triumph. The ferruginous hawk that has been waiting near the burrow takes off, the hapless rodent hanging limply from its talons. With heavy wingbeats the bird flies to its nest among the rocks on a nearby hillside where two downy young wait hungrily for the fresh meat they need for growth.

It is axiomatic in natural communities that where there is food, something will feed on it; where there is prey, there will be predators. The temperate grasslands of southern Alberta and Saskatchewan illustrate the point. An abundance of grasses supports an abundance of small rodents: mice, voles, ground squirrels, and prairie dogs, literally by the thousands per square kilometre in the most productive areas. The abundance of small mammals supports an abundance of predators. On the ground there are shrews, snakes, coyotes, foxes, badgers; in the air, birds of prey — the burrowing owl, short-eared owl, and ferruginous hawk.

The ferruginous hawk is a *buteo,* or buzzard hawk, one member of a world-wide family of large raptors with broad wings and fan-like tails. It measures 56–61 centimetres in length, a bit larger than the rough-legged hawk, a similar species that breeds in the Arctic and winters in southern Canada. Like the rough-legged, the ferruginous hawk is found in two colour phases (pale and dark), each distinctive enough that an inexperienced observer might suppose that there were two species of bird occupying the same environmental niche. Pale-phase birds have brown upper parts streaked with white, white underparts streaked with brown, a white to grayish tail, and extensive orange-cinnamon markings on the shoulders and back. Dark-phase birds are dark brown with a white or gray tail and cinnamon edging on some of the feathers.

Ferruginous Hawk

HIGH DENSITY BREEDING RANGE

LOW DENSITY BREEDING RANGE

Prior to the settlement of the prairies, the ferruginous hawk was fairly common in southern Alberta, Saskatchewan, and southwestern Manitoba. Experts estimate that its Canadian population was over 5,000 breeding pairs — an impressive number for a large predator at the top of the grassland food chain. Today that population is thought to have declined to about 250–300 pairs. A considerably greater number still persists in the United States.

Some of the decline can undoubtedly be attributed to the predatory behaviour of man. The belief that raptors were harmful birds was widespread for many years in the earlier part of this century, and many were shot under bounty regulations. Indeed, although the ferruginous hawk is now protected under wildlife legislation, Alberta did not abolish the hunting season for the species until 1958. Nowadays, most farmers recognize its value in controlling rodents and no longer persecute it. It has been calculated that a breeding pair may kill close to 500 ground squirrels in a single nesting season. This raises a question, as yet unanswered, as to whether the practice of poisoning the common prairie rodents might inadvertently poison the nestlings that are feeding on them in such quantity.

The principal threat to the ferruginous hawk is directly related to its dependence on open, arid, prairie habitat. It is seldom found in woodland locations, or in areas that are subject to disturbance by agriculture. Like many other species of this region, it has diminished in numbers as its habitat has been lost to two types of conversion. On the one hand, with the disappearance of the bison and the control of prairie fires, much of the northern prairie has changed to wooded parkland unsuited to the hawk's needs. On the other hand, more and more of the remaining grassland has come under cultivation, with the result that nests have been disturbed, and prey species displaced.

Generally, where natural grassland has been lost through one or other of these trends, the ferruginous hawk has disappeared; where habitat remains in something close to its traditional condition, the bird remains. It would seem fairly clear, then, that in order to maintain viable populations of this species, large tracts of natural grassland must be maintained. Reserves such as the proposed Grasslands National Park in southwestern Saskatchewan may come to play a crucial role in this story of disappearance or survival.

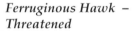

Ferruginous Hawk –
Threatened

Loggerhead Shrike
(*Lanius ludovicianus*)

The bird is the size of a robin, but its plumage is gray and black. A hooked bill and a mask-like, black eye-stripe give it a faintly piratical air as it perches on a thorn bush at the edge of a pasture. Suddenly it cocks its head to one side, its attention drawn to a movement in the short-cropped grass. It drops, pounces, flutters upwards again, a mouse, a small bird, or a large green grasshopper held firmly in its bill. Returning to its perch, it impales the prey on a curving thorn and begins to eat.

The bird is a loggerhead shrike, a predatory songbird of the open countryside, whose widespread decline since 1960, especially in the northeastern portion of its range, has occasioned serious concern among ornithologists and moved COSEWIC, in 1986, to designate it as Threatened across Canada.

In examining the decline of the loggerhead shrike, it is important to note that this species seems to have experienced an equally rapid expansion into eastern Canada a little over a century ago. Its earliest recorded presence as a summer resident in Ontario was in 1860 at Hamilton, while the first individual in Québec was seen in Montréal in 1883, and in the Atlantic provinces, at Milltown, New Brunswick, in 1884. By the early 1900s, the loggerhead shrike was considered to be an uncommon breeder throughout a range that included southern Ontario north to Lake Nipissing and Sault Ste. Marie, much of southern Québec, and a few sites in New Brunswick and Nova Scotia. In certain localities within this range, such as the Kingston area and Manitoulin Island, the bird was described as common.

Before this northeastward invasion took place, the loggerhead's native Canadian territory had been the southern and central portions of Manitoba, Saskatchewan, and Alberta. The most probable explanation for the range extension from the midwestern states into Ontario and beyond appears to be the conversion of forests into farmland. In eastern Canada and adjacent areas of the United States during the mid-nineteenth century, the process created large tracts of open country admirably suited to the needs of a species ordinarily native to the arid grasslands of the Great Plains.

When a species that has successfully established itself in a newly acceptable habitat declines a few decades later with equal suddenness, not only in the new territory but also in much of its previous range, ecologists look for explanations. In the case of the loggerhead shrike, the possible reasons are many and varied. One of the first is loss of habitat. Much of the farmland, especially in southern Ontario and Québec, that was used as marginal pasture early in the twentieth century has long since been reclaimed for other uses: suburbs and super-highways or intensive cash-crop cultivation. In either case, the hawthorn hedgerows that provided hunting perches for loggerheads and protective cover for their bulky nests have been cut down or ploughed under to make way for more profitable uses. Despite these changes, there does seem to be an overall surplus of appropriate breeding habitat in eastern Canada. There is, however, a suggestion that some loggerhead shrikes return to the same nesting sites year after year. If this trait were strong enough, destruction of nesting locations could effectively prevent reproduction by the breeding population in a given area.

Another possible cause of decline is the enormous increase in highway traffic over the past 25 years. Loggerhead shrikes — especially immature ones — are frequently killed on roads. As early as 1920, an American study suggested that 2–7 percent of each year's young were struck by cars as they hunted insects on the warm pavement. Today, with more and faster motor traffic, observers have speculated that the net mortality from this cause may now be much higher.

Toxic chemicals, especially organochlorine pesticides, are undoubtedly contributing to the decline of the loggerhead shrike. Their impact could be either indirect or direct. Indirectly, the toxins could lead to food shortages; directly, the birds could ingest enough poison, if not to kill, then to interfere with successful reproduction. DDE residues have been detected in shrikes at 200 to 400 times the concentrations found in their prey. In other species, elevated levels of DDE have caused eggshell thinning and breakage, with breeding failure as the inevitable result.

Apart from threats associated with human

Loggerhead Shrike

activity, the diminishing loggerhead shrike population may be further stressed by a number of natural factors. Predators such as raccoons and crows will readily eat the eggs and young. Eastern kingbirds and kestrels are known at times to compete fiercely with other species for territory and food. Even weather could be critical. A high mortality among young and adult birds has been associated with periods of cold and rain. And if the warm climate that typified the first half of this century were to be replaced by a trend toward cooler, more changeable weather, then breeding conditions at the edge of the loggerheads' range could cease to be viable.

Whatever the precise combination of limiting factors, their effect on the loggerhead shrike has been extreme. Based on reported sightings, or the lack of them, since 1981, the species may no longer be even a rare summer resident in the Maritimes or in Québec, apart from the extreme southwest corner of the province, near Montréal. The *Ontario Breeding Bird Atlas* estimates the average population in that province during the early and mid-1980s to have been about 50–100 breeding pairs in any year, and notes the disappearance of the loggerhead from many areas where it was formerly considered to be a regular resident.

Only in the Prairie Provinces, which is to say in its original Canadian range, is the loggerhead shrike found in numbers that are the least bit reassuring. Here, too, there have been severe declines since the 1960s and apparent abandonment of northern portions of the traditional range.

Following COSEWIC status designation in 1986, the World Wildlife Fund Canada, the Canadian Wildlife Service, and provincial wildlife authorities sponsored intensive surveys of loggerhead shrike habitat in Manitoba, Saskatchewan, and Alberta during the summer of 1987. The findings confirmed the bird's status as a threatened species.

In Manitoba, 87 percent of loggerhead shrike sightings were in the extreme southwest of the province, which suggests a marked contraction from former range limits. In Saskatchewan, sightings were more widely distributed throughout the southern and central districts, but the preponderance of records came from the south and west. In Alberta, the concentration was in the southeast. In those areas where breeding pairs were found, the rate of reproductive success appeared to be high, although the population trend was nonetheless downward from previous years.

Observers in the three provinces noted the affinity of the birds for very specific habitat situations: caragana shelterbelts; willow thickets near sloughs; stands of thorny buffalo berry. Retention of such settings is often perceived to be incompatible with contemporary agricultural land management practices, and they are becoming less and less common on the prairies. While further research into the various pressures on the loggerhead shrike is needed, one priority would seem to be the implementation of appropriate conservation measures for its preferred habitat in western Canada.

Facing page:
Loggerhead Shrike –
Threatened

The Great Lakes/ St. Lawrence Life Zone

◆

*It is this region that may be
the most crucial testing ground of the
political and social will of Canadians
to restore the quality and balance
of their natural environment.*

The Great Lakes/ St. Lawrence Life Zone

Sometimes referred to as the Mixed-wood Plain, this zone extends from Sault Ste. Marie and Windsor in Ontario, eastward along the St. Lawrence waterway almost as far as Rimouski at the beginning of the Gaspé Peninsula. A region of rolling hills and alluvial plains, it contains large areas of fertile soils that originally supported lush forests of hardwoods mixed with conifers. The climate is continental, with the extremes of heat and cold somewhat moderated by the presence of the lower Great Lakes.

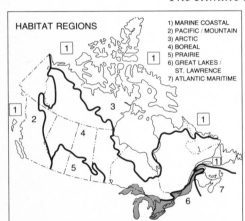

HABITAT REGIONS
1) MARINE COASTAL
2) PACIFIC / MOUNTAIN
3) ARCTIC
4) BOREAL
5) PRAIRIE
6) GREAT LAKES / ST. LAWRENCE
7) ATLANTIC MARITIME

Within this zone, one area merits special mention. In southwestern Ontario an unusually warm climatic subzone extends from the Niagara River to Windsor. Before being cleared for farming, it was a northerly extension of the Carolinian forests, interspersed with occasional remnants of tallgrass prairie, and was characterized by the presence of flora and fauna whose ranges reach far into the southeastern and central United States. For many species this area marks the northernmost limit of their range. Among these are the cucumber tree, eastern prickly pear, Kentucky coffee tree, and others — plants that in times past were important components of the great forests that grew here before European settlement.

Close to half the population of Canada lives in the Great Lakes/St. Lawrence Plain. As a result, no other region of the country has been more drastically altered from its natural state by agriculture, industry, and urbanization, since settlement began in earnest in the early nineteenth century. The mature mixed forests were quickly and systematically cut for lumber and cleared for agriculture. Thus denuded of water-retaining cover, many of the watersheds became little more than flood channels, unsuitable as habitat for the rich assortment of aquatic life that once lived there. Intensive harvesting, habitat destruction, and water pollution have wiped out or endangered numerous species of fish in one of the world's most important freshwater drainage systems. Urban sprawl has covered large tracts of prime land, and pollution by industrial and domestic wastes is a serious threat, not only to wildlife but also to the prospects for continued healthy human habitation.

Not surprisingly, a great many of the wildlife species found here are endangered or threatened. What is more surprising is the quantity of natural habitat that remains, and the number of native species that manage to survive in the face of such severe pressures. Populations of the eastern mole, the gray fox, and the southern flying squirrel are still found here, and the eastern bluebird persists thanks to the efforts of people who maintain nestboxes for this attractive songbird. In part, this zone is a wonderful illustration of the resiliency of nature; in part, it reminds us that where many people live together, concern for environmental protection and quality may more readily be acknowledged as a serious issue. It is this region that may be the most crucial testing ground of the political and social will of Canadians to restore the quality and balance of their natural environment.

Mammals

Eastern Mole	Rare
Grey Fox	Rare
Southern Flying Squirrel	Rare

Birds

Kirtland's Warbler	Endangered
Peregrine Falcon: *anatum**	Endangered
Piping Plover*	Endangered
Henslow's Sparrow	Threatened
Loggerhead Shrike**	Threatened
Caspian Tern	Rare
Common Barn-owl	Rare
Cooper's Hawk	Rare
Eastern Bluebird	Rare
King Rail	Rare
Least Bittern	Rare
Prairie Warbler	Rare
Prothonotary Warbler	Rare
Red-shouldered Hawk	Rare

Fish

Gravel Chub	Extirpated
Paddlefish	Extirpated
Deepwater Cisco	Extinct
Longjaw Cisco	Extinct
Beluga: St. Lawrence ***	Endangered
Blackfin Cisco	Threatened
Shortjaw Cisco	Threatened
Shortnose Cisco	Threatened
Black Redhorse	Threatened
Copper Redhorse	Threatened
Great Lakes Deepwater Sculpin	Threatened
Lake Simcoe Whitefish	Threatened
Margined Madtom	Threatened
Blackstripe Topminnow	Rare
Brindled Madtom	Rare
Central Stoneroller	Rare
Kiyi	Rare
Pugnose Minnow	Rare
Pugnose Shiner	Rare
Redside Dace	Rare
River Redhorse	Rare
Silver Chub	Rare
Silver Shiner	Rare
Spotted Gar	Rare
Spotted Sucker	Rare

Bigmouth Buffalo	Vulnerable
Black Buffalo	Vulnerable
Orange Spotted Sunfish	Vulnerable
Redbreast Sunfish	Vulnerable

Plants: Carolinian

Cucumber Tree	Endangered
Eastern Prickly Pear Cactus	Endangered
Heart-leaved Plantain	Endangered
Hoary Mountain Mint	Endangered
Large Whorled Pogonia	Endangered
Small Whorled Pogonia	Endangered
Spotted Wintergreen	Endangered
American Chestnut	Threatened
American Water-willow	Threatened
Blue Ash	Threatened
Bluehearts	Threatened
Colicroot	Threatened
Kentucky Coffee Tree	Threatened
Nodding Pogonia	Threatened
Purple Twayblade	Threatened
Red Mulberry	Threatened

Plants: Prairie Remnants

Gattinger's and Skinner's Purple False Foxgloves	Endangered
Pink Milkwort	Endangered
Slender Bush Clover	Endangered
Small White Lady's-slipper	Endangered
American Ginseng	Threatened
Pitcher's Thistle	Threatened
Prairie Rose	Rare
Prairie White-fringed Orchid	Rare

Plants: Other

Broad Beech Fern	Rare
Dense Blazing Star	Rare
Dwarf Hackberry	Rare
Few-flowered Club-rush	Rare
Green Dragon	Rare
Hill's Pondweed	Rare
Hop Tree	Rare
Indian Plantain	Rare
Shumard Oak	Rare
Swamp Rose Mallow	Rare
Victorin's Gentian	Rare

*The Peregrine Falcon: *anatum* and the Piping Plover are discussed in the Atlantic Maritime section of this book.

**The Loggerhead Shrike is discussed in the Prairie section of this book.

***The St. Lawrence Beluga is discussed in the Marine Coastal section of this book.

Species listed as Endangered or Threatened in the above table are covered in detail in the accounts that follow; those classified as Extinct, Extirpated, Rare, or Vulnerable, with the exception of the Deepwater Cisco and the Longjaw Cisco, are not.

As of 1989 the classification Rare is being replaced by Vulnerable. See Introduction, page 2, for a detailed explanation.

Kirtland's Warbler
(*Dendroica kirtlandii*)

Kirtland's Warbler

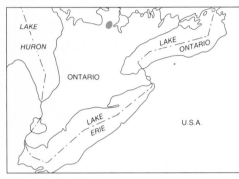

Kirtland's Warbler – Endangered

Five years of intensive observation by participants in the *Ontario Breeding Bird Atlas* project resulted in the only Canadian sight record for the Kirtland's warbler during the period 1981–86. The bird was a male in typical breeding plumage: blue-gray head and back; lemon-yellow breast; black streaks on the sides. For at least 10 days in early July, 1985, it sang on territory in a jack pine forest north of Orillia, Ontario. It was not seen the following year. In fact, only 37 sight records of this species were listed in Canada between 1900 and 1986. Geographically, occurrences have ranged from Lake Winnipegosis, Manitoba, to Montréal, with the vast majority in southern Ontario. One sighting, near Barrie, Ontario, in 1945, was of an adult pair accompanied by at

least one immature bird. All the other records were of individuals, either male or of undetermined sex.

Some species that are rare, threatened, or endangered in Canada are plentiful elsewhere in their North American ranges. The Kirtland's warbler is a rare bird wherever it is found. Its only known breeding ground in the world was discovered in 1903 in the northern portion of Michigan's lower peninsula. There, an annual census of singing males has led researchers to their current estimate of a breeding population that has remained relatively stable at about 200–240 pairs since the early 1970s. Information on the life history of the species has been derived almost entirely from observations of this population.

The Kirtland's warbler is extremely selective in its choice of habitat, nesting only in young jack pine stands growing about two to seven metres tall in well-drained sandy soil. The stands tend to be somewhat uneven, clumps of trees being interspersed with grassy clearings and ground cover of perennials and shrubs such as bracken fern and northern dwarf cherry. The cup-like nest of grass and leaves, lined with vegetable fibres and sometimes deer hair, is hidden under vegetation near the base of a small jack pine that has sheltering branches reaching right to the ground. Four or five eggs are laid in June, hatching after 14–15 days of incubation; the young leave the nest 12–13 days later. Information about fall migration is sketchy, but the species is known to winter in the Bahamas and the Turks and Caicos Islands.

Although the Kirtland's warbler may once have been a regular breeder in Canada, there have been too few documented sightings to permit even an educated guess at its present population, or to consider it as anything more than a rare visitor. One observer recalled the species as having been "not uncommon" in the jack pine forests of the military camp at Petawawa, Ontario, in the upper Ottawa Valley in 1916. Subsequent sightings of singing males were recorded in the Petawawa area in 1939, 1946 (twice), 1977, and 1978. In 1978 an additional singing male was found about 100 kilometres to the east, near the Gatineau River in Québec. Other areas where the species has been seen more than once include Point Pelee (4 times), along the north shore of Lake Ontario from Hamilton to Kingston (11 times), and in the Georgian Bay region near

Barrie (3 times), Orillia, Parry Sound, and Tobermory.

There are extensive stands of jack pine in parts of central Ontario where, at least in theory, the Kirtland's warbler could persist as a breeding species. As noted above, however, the prime breeding sites in Michigan are in stands of short, young trees; in an Ontario survey of potentially suitable jack pine stands, most were found to be too mature. In earlier times, the vitality of jack pine forests was sustained by occasional forest fires. Not only did over-mature trees burn, but the heat of the flames caused their cones to open, releasing seeds to start the next generation. The modern emphasis on forest fire prevention and control has disrupted that natural cycle and rendered potential breeding habitat no longer suitable for the warbler.

In the United States, the Kirtland's warbler is the subject of extensive efforts at preservation. Management procedures have been implemented by state and federal agencies to increase the supply of prime nesting habitat from less than 2,000 hectares in the late 1970s, to as much as 16,000 hectares by 1990.

Any attempt to re-establish the species in Canada would require habitat enhancement initiatives on a similar scale. Realistically speaking, however, it would be a flagrant indulgence in wishful thinking to launch such a renewal scheme before locating at least a small breeding population. The best hope for the moment is to monitor potential breeding sites for the Kirtland's warbler, and to be ready to respond with a constructive strategy should it appear.

Henslow's Sparrow
(*Ammodramus henslowii*)

Henslow's sparrow seems to be a recent arrival in Canada. It was first reported in 1898 when a nest with four eggs was discovered in "a wet, springy place in a meadow" near Lansdowne, about 40 kilometres east of Kingston. In the same year, adult birds were seen and heard near Sarnia and at Jeanette's Creek, Lake St. Clair.

Henslow's sparrow is characterized by a striped head, olive neck, chestnut back and wings, a buffy breast streaked with black, and short, pointed tail feathers. Some authorities speculate that the species was always native to extreme southwestern Ontario, but was just too inconspicuous to be recognized by early settlers in the area. Be that as it may, there is little doubt that it expanded its Canadian range rapidly in the first half of this century, as forests gave way to agriculture. By the 1950s, the small, secretive sparrow was classed as an uncommon local breeding species in Ontario. It had been recorded as far north as Manitoulin Island and as far east as Ottawa, and nesting records from the Hull and Montréal regions indicated the extension of its range into southwestern Québec.

Throughout its range it seeks grasslands interspersed with tall weeds, conditions typical of natural tallgrass prairies, unmowed fields, and overgrown pastures. Often the ground is moist, and matted with dead grasses from previous years. In such locations, males arrive in April or early May and lay claim to breeding territory by means of an unmusical "tse-slik" song. Breeding is often loosely colonial, several pairs nesting in the same field. The females weave nests of grass and leaves, on the ground or in low grass, weeds, or shrubs, and lay three to five small pale-green or cream-coloured eggs, heavily blotched and speckled with browns, purples, and grays. The young hatch in 11–12 days and are cared for by both parents until they are fledged.

Although the Henslow's sparrow may be selective about its nesting conditions, it shows little fidelity to particular sites. Some colonies remain in one spot for years; others use an area once, then abandon it, or return only sporadically. Where locations are used for several years, populations may fluctuate widely. Despite such uncertainties, it is clear that in the past 30 years this species has declined in overall numbers and has withdrawn from large parts of its range in Canada and the United States.

According to the 1957 edition of the *American Ornithologists' Union Check-list of North American Birds*, the Henslow's sparrow ranged from South Dakota and Kansas to the Atlantic coast. By the 1970s, it had largely vanished from the midwest-

Henslow's Sparrow

ern prairies and the eastern seaboard states. It was no longer found in Québec, and in southern Ontario the decline was unmistakable: 74 sightings in 1976; 45 in 1977; 54 in 1978; 15 in 1979; 24 in 1980; and 17 in 1981. The *Ontario Breeding Bird Atlas* (1981–85) listed sightings in 38 (2 percent) of the 1,824 survey squares. Breeding was confirmed in only three squares during the five-year study. The atlas estimates that "in a year of high numbers it is unlikely that the total provincial population [now] exceeds 50 pairs."

Why should a seemingly well-established species experience such a sharp decline? It is generally assumed that the Henslow's sparrow

moved into southern Ontario as agriculture transformed the dominant forest cover into open farmland. The traditional mixed farming rotational cycle regularly left some fields to lie fallow for extended periods, a practice that greatly increased the availability of the sparrow's preferred habitat. The species took advantage of the opportunity. Farm abandonment during the 1940s and 1950s may even have accelerated the process, as areas of marginal pasture and crop land dropped from use and reverted to a natural succession of plant communities.

In the 1960s, three factors altered this pattern. In hinterland areas, many abandoned fields ceased to be suitable as nesting sites, becoming choked with woody growth. Near urban centres, grassland disappeared beneath sprawling subdivisions and highways. On the remaining arable land, agricultural methods became increasingly intensive and mechanized. Pasture and summerfallow in Ontario fell from 1.5 to 0.8 million hectares from 1951 to 1976, while corn acreage nearly doubled from 0.6 to more than 1 million hectares by 1980.

Creation of habitat, as a by-product of human activity, provided an opportunity for the Henslow's sparrow to colonize southern Ontario in the first place. Loss of habitat, also a by-product of human activity, is the most likely reason for its decline. If adequate reserves of grassland nesting habitat can be set aside and maintained at the proper stage of succession, then there is a chance that a small population may survive. For better or for worse, the future of the Henslow's sparrow in Canada is going to reflect the environmental values of Canadians and whether they are ready to accommodate the idea that it is important to reserve space for a small bird—just for its own sake.

Henslow's Sparrow – Threatened

Ciscoes of the Great Lakes

Two of the most widely distributed groups of freshwater fishes in Canada are the whitefish and ciscoes. They are closely related to the salmon, trout, char, and grayling, and like their gamefish relatives, most are prized as food fish, and most show a marked preference for cool, deep,

unpolluted waters.

As a group, these are among the most seriously threatened fishes in Canada. In all, some 18 species of whitefish and ciscoes are recognized. Two of those are extinct. One, the Atlantic whitefish, discussed in the Atlantic Maritime section of this book, is endangered; four are judged to be threatened; and two more have been classified as rare. In other words, half the known species of this subfamily in Canada are listed in one or another of the COSEWIC categories.

The greatest pressure on species of the genus *Coregonus* has occurred in the Great Lakes basin, and particularly on the five species of ciscoes dealt with in the accounts that follow. The ciscoes that appear on the COSEWIC list are, or were, native to the Great Lakes, although one — the shortjaw cisco — has also been reported in a number of inland lakes in northwestern Ontario and Manitoba. Streamlined, silvery fishes measuring as much as 30 centimetres or more in length, they are commonly known as "chubs." During the first half of this century they formed the basis of a substantial commercial fishery. Taken by gillnet, they were smoked and sold as a delicacy in the United States and in some Canadian Great Lakes communities.

Technically, regulations governed the harvesting of each variety of cisco, but because the fish taken were seldom identified by species, the chub fishery was conducted without adequate monitoring or enforcement. At first, nets of a fairly large mesh size were set to take the larger, deepwater species. Exploitation, driven by market demand, increased steadily. As catches of large fish diminished, smaller-mesh nets were set and smaller species became part of the catch. Rather than being reduced to enable waning stocks to recover, the fishing effort was redoubled. Under such pressure, species after species declined to the point of commercial insignificance, until by the 1960s only the bloater and the common cisco, or tullibee, were being taken in quantities large enough to warrant a concerted fishing effort.

Meanwhile, other factors added to the stress on the diminished cisco populations. Important among these was an inexorable degradation of habitat. The years of heaviest fishing pressure coincided with a period of rapid urban and industrial growth in the Great Lakes basin. The ensuing environmental problems were many and varied. Siltation and turbidity came in the wake of deforestation, topsoil erosion, and mineral extraction. Deterioration of water quality reflected an increasingly intensive use of chemical fertilizers, herbicides, and pesticides in agriculture. The discharge of massive amounts of industrial effluent and municipal sewage into the lakes resulted in widespread pollution.

Apart from the direct effects of human activity, natural pressures such as predation, initially by lake trout and later by sea lamprey, and also by introduced species such as the rainbow smelt, may have accelerated the decline as well.

Another factor that may have undermined the viability of some Great Lakes ciscoes is hybridization. Changes in the relative abundance of different varieties may have promoted cross-breeding between the remnants of declining species and other stocks that were still plentiful. Such a trend could cause irreversible dilution of the established gene pools of distinct species, and the replacement of the rarer ones by a variety of hybrids with varied characteristics. Support for this hypothesis can be found in the appearance, since the 1960s, of just such a variety of hitherto undescribed forms of ciscoes.

Finally, the simple arithmetic of species survival cannot be overlooked. As a species becomes rare, its chances of reproductive success are reduced accordingly. Fewer young are recruited into the population to mature and reproduce in their turn. At best, the recovery of a once-numerous population takes a long time. At worst, if the rate of recruitment falls and remains below the natural mortality rate, extinction must certainly follow.

The complex of intentional and inadvertent factors that combined to endanger the ciscoes and whitefish of the Great Lakes illustrates how vulnerable wildlife can be, even when seemingly plentiful. The illustration becomes still more disturbing when considered in the light of one simple fact: many species of the world's flora and fauna have never been identified. For instance, over 300 new fish species were added to Canada's inventory of fresh-water and marine fauna between 1969 and 1984, and still more remain to be discovered. Even among those that are broadly known, there are some, such as the Squanga whitefish, a species endemic to a few lakes in the southwestern Yukon, that have yet to receive enough study to even permit proper taxonomic classification.

Whenever a species becomes extinct, the loss — of knowledge, of genetic diversity, of potential benefit — is immeasurable and irreplaceable. That fact alone emphasizes the extreme care with which the introduction of new human activities to any area should be assessed. To alter or exploit a habitat without prior extensive and meticulous field study is to risk destroying resources, the very existence of which may be unknown. To sacrifice undiscovered or unfamiliar species in the interest of minimal short-term economic advantage is just not worth the price.

Deepwater Cisco
(*Coregonus johannae*)

The deepwater cisco was one of the largest of the Great Lakes ciscoes. It was a silvery fish, tinted with pinkish iridescence, which averaged about 300 millimetres in length and weighed from about 500 grams to a kilogram. It occurred only in the deeper parts of lakes Huron and Michigan and was taken most frequently in nets set at depths of 90–150 metres.

Little is known of its natural history. Judging from the dates when egg-bearing females began and ceased to be caught, it would appear that spawning commenced in mid-August and was terminated by the end of September. Analysis of stomach contents indicated that its principal food items were small fresh-water invertebrates — molluscs, crustaceans, insect larvae, and the like. Its traditional predators would appear to have been the lake trout, the burbot, and most recently the sea lamprey.

Because of its size, the deepwater cisco was a preferred target of the chub fishery that operated profitably on the Great Lakes for about a century, from the mid-1800s to the 1960s. Subject to intense fishing pressure up to and through the 1940s, it appears to have been extirpated from Lake Michigan by 1957. While specific data are not available concerning the disappearance of the Lake Huron population, it would seem that it was wiped out at about the same time, and authorities agree that the species should now be classified as Extinct.

Longjaw Cisco
(*Coregonus alpenae*)

Once abundant in lakes Huron and Michigan, and present in Lake Erie as well, the longjaw cisco was declared Extinct by COSEWIC in 1985. Quite similar in appearance to the deepwater cisco, and only slightly smaller, the longjaw cisco derived its name from having a lower jaw that projected beyond the upper one. In common with other members of the cisco subfamily, it fed on small shrimp and other fresh-water invertebrates, and was fed upon, in turn, by the lake trout and the sea lamprey.

Like the deepwater cisco, the longjaw cisco fell victim to the pressures of commercial exploitation, further aggravated by natural predation and deterioration of habitat. In reviewing the history of the Great Lakes fishery, it is clear that the larger species of ciscoes were the first to be fished heavily. The smaller varieties came under pressure as the catch of the large ones declined and the demand for smoked chub increased. In the 1930s, the longjaw cisco accounted for as much as 30 percent of the total catch. By the 1950s its share had dropped to less than 1 percent, and by the mid-1960s, it had entirely disappeared from the commercial harvest. Extinct status for the longjaw cisco was approved by COSEWIC in April 1985.

Blackfin Cisco
(*Coregonus nigripinnis*)

The blackfin cisco is probably the largest of all the Great Lakes ciscoes, growing to a maximum length of nearly half a metre. It is silver in colour, shading to a dark green on the back, with black fins. Its preferred food is a small fresh-water crustacean, although plant and insect remains and fish scales have been found in a few stomach samples.

Right: Blackfin Cisco – Threatened

Historically, the blackfin cisco was found in deeper water than most species — as deep as 183 metres in lakes Ontario, Huron, Michigan, Superior, and Nipigon. It was a mainstay of the chub fishery for many years, as part of the smoked fish trade.

There have been some reports of this species being found in other lakes of the Precambrian Shield as well, but these appear to have been cases of confusion with either the common cisco or the shortjaw cisco. At present, it seems most probable that it has been extirpated from all the Great Lakes, and that only the Lake Nipigon

population of the blackfin cisco is still extant.

If the Lake Nipigon population is to survive, close protection against commercial fishing would seem to be in order, along with life history studies and population estimates. As noted above, this is another species of cisco for which the scientific identification is somewhat uncertain, and further research is needed to clarify its taxonomic status while this is still possible.

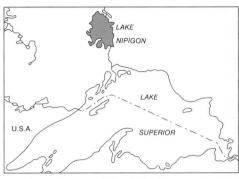

Blackfin Cisco

Shortjaw Cisco
(*Coregonus zenithicus*)

The shortjaw cisco was once common in lakes Michigan and Huron and is thought to have been the most abundant cisco in Lake Superior. Today it is presumed to have been extirpated from lakes Michigan and Huron, the last known specimens having been taken in 1975 and 1982 respectively. In Lake Superior the population has declined drastically, but the species remains relatively common in adjoining Lake Nipigon, and specimens have been taken in a few lakes scattered

across Manitoba, Saskatchewan, Alberta, and the Northwest Territories.

The shortjaw cisco is, on average, a smaller fish than some of the other deepwater members of the genus *Coregonus*. This fact may have protected it, to some degree, from the intense commercial overexploitation that led to the extinction of the deepwater and longjaw species. However, as the larger varieties disappeared from the catch, intermediate species such as this one became the backbone of the fishery. The result of this shift to prominence is evident in a series of population estimates suggesting that chubs of this size class (shortjaw, shortnose, and common ciscoes) made up two-thirds of the Great Lakes stock in the 1930s and 24 percent in the 1950s, but only 6.4 percent in the 1960s. In Lake Superior alone, the proportion of the total catch represented by the shortjaw cisco dropped from over 90 percent in the 1920s to less than 5 percent some 50 years later.

The shortjaw cisco suffered, as did the other deepwater cisco species, from pressures besides the fishery. Predation by sea lampreys is thought to have had a significant impact. Furthermore, as the populations of these species declined, smaller deepwater ciscoes like the kiyi (*Coregonus kiyi*), itself now classified as Rare, and the bloater (*Coregonus hoyi*), as well as introduced species such as the rainbow smelt and the alewife, grew in abundance to the point where they became serious competitors for habitat and food resources, and possibly predators on eggs and fry.

Shortjaw Cisco

*Left: Shortjaw Cisco –
Threatened*

Shortnose Cisco
(Coregonus reighardi)

The shortnose cisco is a smallish, silver-iridescent fish attaining an average length of barely 250 millimetres and a weight of less than 500 grams. Because of its numbers and the high proportion of fat in its body composition, it was one of the most valued chub species in Lake Ontario up to the 1940s and played an important role in the fisheries of lakes Huron and Michigan as well.

Shortnose Cisco

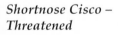

Owing to the same combination of commercial and natural pressures that affected other ciscoes, the population of this species diminished rapidly after the 1940s. It has been extirpated from Lake Ontario since 1964, and from Lake Michigan since 1972. It is rare throughout Lake Huron, except in Georgian Bay, which may now be the sole remaining population centre for the species.

The shortnose illustrates one confusing aspect of the closely related deepwater ciscoes. Putting it simply, they are difficult to identify with certainty. Some scientists have even suggested that the shortnose cisco may be identical to the shortjaw variety. Any study of the deepwater ciscoes of the Great Lakes reveals wide variations in the form of each species, between the population of one lake and that of the next, as well as, at times, striking similarities between supposedly separate species. Furthermore, in recent years it would seem that variant forms of ciscoes are being found with greater and greater frequency.

This has led some researchers to speculate that pressures affecting the population structure of ciscoes in the Great Lakes may be reshuffling genetic characteristics. The hypothesis suggests that several ciscoes may have been conspecific — i.e., they may have been distinctive forms of the same species.

So long as the ecological balance remained more or less in equilibrium, the theory goes, each population would school together, spawn together, and produce offspring with identical characteristics. Once the integrity of those populations was compromised, however, as a result of radical declines in numbers, then interbreeding between members of different populations might become so commonplace that the particular traits that previously served to identify species types might become mixed or lost among a wide variety of hybrid forms.

Shortnose Cisco –
Threatened

Black Redhorse
(*Moxostoma duquesnei*)

The black redhorse inhabits clear, cool, moderately rapid streams that flow over clean sand, gravel, or bedrock bottoms. It is distributed widely, if not commonly, throughout the midwestern United States, but in Canada its range is extremely limited. It has been found in recent years in only three southwestern Ontario locations — upstream sections of the Grand, Thames, and Maitland river systems.

In Canada, this species spawns in late May or early June, each female depositing some 4–11,000 eggs over a gravel or stone bottom in fast-flowing, shallow water. Nearby pools and slower stretches of water serve as nursery areas for newly hatched fry. The fish move to deeper holes with the onset of winter.

Small breeding populations of the black redhorse have been found in the Thames River north of London, Ontario, in the Grand River west of Guelph, and in the Nith River, a

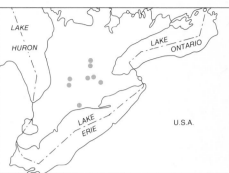

Black Redhorse

Black Redhorse – Threatened

Among redhorse and sucker species, the black redhorse is a relatively small fish, attaining an average adult length of 250–330 millimetres and a maximum weight of about 900–1000 grams. Its attractively streamlined body is normally gray or olive-brown on the back, shading to silver-blue on the sides, and silvery or white below. Fins are slate gray to orange, occasionally tinged with red. During spawning, males display a pale pinkish lateral band and a greenish black coloration on the back and sides, which may account for the reference to black in the common name.

The mouth of the black redhorse, like that of most suckers, is located on the underside of the snout. In feeding, the thick lips protrude downwards, enabling the fish to suck in material from the stream bottom and extract aquatic invertebrates, such as insect larvae and fresh-water crustaceans, from the inedible silt and gravel.

tributary of the Grand, south of Kitchener. In each case, distribution appears to be limited to localized sections of the rivers in question, and this fact is one key to understanding why the species is considered to be threatened.

As noted previously, the black redhorse requires a habitat with low concentrations of silt and a moderately rapid flow of water. Studies of the species in the United States have shown that it will tolerate neither muddy water, nor the slow currents and increased siltation that can result from the damming or impoundment of streams.

Since the Second World War, southwestern Ontario watersheds, including those of the Grand and Thames rivers, have been altered by the construction of dams and impoundments under the direction of regional conservation authorities. Although there is insufficient evidence to establish what the original population and distribution of the black redhorse may have been in Canada, it seems reasonable to theorize that flood control and water conservation measures, by eliminating suitable habitat, may inadvertently have led to a decline in the species. At the time of writing, two new dam sites are proposed in the Grand River system: one at West Montrose; the other north of the town of Ayr. While neither is slated for immediate development, each could, if carried out, have a negative effect on a known black redhorse spawning bed.

Apart from the potential for habitat loss or the damage implicit in such projects, there are other factors that may seriously limit the black redhorse's long-term prospects for survival. Among natural predators occurring in its native waters, the northern pike is believed to prey indiscriminately upon most species of suckers. In addition, other, more common, related species, such as the white sucker, golden redhorse, and shorthead redhorse, occur in the same waters in greater numbers and may offer serious competition for food resources. Furthermore, the upper reaches of the Grand River come under pressure from an active recreational fishery, especially by archers hunting for carp. Few bow fishermen, or other anglers, bother to distinguish between carp — their real quarry — and suckers (including the black redhorse), which are frequently killed and left on the bank to rot.

At present there are no specific protective measures in place for the black redhorse in Canada. The suggestion has been made that a portion of the Nith River system be set aside as a natural history preserve to protect at least one breeding subpopulation. Stricter controls and an aggressive educational effort could lessen the depredations of sport fishermen. In addition, it has been proposed that any dam construction in the Thames or Grand watersheds be undertaken carefully, with a view to avoiding or minimizing negative effects on breeding habitat frequented by the species.

Copper Redhorse
(*Moxostoma hubbsi*)

Suckers and redhorses belong to a large, widespread, and surprisingly little-known family of bottom-feeding, fresh-water fishes. Within this group, the redhorses are typically medium-sized fish with a thick-lipped, sucking mouth set on the underside of the snout. They differ from suckers. Although the genus forms the basis of a modest fishery in areas of abundance, fishermen have ordinarily lumped its various members together for market purposes as suckers or mullet, with no distinction being drawn between species.

Copper Redhorse

Some redhorses are distributed widely throughout eastern and central North America. A few, however, occupy extremely limited ranges, and since habitat suited to their requirements within these areas has been threatened, these species have become quite suddenly vulnerable. The copper redhorse, first officially recognized as a species in 1942, is one of them.

In all the world, the copper redhorse occurs only in a few waterways of southwestern Québec — most notably in the Richelieu and des Milles Isles rivers, and those portions of the St. Lawrence/Ottawa system immediately to the east and west of Montréal. Even in these waters it is rare, with fewer than 250 specimens having been officially reported between 1942 and 1985. Archaeological evidence from sites of native and early European settlements, however, suggests that the fish was more common prior to this century than it is today.

The copper redhorse is a large, heavy-bodied representative of its genus, attaining maximum lengths of up to 700 millimetres and weighing more than 5 kilograms. Its name is derived from its colour, which ranges from coppery gold or olive on the back, to pale off-white on the belly, with copper or dusky fins. It feeds largely on molluscs, which it crushes with an unusual set of teeth located back of the gills in the pharynx, or throat.

Within its limited range, the copper redhorse prefers deep, open waters (4–7 metres) where hard clay or gravel bottoms are swept by moderate currents. Spawning takes place in shallower rapids within these stretches of river. As a rule, the species avoids slow-moving shallows clogged

with heavy vegetation, or areas where the water is turbid or polluted. Its intolerance for these conditions offers a clue to why it has declined in this century to the point where its survival is in serious jeopardy.

The range of the copper redhorse lies within the most densely populated region in the province of Québec. During the past century, human efforts have transformed this area from a vast, wooded lowland watered by a network of clear streams, into a spreading agricultural plain dotted with industrial cities and towns. In the process, increased runoff and soil erosion have muddied the waters and induced greater seasonal fluctuations in flow. Siltation has encouraged the growth of extensive weed beds, reducing open channels and eliminating some spawning grounds. Domestic, industrial, and agricultural pollution has diminished water quality in most of the region's rivers, and acid rain poses a direct threat to the molluscs on which the copper redhorse depends for most of its food.

Since there is little prospect that the land-use patterns that have occasioned these radical changes in habitat in the St. Lawrence lowland will be reversed, it seems likely that industrial and urban expansion will continue to expose the copper redhorse to a very real threat of extinction. In view of that gloomy prognosis, some might be inclined to question why any effort should be expended on its behalf. The answers touch the essence of the whole issue of endangered species.

First, by its definition as a species, the copper redhorse is acknowledged to be unique—the only living means of perpetuating the particular genetic code that makes it what it is. The permanent loss, through human-induced extinction, of even the most obscure and insignificant species impoverishes the biological diversity of the whole earth.

Second, the pharyngeal teeth of the copper redhorse, which presumably enable it to crush the shells of its prey in the act of swallowing them, are a curious example of evolutionary specialization. The study of such oddities can sometimes hold the key to new insights into processes of natural adaptation, selection, and development. When a species disappears, one

more opportunity for gaining scientific knowledge vanishes with it.

Third, species as vulnerable as the copper redhorse, and as closely tied to specific habitats, can serve as indicators of the overall health of the ecosystems in which they live. Their long-term survival symbolizes contemporary society's determination to restore balance to a damaged environment. Conversely, should they die out, their extinction stands as eloquently for society's failure to ensure the triumph of good environmental management over short-sighted greed.

On a broad scale, efforts are being made to minimize and reverse the negative impact of industrial and urban development on sensitive habitats such as the river systems of southwestern Québec. Water quality is being monitored, erosion control and waste management programs are being promoted, and attempts are being made to stop acid rain. But it takes time to overcome the inertia of old attitudes and to achieve tangible progress in ecosystem recovery. As an interim solution, some have suggested that a suitable stretch of pollution-free water be established as a nature reserve, perhaps along the Richelieu River where a viable breeding population of the copper redhorse may still exist. In such a refuge, stocks might be maintained until improved conditions will allow this threatened fish to re-occupy its historic range.

Great Lakes Deepwater Sculpin
(Myoxocephalus thompsoni)

Relatively few people ever see a deepwater sculpin. It is a small fish, averaging only about 70 millimetres in length. Its mottled gray-brown colour, flattened head, and spiny body make it inconspicuous against lake-bottom backgrounds, and no doubt contributed to the invention of the most whimsical of its common names, the deepwater blob. True to its name, it displays a marked preference for the depths — as deep as 365 metres in the case of a specimen taken by trawl in Lake Superior — of the Great Lakes and a scattering of other lakes across central and northern Canada.

Despite its homely appearance and reclusive ways, the deepwater sculpin poses intriguing questions for Canadian zoogeographers. Except that it lives in fresh water, it is indistinguishable from a marine sculpin, *Myoxocephalus quadricornis,* which inhabits cold, salt or brackish waters of the northern hemisphere. In the past many authorities have maintained, in fact, that the two species were identical. The last ice age is probably responsible for this scattered presence in fresh-water lakes of a species with such seemingly close ties to the marine environment. The most widely accepted theory argues that as the glaciers pushed southward, certain arctic marine species, including the deepwater sculpin, were carried along in a body of salt water that flooded across low-lying land in front of the advancing ice. Later, as the glaciers receded, postglacial lakes were formed, the original salinity of their water being steadily diluted by the melting ice.

The most adaptable of the marine species that had been landlocked by this process were able to convert gradually to fresh water.

Today, the deepwater sculpin is found from southwestern Québec, through the Great Lakes, across northwestern Ontario, Manitoba, and northern Saskatchewan, to Great Bear and Great Slave lakes in the Northwest Territories. In most of this range, it appears to be relatively common. In fact, its status as a threatened species applies, for the moment, only to the population in the Great Lakes watershed, because it appears to have been extirpated from Lake Ontario, and perhaps from Lake Erie.

Various explanations have been suggested for this sculpin's disappearance from two large lakes where it was once a common and successful member of the deepwater community. One proposition is that exposure to DDT or other pesticides or contaminants may have been sufficient to eliminate the species from the most severely polluted of the Great Lakes. Others suggest that predation or competition from native or introduced species may have played a part in the deepwater sculpin's decline. On the other hand, the lake trout and the burbot are the only native, predatory fishes known to feed regularly on deepwater sculpin, and there is no indication so far that sculpins in other lakes have suffered from their depredations. In fact, there is evidence that the species has made a comeback in Lake Michigan in recent years, after a marked decline during the 1960s. Continued research may reveal reasons for this fluctuation in numbers, and whether a similar recovery may be anticipated in the lakes from which it has disappeared.

Great Lakes Deepwater Sculpin

Left: Great Lakes Deepwater Sculpin – Threatened

Lake Simcoe Whitefish

(Coregonus clupeaformis)

For many an angler who grew up in south-central Ontario, the Lake Simcoe whitefish was a favourite quarry. Some might troll for lake trout or wait eagerly for the April spawning of the yellow perch. But for sheer popularity, the whitefish was the most sought-after species in Lake Simcoe, especially in winter, when it was the target of as many as 80 percent of the anglers whose fishing huts spread in impromptu settlements on the frozen lake, virtually from freeze-up to spring thaw.

The fish they were after has a sleek, silvery body with a dark back, averages about 380–500 millimetres in length, and ordinarily weighs 0.5 –2.0 kilograms, although a record 42-pound (19-kilograms) specimen was caught in Lake Superior about 1918. It is highly regarded for the table, having palatable flesh and a low incidence of infestation by parasites.

The lake whitefish is the most widespread member of the genus *Coregonus* in Canada, inhabiting large lakes and rivers from New Brunswick westward through the Great Lakes to interior British Columbia, the Northwest Territories, and the Yukon. Within this range, an isolated population is found in Lake Simcoe, a large inland lake located between Georgian Bay and Lake Ontario. While the lake whitefish is not endangered on a nation-wide basis, this isolated

population has declined alarmingly since the 1960s, and in 1987 was judged by COSEWIC to merit classification as Threatened.

The Lake Simcoe whitefish has been separated from other populations of the species for the past 7,000 to 10,000 years by geographic barriers. Although the Trent Canal system was constructed during the nineteenth century as a navigational link between lakes Simcoe and Ontario, its many locks effectively preserved that isolation. Lake Simcoe, with a pH reading of 8.3, provides an alkaline, fresh-water environment that is unique in Canada. In consequence, the Lake Simcoe whitefish stock has developed genetic characteristics distinctly different from those of other, nearby populations. Any indication of a threat to its continued health and vitality would therefore be cause for concern.

Just such an indication appeared in the late 1970s when a study revealed that the Lake Simcoe population of the whitefish had fallen to an estimated 250,000 fish — a decline of 40 percent since 1972, and 83 percent since 1963–65. As an immediate response, seasonal restrictions and a possession limit of two Lake Simcoe whitefish per angler per day were introduced by the province of Ontario in 1977, the first time that such protection had ever been deemed necessary for this population. Another disturbing observation accompanied the reduction in population; the size of whitefish being taken was found to be increasing to such an extent that the mean weight of fish taken from 1977 to 1983 was close to 1.5 kilograms, compared with only half a kilogram in 1966–67. The increase in mean size was a sign that very few young fish were being recruited into the population, and that the age structure of the population was shifting toward older, larger individuals. If such a trend were to continue, population collapse and imminent extinction might be anticipated.

In response, the Ontario Ministry of Natural Resources began an experimental program of hatchery rearing and restocking, with a view to maintaining the population until natural reproduction could be restored. Since 1982, eggs have been collected and fertilized, using Lake Simcoe whitefish parent stock captured each year during the November spawning run.

Conservation efforts on behalf of a species or population can only hope to succeed if the reasons for its decline are understood and are susceptible to correction. In the case of the Lake Simcoe whitefish, unlike that of the extinct and threatened ciscoes of the Great Lakes, excessive fishing does not appear to have been a critical factor. Rather, habitat deterioration and predation by the rainbow smelt seem to have been the primary negative influences.

The habitat of the whitefish has undergone changes that reflect the transformation of the Lake Simcoe shoreline and watershed by deforestation, agriculture, and urban development. Each of these human activities has contributed to erosion, which in turn has led to some siltation of the near-shore gravel shoals used by the whitefish for spawning. Associated with this trend is an increase in the level of dissolved nutrients in the water, a result of municipal sewage disposal and the runoff of agricultural fertilizers. Taken together, these factors may encourage algal blooms and an accumulation of vegetable matter, the decay of which could reduce the availability of oxygen to developing whitefish. Studies seem to support the hypothesis that both siltation and low oxygen levels, possibly in combination with chemical contaminants, have significantly diminished the quality of the Lake Simcoe gravel shoals as whitefish spawning habitat. This in turn could seriously jeopardize the chances for survival of whitefish eggs and young.

Lake Simcoe Whitefish

A second possible factor in the decline of the whitefish is the addition of the rainbow smelt to the faunal community of Lake Simcoe. How smelt got there is unknown, but it is suspected that they were introduced by man, perhaps as live bait released by anglers. Smelts had never been taken in the lake prior to 1961, but their numbers have expanded rapidly since then. Over 1,000 were taken by ice-fishing in 1966, and this harvest rose to a peak of 234,865 in the winter of 1973. Although a direct link between the increase of smelt and the nearly simultaneous decline of the Lake Simcoe whitefish has not been established, evidence from other lakes indicates that the rainbow smelt does prey on the larvae of lake whitefish and other *Coregonus* species.

Since the threat to the Lake Simcoe whitefish was recognized in the mid-1970s, several management counter-measures have been taken by the Ontario government, in addition to the season and possession limits, and the hatchery program already mentioned. Water quality controls on domestic sewage discharge have been implemented, and efforts made to minimize nutrient inputs from farming. Yearling whitefish derived from Lake Simcoe parent stock have shown good rates of survival and growth when planted in the lake. By 1985 it was recommended that the stocking rate be increased to 100,000 per year. This interim measure would maintain the genetic stock of the Lake Simcoe whitefish at a minimum population level while further efforts were being made to re-establish a self-sustaining breeding population.

Margined Madtom
(*Noturus insignis*)

The madtoms are the smallest members of the catfish family in Canada, seldom reaching much more than 10 centimetres in length. As a group they tend to be secretive, nocturnal bottom-dwellers, favouring relatively warm fresh-water lakes and streams. The common name, madtom (and its French counterpart *chat-fou,* or mad cat), is thought to be derived from their prominent barbels, or whiskers, and their frenzied attempts to escape when disturbed.

Margined Madtom

Within this little-known group of fishes, one species, the margined madtom, named for the dark band along the margins of its fins, is harder to find in Canadian waters than its fellows. Although not uncommon in the northeastern United States, this little fish had never been taken in Canada until August 1971, when four specimens were collected in a stream linking Lac à la L'Outre and Lac la Pêche in Gatineau Park, some 45 kilometres northeast of Ottawa.

The find was considered significant, if only because its location lay about 200 kilometres north of the previously recognized range limit of the species, which was thought to be in New York State. In subsequent years, several more were caught along the same stream, and then, in May of 1976, a margined madtom was collected from the Fall River in Lanark County, Ontario, 85 kilometres southwest of Ottawa. The presence of specimens from two quite separate locations in the Ottawa River watershed prompted an obvious question: How did they get there?

There were two possibilities. One is that the margined madtom was introduced to the area. Madtoms of various species are popular bait fish in some parts of the United States, although their use for this purpose is not legal in either Ontario or Québec. It is easy to imagine that American anglers might have brought supplies of the little catfish on fishing excursions to Canada, and unthinkingly released them in habitats where they managed to survive as marginal populations.

Right: Margined Madtom – Threatened

A second possibility is that the isolated Canadian populations of the margined madtom are relics of a time, some 8,000 to 10,000 years ago, when the waters of interconnecting postglacial lakes provided a route by which southerly species of fish might have spread into northern areas. Small breeding populations that successfully established themselves during this period would have become isolated as the water level fell, but could have survived to the present day in favourable locations. The margined madtom must have clean, swift water, flowing over a stream bed of rubble, boulders, or coarse gravel. Documentation of the species' requirements in the United States indicates that it will not tolerate even slight changes from these conditions.

No margined madtom specimens have been taken in Canada since 1982. While the reason for this is uncertain, a report filed in 1986 states that an increase in the number of beaver dams along the stream in Gatineau Park was resulting in slower water flow and a build-up of silt over the pebble bottom. Such changes could be sufficient to render that area unsuitable as habitat for the margined madtom.

There is also a possibility that scientific interest contributed to the depletion of the species. If the two known populations in Canada were truly isolated and very limited in size, then the collection of about 50 specimens could conceivably have reduced the number of breeding adults in those areas to a point below the critical level necessary to maintain a viable population.

In April 1989, COSEWIC designated the margined madtom as a threatened species. This reflects the possibility that it no longer exists in the Canadian waters where it was discovered, while acknowledging that with limited resources for field research, other populations of such a rare and economically insignificant fish might go undiscovered in other, similar locations.

Cucumber Tree
(Magnolia acuminata)

The cucumber tree, a member of the magnolia family, reaches the northern limits of its natural range in extreme southern Ontario, its presence contributing to the Carolinian aspects of the region. It is locally common in mountain valleys of the Carolinas and Tennessee and has a more or less continuous range northward into Canada. Like its close cousin, the tulip tree, also native to southern Ontario, the cucumber tree can attain great heights — well over 30 metres on good sites. Sharing similar large yellowish flowers, a common habitat, and tree form, the two species can be easily confused. The shape of the leaves

and the structure of the fruit, however, separate them easily.

Prior to the clearing of extensive areas of natural forested ecosystem for agriculture, the cucumber tree was locally abundant near the city of St. Catharines, and also in the Haldimand/Norfolk area at and just north of Long Point. The tree is now so rare, however, that it has been placed on Canada's endangered species list.

Today, only three woodlots remain where small, viable populations of seedlings or trees are found. There are six additional known sites where this species occurs, but each contains only one or a few nonreproducing trees. Some isolated trees do set seed, suggesting that the protection of even nonreproducing trees is important.

A surviving individual has been reported from the National Wildlife Area at Long Point, where intense and sustained deer browsing is having a devastating effect upon natural communities.

Although existing provincial legislation is less than fully effective in protecting trees on private woodlots, the immediate threats to this species have been lessened by cooperation with the Ontario Ministry of Natural Resources and the Carolinian Canada Landowner Stewardship Program.

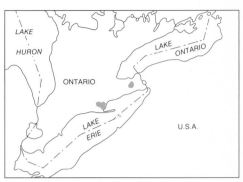

Cucumber Tree

Left: Cucumber Tree – Endangered

Cucumber Tree

Eastern Prickly Pear Cactus
(Opuntia humifusa)

Cacti are practically synonymous with desert. It is surprising to learn, therefore, that four species of these peculiar, fleshy, spiny desert plants are actually native to parts of southern Canada.

Like almost all cactus species, those in Canada grow in open, dry sites such as prairies, dunes, exposed rocky ridges, or semi-open dry woodlands in rocky or sandy soil. Here, drainage is excellent and the plants are exposed to plenty of sunshine and hot soil temperatures during the summer.

Probably the rarest of Canadian cacti is the eastern prickly pear — so named because it is

native to eastern North America and because its fruit is large, succulent, and pear-like in shape. In Canada, colonies are found at only four natural sites in extreme southwestern Ontario. One is on Pelee Island, while the largest and most secure colonies are found in the sandy soils of Point Pelee National Park, where they benefit from the protection afforded by the park.

The park population was initially recorded in 1882 during the first known visit of a botanist to the point. At present, at least 13 sites are confirmed in the park. One of these — the "cactus field" — is well known to visitors, and contains many spreading colonies carefully managed and monitored by park staff. It is said that some years ago a park warden, fearing the loss of this species in the park, quietly spent

Eastern Prickly Pear Cactus

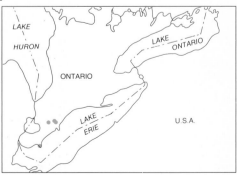

some time establishing new colonies in appropriate habitat within the park.

Spectacularly photogenic, its bright yellow flowers emerge early in midsummer. The fruits are at first green, but turn red, soft, and sweet in the fall, often persisting into the winter or spring. Each fruit contains several dozen seeds, but most reproduction is thought to be by vegetative means. Pads placed on damp ground will readily develop roots. Nevertheless, bees and beetles frequently visit the flowers, and cross-pollination appears to be essential for seed development.

The fruits are a favourite food of rabbits, but chipmunks, squirrels, and birds are also thought to eat them from time to time. The stone-like seeds remain intact after being eaten and pass through the digestive tracts of animals. This may be the primary means of spreading the plants to new sites.

The greatest threat to the survival of the two known Canadian populations of the eastern prickly pear comes from people who think nothing of removing plants from the wild to transplant into home gardens. The plant's ecological requirements pose another major problem for the survival of natural populations. Like most other cacti, this species is not tolerant of shade. The Canadian sites where the plant is found today are sunny and open. But in many of these areas, natural forest succession will likely result in the shading out of colonies — with the inevitable local extirpation of the species. This predictable long-term fate for the eastern prickly pear is particularly evident at Point Pelee, where tree seedlings are emerging in open sites, or where natural succession in old fields is seeing the re-establishment of natural overhead canopies of Carolinian forest.

At Point Pelee today, park managers have made the decision to retain a small area of suitable habitat for the prickly pear. Tree seedlings are removed by hand, and fire may be used in future to maintain the required open habitat.

The preservation of the eastern prickly pear cactus requires that suitable habitat for it be maintained in parts of Point Pelee National Park, and that people stop digging up the tiny Pelee Island colony. Its preservation should be seen as an attempt to retain as many examples as possible of the world's diminishing diversity.

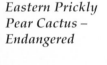

Eastern Prickly Pear Cactus – Endangered

Heart-leaved Plantain
(Plantago cordata)

Mention the word plantain to a gardener or farmer and the mind conjures up images of low, round-leaved weeds of roadsides, yards, lawns, gardens, pastures, and fields. The sight of a plantain among the carrots or broccoli is a warning to the conscientious gardener that unless removed, the next season will see it multiplied a hundredfold. The reputation of the weedy plantains to thrive in disturbed places is deserving of special admiration. It comes as a surprise, therefore, to learn that in Canada one plantain species, the heart-leaved, is endangered, and that its behaviour is the very opposite to that of its weedy cousin. This unique species is an aquatic and lacks even the slightest semblance of

considered to be endangered in many states. Historical records show it to have been present in four other Ontario sites where it is no longer found. The only known remaining Canadian colony was recently rediscovered along a creek in the Ipperwash Military Reserve, where there are some 300 plants in an area not immediately threatened. Considered by local Indian people to have medicinal properties, knowledge of the Ipperwash colony had in fact been retained by members of the Potawatomi Indian community at Kettle Point.

The heart-leaved plantain requires edges of cool, shaded streams that run through natural canopied climax hardwood forests. At Ipperwash, it grows under species such as sugar maple, red maple, beech, basswood, and bur oak.

Heart-leaved Plantain

Heart-leaved Plantain – Endangered

weediness — so much so that when the sites where it grows are disturbed, it has difficulty maintaining a foothold. Its very large heart-shaped leaves and its height — up to half a metre — readily distinguish it from any of the weedy plantains.

The heart-leaved plantain is a native of the eastern United States and southwestern Ontario, but nowhere is it abundant. Its few populations are separated by hundreds of kilometres and it is

Obviously, the Ipperwash colony is valuable genetically, for not only is it the last known in Canada, it is also the northernmost colony in North America. The plants could readily provide a source of seed for the re-establishment of wild colonies in known former sites in Ontario. The rehabilitation of natural colonies of endangered species such as this could be achieved by making agreements with landowners, and by following a program of environmental restoration.

Hoary Mountain Mint
(Pycnanthemum incanum)

Hoary Mountain Mint

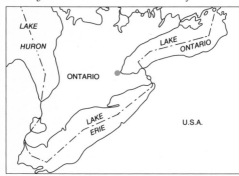

The only Canadian colony of the hoary mountain mint is found near the rim of the warm, south-facing slopes overlooking Burlington Bay at the western end of Lake Ontario. A species whose main natural range is in the eastern United States, only 41 stems of this relict population remain at the site, according to a recent survey, and COSEWIC has declared it to be endangered.

A relative of well-known herbs such as catnip, sage, and the common garden mint, this species too has a distinct, fragrant scent.

As the remaining plants grow on private land, the most immediate threat to their survival is complete habitat destruction. As well, several species of introduced shrubs are spreading in the area and may adversely affect the plant's habitat. Most of the nearby areas where plants might have grown in the past have already been converted to various human activities.

Large Whorled and Small Whorled Pogonias
(Isotria verticillata and medeoloides)

Large Whorled Pogonia

Among the rarest of Canadian orchids are two closely related species — the large and small whorled pogonias — so called because all their leaves are arranged in a single whorl near the top of the stem. When not in flower, both can be easily confused with Indian cucumber-root, a common species that grows in much the same kind of wooded habitat. As with many other rare Canadian species, these two orchids are found in the warm Carolinian zone of extreme southern Ontario.

The small whorled pogonia is so rare that in all of its native range in eastern North America, only some 30 tiny colonies exist today, with the total estimated number of plants at around 1,500. Canada's only colony was recently found in a wood-lot in Elgin County, and even this has not reappeared in recent years. Botanists speculate that this pogonia might lie dormant for years and reappear from time to time, but in fact little is known about its growth behaviour.

As for the large whorled pogonia, only three colonies are known in southern Ontario today. The main portion of its range is from Florida to New England and Michigan, where it can sometimes be very abundant locally. Once established, colonies have the capacity to spread by underground rhizomes.

Both species also reproduce sexually. Flowers of the small whorled pogonia are yellowish green and are known to be automatically self-pollinated. Those of the large have purplish sepals with a white to yellowish-green lip and are cross-pollinated by solitary bees. Neither species has nectar guides or nectar. In the United States, where the two grow close together, it has been found that flowering in the small occurs one to two weeks earlier than in the large.

Both these species are now protected under Ontario's Endangered Species Act.

Left: Small Whorled Pogonia – Endangered

Spotted Wintergreen
(*Chimaphila maculata*)

The spotted wintergreen, a member of the heather blueberry family, is another endangered Carolinian species of southwestern Ontario. Widely distributed in the eastern United States, it is also found in the mountains of Mexico south to Guatemala. Only three small colonies containing

about 5, 15, and 40 stems respectively are known in Ontario: two are in the Haldimand/Norfold region within the St. Williams Provincial Nursery and are located about a kilometre apart. The third is to the north in Wasaga Beach Provincial Park, along the southern shores of Georgian Bay.

This low evergreen herb with its woody rhizomes and dark green shiny leaves with white veins thrives in dry to moist, sandy, oak-pine woods. Flowers are showy white or pinkish. The anthers produce heavy sticky pollen that matures well before the stigma of the same flower is ready to receive pollen. The difference in maturation time of the sex organs of the flower, and the presence of pollen that is so adapted to carrying by insects, indicate that the flowers are cross-pollinated.

Plants of each colony spread vegetatively and may indeed represent only a single individual. Some stems do flower and capsules are set, but it is not known whether seed is produced. It is likely that once a new colony is established, spread is mainly by underground rhizomes.

The colourful folk name *sipsisewa* was applied to this species by some Indian tribes, neatly distinguishing it from the closely related and widespread Canadian species called *pipsisewa*.

The principal threat to all colonies is that of habitat modification or destruction. The low number of stems in the three known colonies also places the populations at serious risk of extirpation.

Spotted Wintergreen – Endangered

American Chestnut

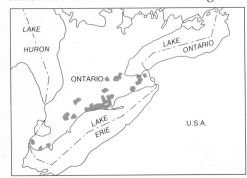

American Chestnut

American Chestnut –
Threatened

American Chestnut
(*Castanea dentata*)

The loss of great stands of the American chestnut from the forests of eastern North America to a fungal disease early in this century was one of the most tragic events affecting the integrity of woodland ecosystems in this part of the continent. The chestnut was an important tree in many parts of the deciduous upland forests, providing a consistent and abundant supply of nuts that sustained many animal species and some birds.

Although now a threatened species, the chestnut is still found throughout most of its former range, but larger individuals are scattered and the blight continues to kill young trees growing from seed or sprouting from old stumps and roots. A new ray of hope has recently arisen from the appearance of less deadly strains of the blight. Some Ontario trees that are infected with it have survived and bear fruit.

Parts of southern Ontario once offered excellent habitat for the chestnut, and even today, large remnant stumps can be seen near Aylmer in the Backus Woods, now protected as a nature sanctuary. There are 49 known sites in Ontario where at least one individual with a minimum of 10 centimetres diameter at breast height is found in woodlands where its ancestors flourished. One stand contains several hundred saplings and stump sprouts that have some resistance to the disease. Here, root sprouts often attain a size of 10–15 centimetres diameter at breast height before blight cankers appear. A dozen or so populations contain trees over 40 centimetres in diameter, and in such places, cross pollination is successful and some seedlings are almost invariably present.

Like so many other tree species of southern Ontario, the chestnut is monoecious, meaning that both male and female catkins occur on the same tree. For seed to set, however, cross pollination must occur, and several larger trees need to be present in a colony before spread by seeds is possible. Seeds are actively dispersed by squirrels and birds.

Present and future threats to the chestnut come from continued habitat destruction — mainly the clearing of woodlots. Some of the private woodlots where chestnut is found are managed under agreements with the Ministry of Natural Resources, and care is taken to protect chestnut trees during cutting operations. Given sufficient time, it is possible that resistant strains of the tree will arise. It is essential, therefore, to preserve the genetic diversity of this majestic species, and this means that every population, however small, is important and should be preserved. Even isolated or blighted trees contain diverse genetic material important for the long-term survival of this species.

American Water-willow
(Justicia americana)

The American water-willow is the northernmost member of the large, tropical acanthus family, which includes many favourite ornamental and greenhouse plants. It is an aquatic herb, growing in saturated gravels, sands, or organic matter along streams, and is completely at home in water 15–50 centimetres deep. Its stout stems can grow 20–100 centimetres high, and produce white or violet flowers, which form elongated tubes with two lips.

Widespread in the eastern United States, it has been recorded historically in 10 Ontario localities along lakes Erie and Ontario, and at 15 places along the St. Lawrence River in Québec. The northernmost colony was at Grosse-Isle, north of Montréal. Most Ontario colonies have not been seen in years, while only 11 were recorded in Québec in 1983, the last time a count was taken.

Water-willows can reproduce vegetatively, by means of rhizomes and runners, or sexually via seed production. Seeds can be carried on the surface of the water to new sites where suitable conditions exist. It is often the first plant to colonize gravel bars and is important in stabilizing banks, enabling other species to grow.

The plant has been designated as Threatened because of the relatively few colonies known historically, and because of the generally sensitive nature of shoreline habitat. Except for those in Point Pelee National Park, all American water-willow colonies grow on private land where, along with so many other plants, they are vulnerable to the threats of land development.

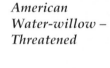

American Water-willow

American Water-willow – Threatened

Blue Ash
(Fraxinus quadrangulata)

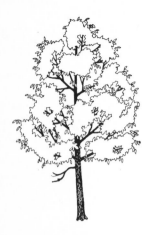

Blue Ash

*Right: Blue Ash –
Threatened*

Blue ash is so named because a blue dye can be extracted from its inner bark. This threatened species is most easily distinguished from other ashes by its square young stems, of which the corners may be strongly winged. Hence, it is sometimes called four-angled ash.

Reaching its northern limits in extreme southern Ontario, it is an important element of the Carolinian forest ecosystem. Its main range is the central United States, but nowhere has it even been common. In Canada it is restricted to dry ridges and shoreline areas of the Erie Islands, Point Pelee, and to three river and creek floodplains. Less than 20 populations are known to exist in what remains of natural sites in the region. At some of these there is excellent reproduction, while at others, only older trees are present. A key to spreading and reproduction in this species is the presence of open sunny areas, since young plants cannot tolerate heavy shading.

Two populations are fairly secure. One lies within Point Pelee National Park and the other is at Lighthouse Point Nature Reserve on Pelee Island, owned by the province.

Threats to the survival of the blue ash are varied. Some populations are threatened by stone quarrying, others by road widening, forest clearing, or as a result of forest management agreements that do not recognize the need to maintain viable populations of rare species on private land. Some conservation authorities and Ministry of Natural Resources foresters are now aware of this need, providing one small sign of hope for the survival of this Carolinian species.

Bluehearts
(Buchnera americana)

Bluehearts

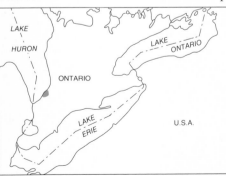

Although bluehearts is related to 100 tropical and subtropical species, it alone, within its genus, managed to develop the necessary adaptations to survive in a cold northern climate. With their unique genetic makeup and their ability to evolve readily into new varieties and species and radiate into new niches in a temperate or even arctic climate, species like bluehearts are extremely valuable to the future biological diversity of natural ecosystems.

Bluehearts is a rare and declining species throughout much of its range, which extends from Oklahoma eastward to the Carolinas. Populations south of this area are of uncertain status, while the northern states harbour only a few scattered colonies. The Canadian populations occur along a 12.5-kilometre stretch of sandy Lake Huron shoreline from Pinery Provincial Park to Ipperwash, Ontario, where approximately 2,200 plants were counted in 1981. There can be no question of the genetic uniqueness of the Canadian plants; the next population to the south is 800 kilometres away at the south tip of Lake Michigan, while the main range of the species is some 1,300 kilometres away.

A lovely perennial wildflower with a spike of deep purple flowers, its habitat in Ontario is limited to moist, sandy soil in prairie openings, and wet interdunal depressions. The littoral meadows on both private and federal lands near Port Franks support the largest colonies.

Because the interdunal shoreline ecosystem

Bluehearts –
Threatened

that bluehearts requires for survival is fragile and sensitive to disturbance, the future of this species in Ontario is coming into greater jeopardy with each passing year. Recreational activi-

ties are bound to place increasing pressure upon these fragile habitats, and bluehearts will survive in Canada only if more people learn how to care for the integrity of natural ecosystems.

Colicroot
(*Aletris farinosa*)

Colicroot is a showy perennial of the lily family, distinguished by a flat, yellowish-green, basal rosette of narrow, blade-shaped leaves, from the centre of which rises a stalk, some 30–100 centimetres in height, bearing a spike of white tubular flowers.

The plant derives its common, English name from the herbal lore of pioneer days when a bitter tonic, made by pounding the roots and mixing them with water or alcohol, was a remedy for

colic. This and other medicinal applications have little practical value now, for one simple if unfortunate reason. Nowhere common, colicroot has become so rare in Canada that it must be protected from exploitation.

A native of the Carolinian zone of southwestern Ontario, colicroot is currently known to persist at only 17 sites near the shores of Lake St. Clair, the Detroit River, and Lake Erie. Its extirpation from 15 other known locations in this area, as well as continued threats from agricultural and residential development, and unrestricted

Colicroot

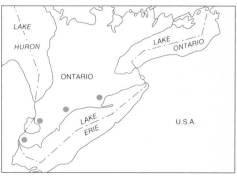

trail-bike traffic, all support its designation by COSEWIC as a threatened species.

The region where it grows in Canada is characterized by hot summer and mild winter temperatures, and a long frost-free period, conditions which favour the survival of flora that are usually associated with a more southerly ecosystem. The colicroot prefers moist, coarse-textured sand or sandy loam with neutral to somewhat acid pH conditions. Intolerant of shade, it has some tendency to colonize areas where the soil has recently been disturbed. Otherwise, it is found in remnants of tallgrass prairie, old fields, and deciduous woodland edges.

The most encouraging aspect of colicroot's present status is that several previously unknown colonies have been discovered in recent years. This fact offers grounds for a cautious optimism that additional populations may yet be found.

Right: Colicroot –
Threatened

Kentucky Coffee Tree
(*Gymnocladus dioica*)

Kentucky Coffee Tree

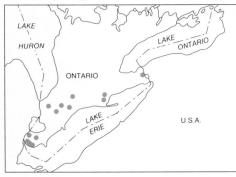

Most people are familiar with herbaceous legumes — beans, peas, wild clover, vetches, and lupines. But the legume family also includes some very large trees, especially in the tropics. One of these, the Kentucky coffee tree, now a threatened species, is native to the Carolinian zone of extreme southern Ontario. Because of extensive destruction of the Carolinian forests for agicultural purposes, in its wild state it is now among the rarest of all Canadian trees. However, it has been extensively planted as an ornamental.

Seldom abundant, it has a rather peculiar distribution centred in the American Midwest. Rich, moist woods and edges of floodplains are its usual habitat, although it sometimes occurs on dry ridges.

The Kentucky coffee tree is so named because, according to early accounts, its dried beans made a brew similar in taste to coffee. It has gracious, widely spaced branches and immense leaves with leaflets arranged in feather-fashion. Its greenish-white flowers are very fragrant, and the

Right: Kentucky
Coffee Tree –
Threatened

fruit, a large brownish pod, often hangs on the tree all winter.

In Canada today, only about 25 stands remain in the wild. These range in size from 1 to about 200 individuals. They survive along roadsides, ditches, fence lines, and railroad rights-of-way, although less than half occur in natural woodlands where their future is more secure.

Kentucky coffee trees are either male or female, and they can spread clonally by underground suckers. Once a seedling becomes established, an entire stand can develop from it and be of only one sex. Unless trees of the opposite sex are located nearby, female trees will not set seeds. Indeed, only three of the wild populations (Canard River, Dover Township in Kent County, and East Sister Island on Lake Erie) are known to bear seed; the others are maintained clonally. The Canard River population is of more than usual interest because three small stands are present some distance downstream, suggesting that natural regeneration can take place by seed disseminated by flowing water.

Another trait of the Kentucky coffee tree is the intolerance of its seedlings to shade. Young shoots can survive only in places where the overhead canopy does not shade out the ground, and this may be one of the reasons why it grows in floodplain sites.

The main threat to the survival of natural populations of this beautiful tree is destruction of its habitat for agriculture — drainage, channelization, and outright removal of the natural ecosystem on which this species depends for life. Forest manipulation through selective cutting could also be a threat. It is worth noting, however, that this species has never been particularly abundant, and existing populations are very persistent, suggesting that with awareness and care, most may survive and perhaps even expand in the future.

Kentucky Coffee Tree

Nodding Pogonia
(*Triphora trianthophora*)

This rare and beautiful orchid, a native of mature deciduous woodlots, occupies an extensive territory from southern Maine to the Gulf of Mexico. In Canada, however, it is known in only two locations, in the counties of Essex and Kent deep in the Carolinian belt of extreme southwestern Ontario. It appears that even here the species is at the northern edge of its range, for while earlier records refer to its having been found at another Ontario site, there is no convincing evidence of its ever having been widespread in the province.

The generic name, *Triphora* (which means "bearing three"), refers to the fact that the plant usually bears three flowers, although the number may vary from one to seven. A common name is the three birds orchid, and indeed, the flowers are reminiscent of birds, with graceful sepals spread like wings on either side of the delicate pink petals.

The nodding pogonia is not an easy plant to find, even in locations where it does grow. Its stems and leaves rise from an underground tuber in deep leaf litter which often obscures them from view. Furthermore, each flower blooms for only a few hours before withering; to find the plant requires good luck as well as a good knowledge of where to look.

Of the two known Canadian locations, one is in a privately owned woodlot in the general vicinity of Point Pelee National Park, while the other is in Rondeau Provincial Park. The first station was discovered in 1950. In 1956, officials became concerned that it might be wiped out by grazing livestock. Consequently, several clumps of the plant were transplanted elsewhere in the park in the hope that they would establish themselves in these new locations. Strangely, although the transplanted clumps apparently died out after a few years, a large new site was discovered in 1966, about one kilometre away. Since then, other sites have also been found in the park, and in 1986 the total number of flowering nodding pogonia plants within its boundaries was estimated at about 1,500.

Accurate population figures are difficult to determine because of the plant's erratic flowering habits. One year it blooms prolifically; for the next several years it may diminish, or disappear entirely, only to reappear in profuse bloom the year following. At the largest Rondeau station, for example, the population has fluctuated from a high of nearly 1,350 to a low of just over 100 visible plants. One reason for this is that the plant's tuber derives nourishment from its association with an underground fungus and therefore, like many other orchids, is less dependent than most flowering plants on food produced in

Nodding Pogonia

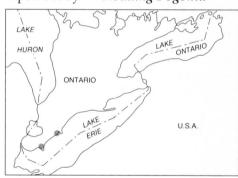

Nodding Pogonia –
Threatened

its leaves by the process of photosynthesis.

Any species that occurs at so few sites is vulnerable to sudden or radical changes in its habitat, but the principal threat to the nodding pogonia comes from grazing — by livestock in the private woodlot, and by a large population of white-tailed deer in the provincial park. In 1986, for example, one clump of 77 stems was eaten by deer. Although the tubers presumably remained beneath the surface of the soil to reproduce in another year, the buds and flowers and all but one of the developing seed capsules were destroyed. The event demonstrated all too effectively just how precarious a species's hold on survival may be once its numbers are diminished to a critical level.

Purple Twayblade
(*Liparis liliifolia*)

Purple Twayblade

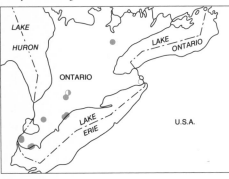

○ PRE 1925

◐ 1950–1964

● POST 1964

The purple twayblade is another rare and beautiful native wildflower that is under intense pressure from the encroachment of human activities on its natural habitat. Although it is fairly common in the eastern and midwestern United States, the Canadian range of this wild orchid is extremely limited. Eleven of the 12 sites where it is known to grow in Canada are in the Carolinian zone along the north shore of Lake Erie, while the 12th is north of Toronto in the Regional Municipality of York. At none of these stations does the plant appear in great numbers; 6 of the stands consist of 3 specimens or less, and the largest has been reduced in the past decade from over 300 to a mere 34.

The purple twayblade is small, but showy. A list of six different common names in English, including lily twayblade, large twayblade, purple scutcheon, and mauve sleekwort, attests to its having been widely known to early settlers. Its single stem rises from between two glossy, light-green, oval leaves to a height of about 12–25 centimetres, bearing anywhere from 5 to 30 or more flowers. The flowers have exceedingly narrow lateral petals and, by contrast, a long

broad lip, violet-mauve in colour and delicately streaked with a network of reddish-purple veins.

First officially recorded in Ontario as recently as 1960, this species may once have been more widespread in the province. It prefers a fairly dry, sandy loam near the edge of oak or mixed hardwood stands, a type of site that was quite common in the Carolinian zone before so much of the tallgrass prairie and savannah was converted to farming or urban development. Typically, it is found in areas of secondary growth in the wake of fire or some other habitat disturbance. In common with many plants found in successional communities, it is intolerant of dense shade, and if the surrounding trees are permitted to grow unchecked, purple twayblade colonies will gradually lose their vigour and die out as the forest canopy thickens.

It is not only natural succession, however, that threatens the habitat and consequently the survival of this flower. Several hundred individual plants have been lost to development over the past 10 years. Land clearance for a variety of purposes — agriculture, housing, recreational parkland — has resulted in the extirpation of some colonies. One site was wiped out by a combination of increased shade, predation by slugs, and aerial spraying of herbicide. With the known Canadian population of the species reduced to little more than 120 plants, the loss of even a single specimen — to scientific collection for an herbarium, for example — is a potential contributor to extirpation.

Positive conservation measures are required

Purple Twayblade –
Threatened

if the purple twayblade is to be saved as a native Canadian wildflower. Eleven of the 12 sites where it is known to grow are on private land, potentially subject to habitat-destroying changes. It is important that not only the landowners but the general public in these areas be informed of the scarcity of this orchid, and the value of preserving and restoring its numbers. Purchase of sites as nature reserves could make the task of species protection considerably easier. Site management, in the form of selective removal of trees to allow sunlight into areas of dense shade, might be advisable at some locations. Attempts to raise more stock from seed have met with some success to date, and offer a modest hope that new colonies could be established, or old ones restored. Finally, if it appears inevitable that a site where the species occurs will be lost, then it would seem preferable to attempt to transplant the stand, rather than let it be destroyed.

Red Mulberry
(*Morus rubra*)

Almost everyone has heard of the mulberry tree, made famous by the silk industry of China. The native Chinese tree is called the white mulberry. Thanks to its fine ornamental qualities and the delectable jams that can be made from its fruits, it has been introduced to many parts of the world. In southern Ontario, the white mulberry has invaded roadsides, fence lines, and native woodland, where in many places it now grows aggressively right next to the red mulberry, a similar tree and a native of eastern North America.

In the forest, red mulberry is an understorey species. Reaching the northern limits of its range in southern Ontario, it is a typical rare Carolinian species. Populations are known at only six sites centred in two regions — the Niagara area and southern Essex County, or the "toe" of Ontario, including Point Pelee National Park.

The introduction and naturalization of the white mulberry is threatening to the red because the two readily interbreed and produce hybrids, and it is feared that the white may in time completely swamp the red through repeated cross-pollination. There are, in fact,

Red Mulberry

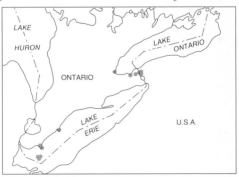

121

Red Mulberry

Red Mulberry –
Threatened

already some places where only whites and hybrids are found. Among Canada's threatened species, the red mulberry is therefore unique in that the most immediate threat to its survival is not habitat loss but rather genetic swamping through hybridization.

Another aspect of the red mulberry's vulnerability is that, like the white, it is wind pollinated.

This means that the survival of any population of red mulberry can be greatly enhanced by removing nearby whites, particularly from the direction of prevailing winds. Clearly, many years of management, involving the removal of plants carrying white mulberry traits, would be necessary to achieve such an objective.

Right: Gattinger's
Purple False
Foxglove –
Endangered

Gattinger's and Skinner's Purple False Foxgloves
(*Agalinis gattingeri* and *skinneriana*)

to white; Gattinger's are pink to pink-purple, with yellow lines and red spots on the throat. Both species have the unusual characteristic of being partially parasitic on the roots of other plants.

Although the two species are widely distributed in the United States from Michigan and Minnesota south to Louisiana, both are rare, and in Ontario their range is so extremely limited and

Gattinger's Purple
False Foxglove

Remnants of the prairie ecosystem in southern Ontario harbour a variety of species that are foreign to the adjacent deciduous forests. Gattinger's and Skinner's *Agalinis*, or purple false foxglove, are two rare wildflowers that fall into this category. Both plants are annuals with slender ridged stems, narrow opposite leaves, and upturned, bell-shaped flowers. Gattinger's foxglove tends to be a more generously branching plant than Skinner's. The flowers of Skinner's purple false foxglove are pale pink

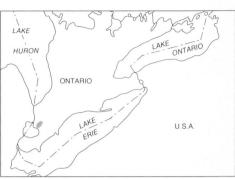

Skinner's Purple
False Foxglove

vulnerable that they have been declared Endangered. Gattinger's foxglove occurs at 10 Canadian stations, all of them within the boundaries of the Walpole Island Indian Reserve. There are 12 known stands of Skinner's, 11 of them on the Walpole Island Reserve, and 1 at La Salle, on the outskirts of Windsor.

Populations of each species range in number from a few plants at some sites, to a few thousand at others. Of critical importance with regard to protection is the fact that in seven locations, the two species co-exist in close proximity to each other. Major alterations of habitat conditions at any of these sites could thereby destroy important stands of both these plants.

Apart from the simple fact of their rarity, the main risk to both species stems from the exposed position of a number of the known stations. Several are close to roads and buildings. All populations are at least potentially vulnerable to land development for housing or agriculture. Certain sites have been recommended for preservation as critical habitats. It is hoped that such identification, coupled with appeals to the owners of land on which the sites are located, will assure the preservation of these two charming and endangered wildflowers.

Left: Skinner's Purple
False Foxglove –
Endangered

Pink Milkwort
(Polygala incarnata)

Pink Milkwort

An annual wildflower, the pink milkwort is often abundant in the dry sand prairies of the eastern and central United States. In contrast, only two small colonies are known in Canada, at the mouth of the St. Clair River in extreme southwestern Ontario. Both are on the Walpole Island Indian Reserve, comprised of Walpole and Squirrel islands, where some years ago only 100 and 12 plants respectively were counted. Historically, the species once existed on the Windsor prairie and at a site near Niagara Falls, but it has been extirpated from both these areas.

The continuing survival of this colourful wildflower at the two locations on the Walpole Island Indian Reserve appears to be dependent upon three factors. First, the marshes and associated prairie openings must be preserved from the encroachment of forest growth by periodic burning. Second, excessive collecting by botanists, a serious problem at the Squirrel Island site, must be stopped. And third, these two unique ecosystem remnants must be maintained in their natural state, a critical factor in an area that has seen most of its natural ecosystems destroyed through conversion into cornfields.

Left: Pink Milkwort –
Endangered

Slender Bush Clover
(Lespedeza virginica)

The slender bush clover, a slender herbaceous legume of dry, open habitats, is native to the eastern United States. One small colony was recorded in Leamington, Ontario, in 1882, by the Canadian botanist John Macoun. It grew, along with many other wildflowers and grasses, in what must have been a beautiful remnant prairie. What was a locally rare ecosystem has since been destroyed by the expansion of Leamington.

Slender Bush Clover

Over 90 years later (in the late 1970s), two other colonies of this native bush clover were discovered in prairie-like sites near Windsor. One of these has since been completely lost due to trail-bike activities. Because only about 150 individuals remain at the other site, the species has been declared Endangered in Canada. Privately owned, the remaining site is being variously affected by human activities.

Right: Slender Bush Clover – Endangered

Slender bush clover plants are wand-like. The tiny leaves are close to the stem, while the small red flowers are packed together into heads —

somewhat akin to clover. The species has an interesting peculiarity: two types of flowers. The flowers in the head, while not showy, are relatively large and open; another set of tiny flowers, found lower down on the stem, are self-pollinating and never open at all.

The continuing survival of this endangered species appears to be tied to periodic burning of the area where it lives, which has helped maintain the open habitat required by most prairie plants. There is also an attempt underway to gain permanent protection of the habitat through land purchase.

Small White Lady's-slipper
(Cypripedium candidum)

The discovery that a nearby fen, bog, or fragment of native prairie is the home of a rare orchid makes many people ask whether the place is protected. Fortunately, for the small white lady's-slipper, the answer is a partial yes.

One of Canada's rarest lady's-slippers, the small white is an exquisitely fashioned floral gem whose white inflated lower lip petal resembles an imaginary slipper. This species is considered to be so precious by those who care about its survival that the exact location of its few remaining wild colonies is a guarded secret.

The small white lady's-slipper is a native of

eastern North America where it was especially abundant in low, open prairies of the central Midwest. In Canada, it survives in four places in southern Manitoba and two in southern Ontario. A Saskatchewan colony once existed in the late nineteenth century near Indian Head. In Ontario, it was formerly known in six counties, but is restricted today to very small sites in Lambton and Hastings.

Lady's-slippers are peculiar in that it may take up to a dozen or more years for a plant to grow from seed to a flowering individual. Consequently, most plants in some colonies are not in flower. Stems occur singly or in clumps, with up to several dozen shoots emerging from an underground rhizome.

The beautiful flowers are objects of enchantment to small bees, which are attracted by a combination of colour, fragrance, and a promise of nectar. Seeking nectar, a bee enters the flower through the large hole at the top. There is no nectar, however, and the bee cannot escape through the entry passage because the upper surface of the shiny petal is so waxy and slippery that a bee simply cannot obtain a foothold. Indeed, the slipper provides a one-way passage for pollinators, which always enter through the opening at the top, but are forced to exit through either of two openings at the base of the flower, where hairs and rough areas offer a foothold. Going through the passage, the bee brushes first against the stigma and then the anther sacs, thereby carrying pollen away to another flower. Although the slipper provides no reward for the bee, the bee unwittingly cross-pollinates the flower in the process of visitation. One of the characteristics of all cross-pollinated lady's-slipper species is that many or most flowers remain unpollinated. This is because bees, being relatively intelligent insects, soon learn of the futility of visiting lady's-slippers and go on to seek nectar from other nearby flowers.

This species provides another compelling reason for protecting the rare natural ecosystems in which rare species are found. Almost inevitably, other rare or beautiful species occur either in the same spot or very near to it. In the Hastings County site, for example, 4 other lady's-slipper species — the yellow, ramshead, showy, and moccasin-flower — as well as the dragon's-mouth are found within a five-minute walk of the small white. The same is true of the colony at Lambton County where at least 10 other rare plant species grow at the same site, one of which — the bayberry — is found here and nowhere else in Canada.

Small White Lady's-slipper

In 1977 the small white lady's-slipper was officially designated as Endangered in Ontario under the provincial Endangered Species Act. The Hastings County colony is now partially protected by a provincial nature reserve, while in Manitoba, one site has been purchased by the provincial parks department.

Small White Lady's-slipper – Endangered

American Ginseng
(Panax quinquefolium)

The taxonomist's name for American ginseng provides a descriptive clue as to why this is a threatened species. *Panax* combines two Greek root words: *pan* means all, and *akos* means cure; *quinquefolium* is Latin for having five leaves. Hence, *Panax quinquefolium* claims the distinction of being the five-leafed cure-all.

Ginseng is a perennial herb that grows in rich, moist, shady sites in deciduous forests. Above ground, it reaches a height of 20–70 centimetres, the single stem being topped by a flower stalk

American Ginseng –
Threatened

and 1–4 palmate leaves or prongs, each consisting of 5 leaflets. Its greenish-white flowers produce a cluster of berries that are bright red when ripe. Beneath the ground, a gnarled rhizome extends down to a thick, forked, storage root.

The ginseng life cycle does not favour prolific growth, even under ideal conditions. Although individual plants may live for 50–60 years, they produce no seeds until they are 5–8 years old. Even then, production is sparse, especially in dry years, and during the 18–22 months required for germination, the seeds are vulnerable to predation by birds and rodents, and also to fungus.

The species is widely but sparsely distributed throughout eastern North America, its range extending northward into most of southern Ontario and the southwestern counties of Québec. Field research in 1987 confirmed the presence of 51 stands in Ontario and 15 in Québec, with populations ranging from as few as 1 or 2 plants, to more than 3,000 at one site. Other populations are known to exist, and more may yet be found in areas of suitable habitat that have not been fully explored.

Ordinarily, such a widespread plant would not qualify as a threatened species under COSEWIC criteria. It is ginseng's reputation as a cure-all and, in consequence, its position as the object of an active commercial trade, that put its survival at risk. Long before Europeans came to North America, native herbalists used ginseng to treat coughs, headaches, rheumatism, and a variety of other conditions. A Jesuit priest, Louis-Joseph Lafitau, found the species growing in the Montréal area in 1715. Given the presence of his order in the Far East, Fr. Lafitau was presumably aware that ginseng root was prized in China for its medicinal and tonic properties. It is reported that by 1720 the harvesting of wild American ginseng for export to the Orient was a lucrative enterprise in New France, second only to the fur trade in value.

Since 1973, when ginseng was listed under Appendix II of the Convention on International Trade in Endangered Species (CITES), the province of Québec has prohibited its export. In Ontario, however, at least as recently as the early 1980s, diggers were still collecting and exporting about 140 kilograms annually. An unknown quantity is also collected in both provinces for domestic sale. A wholesale price of about $440 per kilogram for well-grown wild roots provides a strong incentive for this trade, and indications

are that many more plants are being gathered than the population can withstand.

It is interesting to note that ginseng was actually protected in Ontario under legislation passed in 1891, which prohibited harvesting between January and September in order to allow an adequate season for the production and dispersal of seeds. This protection appears to have been inadvertently removed in 1950 under an omnibus bill aimed at cancelling laws that were considered to be antiquated.

Although unregulated harvesting has clearly reduced the abundance of native ginseng in Canada, and may constitute an immediate threat to the survival of specific populations, it would be unfair to lay the blame for the decline of the species exclusively on collectors. A 1980 survey of known ginseng diggers in Ontario indicated that many of them were conscious of the need for conservation measures, that they waited to harvest until after fruit had set, and that they took the trouble to gather and plant seeds in areas where they dug. The pressure on wild plants may also be reduced to some extent by commercial growers who are able to bring ginseng root to market at a considerably lower cost.

Over the years, loss of deciduous woodland habitat to agriculture and urban expansion has undoubtedly been responsible for the greatest decline in ginseng populations in Canada. The process continues to the present day. Grazing by cattle or the clearing of forest for development purposes can readily destroy a colony of plants. Indeed, ginseng is so attuned to the shady twilight of the forest floor that even woodlot management practices such as selective cutting of mature trees can retard or terminate its growth if too much light is allowed to penetrate the treetop canopy. In addition, it is susceptible to a variety of plant diseases.

If, in the presence of these stresses, the wild ginseng harvest is allowed to continue unabated, then the survival of this species will be seriously threatened. On the other hand, there are enough healthy populations still extant that a program to protect habitat, to preserve key colonies in nature reserves, and to regulate harvesting on a sustainable-yield basis, should be sufficient to preserve the five-leafed cure-all for future generations.

American Ginseng

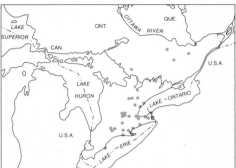

Pitcher's Thistle
(*Cirsium pitcheri*)

Pitcher's Thistle

Some endangered species of wildlife are at risk because of excessive harvesting; for others, the chance of survival may be diminished by changes in climate or habitat. Plants such as the pitcher's thistle, however, are often victims of indifference, no one noticing their scarcity until they are almost gone.

Outside of Scotland, whose floral emblem is the thistle, most people regard the spiny members of the genus *Cirsium* as common weeds. At least within living memory, however, pitcher's thistles have been so few and so isolated that not many people would even recognize the species, let alone treat it as commonplace. The slender plants grow in stands of a few dozen to a few hundred on dunes along the shores of the upper Great Lakes. In 1987 they were found at five sites on Manitoulin Island. Other Ontario records in recent years bring the total number of Canadian stands to about a dozen, of which the northernmost is at Pukaskwa National Park on the north shore of Lake Superior. The species has been extirpated from at least three locations in the past 40 years.

Pitcher's thistle is a graceful and attractive plant. Its central stem rises to as much as a metre in height, supporting from 1 or 2 to as many as 125 composite flowering heads, each consisting of 20 or more tiny, creamy-yellow flowers. The stems and deeply divided, spine-tipped leaves are green, overlaid with a white coat of woolly hairs. A deep taproot holds each plant firmly in place in its desert-like habitat.

Growing in open beach and dune locations, the species faces the natural hazards of an exposed habitat: burial or exposure resulting from an accumulation or loss of sand; destruction by ice scouring in winter; washouts by wave action during summer storms. In addition, larvae of the plume moth feed on the plant, reducing seed production. The greatest hazard of all, however, is human in origin. It comes from lakeshore recreational development.

Affluent urban societies place a premium value on natural locations where people can "get away from it all." Since 1950, much prime lakeshore and wilderness land in southern and central Ontario has been transformed into recreational parks and vacation subdivisions. Pitcher's thistle occurs in locations that are highly attractive for such purposes. Without any malicious intent, holiday visitors to these sites can do enormous damage; all-terrain vehicles crush the plants and damage the delicate structure of the dunes where they grow; access roads and cottage construction may inadvertently wipe out entire stands. In the 1987 survey mentioned above, dead and damaged plants were observed in ATV tracks at four out of five sites.

All known stations where the species persists, except those at Pukaskwa National Park and Pinery and Inverhuron provincial parks, are on privately owned land where the likelihood of further recreational development is high. Protective measures such as the creation of nature reserves, as well as educational efforts to heighten public awareness, are urgently needed if the survival of this graceful but threatened beach plant is to be assured.

Pitcher's Thistle –
Threatened

The Atlantic Maritime Life Zone

◆

As one of the more densely populated life zones in the country, the human social and economic uses of the Maritime region have had a profound influence on natural ecosystems.

The Atlantic Maritime Life Zone

The Atlantic Maritime life zone consists of New Brunswick, Nova Scotia, Prince Edward Island, and the Gaspé Peninsula of Québec. The glaciers of the last ice age retreated from this zone less than 10,000 years ago, having stripped the hills and coastal plains of much of their topsoil. Although there are some pockets of deep, fertile land, typical Maritime soils are rocky, poorly drained, acidic, and low in fertility, suited to a limited range of plant life.

The climate of the Atlantic Maritime life zone is generally cool, moist, and temperate, the extremes of continental temperature ranges being moderated by the surrounding masses of seawater. For several centuries prior to 1200 A.D., the region experienced a much warmer period, followed from 1200 to 1900 by a phase that was cold and harsh enough to be popularly called the "Little Ice Age." During the twentieth century, the general trend has been a return to somewhat warmer conditions.

The typical vegetation is Acadian forest, an association of mixed broadleaf and conifer trees that covers about 60 percent of the land area. At higher elevations, or where soils are very thin, the forest gives way to tundra-like barrens. Where the coastal plain is relatively wide and low, fresh-water wetlands and river estuaries marked by extensive areas of tidal salt marsh support a rich diversity of plants.

Wildlife species in the Maritime zone are largely similar to those found in the adjacent Boreal zone. Beaver, mink, muskrat, and white-tailed deer are among the principal species of mammals, and one local rarity of interest is the Gaspé shrew. The large areas of salt marsh and other wetlands provide excellent habitat for waterfowl. Offshore, among the windswept dunes of Sable Island, is the sole nesting ground of the Ipswich sparrow (a subspecies of the savannah sparrow), but perhaps the most distinctive avian feature of the region is its vast colonies of sea birds.

Finally, the human social and economic uses of the Maritime region have had a profound influence on natural ecosystems. The region contains only about 8 percent of Canada's human population, but with a land area comprising less than 2 percent of the national total, it is one of the more densely populated life zones in the country. Historically, it has been subject to intensive settlement and resource development for close to four centuries — much longer than most parts of Canada. Industrial and municipal effluents, oil spills, ground-water contamination, acid precipitation, and pollution by toxic chemicals all add to the complex of stresses that human activity places on the Maritime life zone.

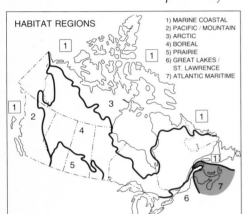

HABITAT REGIONS

1) MARINE COASTAL
2) PACIFIC / MOUNTAIN
3) ARCTIC
4) BOREAL
5) PRAIRIE
6) GREAT LAKES / ST. LAWRENCE
7) ATLANTIC MARITIME

Mammals

Eastern Cougar	Endangered
Maritime Woodland Caribou	Threatened
Gaspé Shrew	Rare

Birds

Peregrine Falcon: *anatum*	Endangered
Piping Plover	Endangered
Roseate Tern	Threatened
Cooper's Hawk	Rare
Eastern Bluebird	Rare
Ipswich Sparrow	Rare
Red-shouldered Hawk	Rare

Fish

Atlantic Whitefish	Endangered
Shortnose Sturgeon	Rare

Plants

Eastern Mountain Avens	Endangered
Furbish's Lousewort	Endangered
Pink Coreopsis	Endangered
Water Pennywort	Endangered
Golden Crest	Threatened
Plymouth Gentian	Threatened
Sweet Pepperbush	Threatened
Lilaeopsis	Rare
Gulf of St. Lawrence Aster	Vulnerable

Species listed as Endangered or Threatened in the above table are covered in detail in the accounts that follow; those classified as Rare or Vulnerable are not.

As of 1989 the classification Rare is being replaced by Vulnerable. See Introduction, page 2, for a detailed explanation.

Eastern Cougar
(Felis concolor couguar)

Surely no creature on Canada's endangered species list is more elusive than the eastern cougar. Historically, it ranged across central Ontario and southern Québec, and east to New Brunswick. As early as 1908, however, it was declared to be extinct in Ontario, and many mammalogists subsequently concluded that the verdict could be applied throughout eastern Canada and the northeastern United States. There was just one problem. While the experts insisted that the eastern cougar was gone forever from its former haunts, people who lived in hinterland areas persisted in reporting the presence of panthers, pumas, painters, catamounts, and mountain lions — whatever name local tradition had attached to the big cats.

The late Bruce S. Wright, who for years headed the Northeastern Wildlife Station at Fredericton, New Brunswick, was one biologist prepared to challenge the opinion of his colleagues and give credence to the popular reports. From newspapers, journals, and interviews, he established a list of 304 reported sightings in Québec and the Maritimes between 1900 and 1971. Since then, there have been well over 200 additional reports in Atlantic Canada, and about 150 in Ontario. No recent sighting has been accompanied by definitive evidence such as a specimen, living or dead, or a clear sequence of photographs. The easternmost Canadian specimen taken in recent years was a two-year-old male killed at Stead, Manitoba, about 52 kilometres northeast of Winnipeg, in December 1973, but it appears to have been of the western *missoulensis* subspecies, not an eastern cougar. Tracks, scats, and hair samples found in the eastern provinces have been inconclusive.

Although the last cougar to be killed in eastern Canada was shot in Kent County, New Brunswick, in 1932, Wright was wholly convinced that a marginally viable breeding population of 25 to 50 individuals was sustaining itself in the more remote wilderness areas of the province, and even expanding into Nova Scotia. Many scientists still doubt this hypothesis, preferring to wait for physical evidence in the form of a living or dead specimen of guaranteed origin. Nonetheless, scientific opinion now tends to

Eastern Cougar

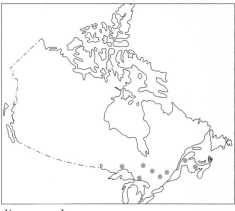

*Eastern Cougar –
Endangered*

favour the view that it is possible, if not proven, that a few eastern cougars survive in New Brunswick, and perhaps in Ontario, Québec, and Nova Scotia as well. The possible existence of the eastern cougar has been officially acknowledged through its designation by COSEWIC in 1978 as an endangered species, and its protection under the laws of the provinces in which it is thought to live. So little is known of the natural history of this particular subspecies, however, that any summary account of its general biology must be largely speculative.

Studies elsewhere in North and South America describe the cougar as a large cat with a body length of 150–275 centimetres, a tail length of 53–90 centimetres, and a body weight of 36–103 kilograms. Its long slender body is surmounted by a small head with rounded ears. Seen in profile, the hindquarters are noticeably higher

than the shoulders. The colour of the short rough coat varies from gray or brown through shades of cinnamon and buff, darker along the back, and white on the chest, throat, and chin. Although black individuals are said to be rare, fully 20 percent of the sightings reported in Atlantic Canada from 1976–87 were alleged to be of black animals, suggesting that this might be a more common colour variant in the eastern cougar.

Cougars are solitary animals, each occupying an established home territory that it marks by scratching on trees, urinating, or leaving scats at boundary points or scrapes. Size of territory seems to vary considerably in relation to the population density of prey. The species is remarkably adaptable to different types of habitat, and distinct subspecies have been described in association with areas as diverse as the Rocky Mountains, Florida everglades, Brazilian jungles, and Mexican deserts. Two factors, however, seem to be common requirements in all habitats that sustain cougars. The first is an abundant supply of food; the second is an absence of major disturbance by human activity.

Food supply for eastern cougars can be equated with white-tailed deer, although evidence from other areas suggests that the cats will prey on caribou, moose, and elk, as well as smaller mammals such as porcupines, rabbits, skunks, beaver, and even mice. In this century, there has been a significant increase in the deer population of much of eastern Canada, a response to the expansion of favourable habitat in the wake of logging and farm abandonment. In New Brunswick and Nova Scotia, for example, deer densities in about 23 percent of the province are comparable to those known to support a stable cougar population in Idaho. In New Brunswick and Nova Scotia, too, it is interesting to note a fairly close correspondence between areas of high deer density and locations from which cougar sightings are most frequently reported. The same areas tend to be among those least disturbed by urban or industrial development.

So long as there is adequate food, threats to the survival of cougars tend to be of human origin. Hunting, especially by parties with tracking dogs, and trapping, appear to have been the principal causes of the near extermination of the eastern cougar throughout its range in Canada and the United States. Loss of habitat has been cited as a significant factor in reducing numbers and preventing recovery. In the Florida ever-

glades, where a small remnant population of cougars has been studied closely for the last several years, at least seven have reportedly been killed by motor vehicles since 1979. On the other hand, since nothing is known about the mortality of the eastern cougar in Canada during the past half century, it is virtually impossible to pinpoint particular factors that might affect their welfare in this country.

In the face of so much uncertainty, what grounds remain for supposing that the eastern cougar has not been extirpated? To begin with, the flow of reports from people who believe they have seen the great cats continues unabated. While some verge on fantasy, many are submitted by reputable witnesses — woodsmen, wildlife technicians, veterinarians — whose judgment is hard to question or refute. Then, too, cougars are extremely solitary animals. Other Canadian members of the family *Felidae*, such as bobcat and lynx, are relatively plentiful in many parts of their range; yet they are seldom seen or photographed in the wild. A cougar sighted within the 225-hectare enclosure of a wilderness park in Seattle, Washington, managed for three full days to elude capture by a large party of park employees, game department officers, and others, and a pack of six trained cat hounds. In view of such experiences, it is not inconceivable that a small, stable population of the eastern cougar could remain largely undetected in the rugged, sparsely populated wilderness areas of eastern Canada.

Maritime Woodland Caribou
(*Rangifer tarandus caribou*)

Anyone who in recent years has watched television footage of the hundreds of thousands of woodland caribou that make up the vast George River herd in northern Québec and Labrador might be forgiven for wondering why such an abundant species should be listed as Endangered. And indeed, that particular population faces no immediate danger. South of the St. Lawrence River, however, the story is different. Two

centuries ago, woodland caribou roamed the highlands of the Maritimes and the Gaspé Peninsula by the thousands. Today, only a few hundred remain. It would be hard to find a more striking illustration of how rapidly events may conspire to extirpate a plentiful species from a particular territory.

The caribou of North America and the reindeer of Europe and Asia are widely considered to belong to a single, circumpolar species. When populations occupy geographically separate territories, however, they may differ enough for biologists to classify them as distinct subspecies. The correct classification of some of the major Canadian caribou herds is a subject of continuing scientific debate, but at present there is general acceptance of at least a basic division into three main subspecies: the Peary caribou, which inhabits parts of the Arctic archipelago; the barren-ground caribou, which ranges across most of the Northwest Territories; and the woodland caribou, which occupies the most southerly range.

All caribou are physically well-adapted to life in the arctic and subarctic regions where they occur. A thick coat of buoyant, insulating fur helps preserve body heat. Their feet alter with the seasons; they walk the summer barrens on

Maritime
Woodland Caribou –
Threatened

within Gaspé Provincial Park, their status as the sole surviving remnant of a once-abundant Maritime population is precarious enough that COSEWIC has designated them as Threatened.

The ecological process of extirpation is seldom simple, but some understanding of it may be gained by examining the events that led to the disappearance of the woodland caribou from the Maritimes, and the factors that make its recovery in that region highly unlikely for the foreseeable future.

soft, enlarged, shock-absorbing pads, but traverse the winter landscape on broad horny hooves that protect the shrunken pads against cold and enable the animals to dig through as much as 50–100 centimetres of snow in search of food. The muzzle and teeth are ideal for cropping the tough, ground-dwelling lichens typical of northern tundra and taiga grazing grounds.

The woodland subspecies is the largest caribou in North America. It is found in lichen-rich areas of mature boreal forest and associated bog and muskeg regions across Canada from British Columbia to Newfoundland, and is especially abundant in northeastern Québec and northern Labrador. South of the St. Lawrence River, the woodland caribou has disappeared from most of its former range. There is a small herd in the Shickshock Mountains of the central Gaspé, and despite virtually total protection of these animals

The first inferences about the presence of woodland caribou in the Maritimes are based on archaeological research. During the late 1950s and early 1960s, excavations at a number of sites in Nova Scotia revealed continuous occupancy by native people for several centuries. Identification of bone fragments found at these locations gave some indications of which animals were plentiful during this extended period of time. White-tailed deer remains were found at the earliest levels, as far back as 160 B.C., while caribou bone fragments dated from much later, around 1100 A.D. and after. From this, it has been suggested that caribou were rare or nonexistent in Nova Scotia before the so-called Little Ice Age (circa 1200–1800 A.D.), but replaced deer when the climate became colder and more consistently subarctic.

References in the journals of seventeenth- and

eighteenth-century settlers certainly suggest an abundance of caribou and an absence of deer in the mature Maritime forests. But with European settlement came a demand for farmland, and one of the most effective means of clearing forest was fire. By 1801, Titus Smith, who made a walking tour of the area in that year, noted that "the Caribou are more numerous than the Moose, but are very few compared to what they have been heretofore, owing to the fires, which have burnt over the open barrens and destroyed the Reindeer moss which is their principal food." Besides the loss of habitat, Smith noted that excessive hunting during the preceding twenty years had "greatly diminished the Caribou."

An observer in 1830 stated that "the Caraboo [sic] is still found most numerous . . . and usually in large herds," but as early as 1855, Lieutenant C. Hardy of Halifax wrote that it was "so seldom met with now in Nova Scotia that it may be considered on the verge of extinction," and by 1900 the report of the Game and Inland Fishery Protection Society stated bleakly that "a few still exist, a remnant of the numberless herds which used to roam over our bogs and barrens half a century ago." By 1914, there were no more woodland caribou in mainland Nova Scotia. A decade later, they were gone from Cape Breton and New Brunswick as well.

A complex set of human-related factors had combined to extirpate the most numerous ungulate in the Maritimes. Fire had destroyed the mature forests where the woodland caribou took shelter, and the lichen-producing barrens where they grazed. Settlement and roads had split the herds and disturbed traditional calving and rutting grounds. Lumbering, like fire, had further reduced available range and food supplies, and throughout the period, the biggest and the best animals had been shot or snared to satisfy social and economic demands for meat and trophies.

The extirpation of the Maritime woodland caribou is probably irreversible. In 1939, and again in 1968–69, two attempts were made to reintroduce the species to Nova Scotia. Both failed. The Canadian Wildlife Service conducted a field study of the second failure, which concluded that a new factor had arrived with the twentieth century — the white-tailed deer. Two centuries of forest fires, clear-cut logging, and agriculture had created habitat conditions in the Maritimes that favoured the deer, and from the late 1800s onward, it effectively re-colonized the region,

after being virtually absent during the several hundred years when the caribou predominated.

The white-tailed deer often carries a parasitic worm called *Paralaphostrongylus tenuis*, commonly known as the brain worm because of its habit of burrowing up the nervous system and into the brain of its host. The deer has adapted to the presence of this parasite, but research has shown that a caribou can die in as little as four months after infestation by the worm. For this reason, it seems almost certain that caribou and deer can never co-exist on the same range.

Although the Maritime woodland caribou died out under the impact of human activity, it can be argued that its survival south of the St. Lawrence was an anomaly. The species is superbly adapted to subarctic conditions on the borderline between boreal and barren-ground zones. Even without the profound environmental changes wrought by European settlement, the climatic warming trend which ended the Little Ice Age during the nineteenth and twentieth centuries might well have accomplished the same end more slowly by eliminating the last vestiges of true boreal habitat from the Maritimes.

The Mont Albert area in the Gaspé Peninsula sustains its small relict herd of woodland caribou on territory that has been described as: ". . . a region of transition between the eastern mixed forest and the northern conifer forest. At altitudes of 2,000–2,900 feet, a zone of taiga is found, and at 3,000 feet the trees do not reach more than 6'–7'. At high altitudes . . . we find an arctic alpine vegetation which may be compared to the tundra of the arctic region."

Apart from the Cape Breton Highlands plateau, there is probably not another location in the Maritimes that provides equally appropriate caribou habitat over a large enough area to sustain a viable population.

North of the St. Lawrence, the future is promising for the woodland caribou. Across much of the boreal zone, from Newfoundland and Labrador to the Yukon, populations are stable or increasing. South of the river, however, the once-plentiful Maritime herds will roam only in history books and in the forests of the imagination.

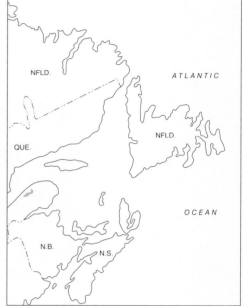

Maritime Woodland Caribou

Peregrine Falcon
(*Falco peregrinus anatum*)

Peregrine Falcon

On August 8, 1987, a crowd of 250–300 people gathered at Mary's Point, New Brunswick, for the official dedication of the Shepody Bay International Shorebird Reserve at the upper end of the Bay of Fundy. Obligingly, a flock of 40–50,000 semipalmated sandpipers roosted impassively on a narrow strip of beach some 50 metres away. Suddenly, the calm of the sandpipers was replaced by an air of alertness and alarm. Within seconds, the entire flock sprang into the air in a dazzling display of synchronized evasive flight. For a moment, it was unclear what had caused the instant panic; then it became apparent, as a dark winged form dove into the mass of fluttering shore birds and veered up and away, a single sandpiper dangling from its powerful talons. The fortunate human observers had just witnessed a breathtaking display of the predatory skill of the peregrine falcon. What made the experience especially remarkable was the fact that this bird was one of the first free-flying, adult peregrines to summer in the Maritimes since their extirpation as a breeding species of the region more than 30 years before.

The peregrine is a powerful, crow-sized falcon that has been clocked, in a dive, at speeds of close to 300 kilometres per hour. It ordinarily nests on inaccessible cliff ledges, usually close to coastal or wetland areas where shore birds, sea birds, or waterfowl gather. Occasionally, it will nest on the roof of a tall city building and prey upon rock doves in nearby parks. One such pair were regular residents of an office building in downtown Montréal for many years.

Three subspecies of the peregrine falcon occur in Canada: *Falco peregrinus tundrius,* across the wide arc of tundra from the Mackenzie delta to Hudson Bay and Ungava, and north to Baffin Island; *Falco peregrinus pealei,* along the Pacific coast from the Aleutians to the Queen Charlotte Islands; and *Falco peregrinus anatum,* historically the most widespread race, breeding across Canada from the tree line south and east to the Atlantic coast. It is primarily with the third of these, the *anatum* subspecies, that this account is concerned.

It was in the early 1960s that evidence began to be compiled documenting a decline among peregrine falcons in eastern Canada and the United States. The outlook was disturbing enough that, following a conference in Wisconsin in 1965, it was decided to undertake North American surveys for breeding peregrines every five years. The 1975 results indicated how serious the problem was. Of more than 50 known nest sites surveyed in Ontario, southern Québec, southern Labrador, and the Maritimes, not one was active. Only in Alberta, the Yukon, the Northwest Territories, and possibly the interior of British Columbia, was there evidence of an active breeding population of the *anatum* race in Canada. Throughout the East, it appeared to have been virtually extirpated.

The cause of this rapid and severe decline was traced to the buildup of DDT and other organochlorine pesticide residues in the body tissues of the birds. Raptors, because they occupy the uppermost link in the food chain, are especially vulnerable to toxic chemicals, which they ingest in dangerous concentrations with their prey. Although the amounts may not be sufficient to kill the adult birds, they do result in eggshell thinning and breakage, reduced nesting success, and ultimately, nonbreeding and abandonment of breeding territory. It was arguably too late to determine beyond question if this had happened to the *anatum* peregrines of eastern Canada, but it seemed very likely, as tests on *tundrius* birds and eggs in Ungava and the Arctic confirmed that pesticide residues were causing problems in that northern population as well.

An immediate concern, once the nature and scale of this threat to the peregrine falcon were understood, was to ensure that the *anatum* race should not be lost. As early as 1970, the Canadian Wildlife Service took 12 nestlings into captivity to maintain a gene pool and provide the initial stock for a captive breeding program established at Wainwright, Alberta. Subsequently, captive breeding programs were started in Saskatchewan and Québec as well.

Because the falcons had been inadvertently wiped out as a result of human intervention in the environment, there was a strong sense of commitment to the idea that the original range should be restocked where possible. Beginning in 1975, experimental releases were made using

the technique of fostering, or placing captive-hatched nestlings in the nests of wild parents. The method was successful in northern Alberta, where wild birds were still nesting. It obviously could not work, however, in those regions from which the peregrine had already been extirpated.

Another technique, known as "hacking," was borrowed from the ancient sport of falconry, and has been employed in a joint federal/provincial peregrine recovery program at some 15 sites across southern Canada. Hacking involves raising young, unfledged birds in an artificial nest box at a site that might normally be chosen by nesting peregrines, and releasing them when they reach the stage of development at which they would ordinarily be expected to fledge, or fly, in the wild. Thereafter, experience has shown that there is a good chance of the birds' returning, breeding, and restocking the area naturally.

The procedure does not re-establish a breeding population immediately. Risks such as shoot-ing, predation by great horned owls, bad weather, and inexperience at capturing prey contribute to a mortality rate among the fledglings that may be higher than 50 percent for first-year birds, and 15 percent per year thereafter. Since peregrine falcons do not often breed before their third or fourth year, as many as two-thirds of the young released from a given site each year may be lost before reaching sexual maturity.

Some of the first hacking in eastern Canada took place atop government office buildings in Hull, Québec. Between 1976 and 1986, 63 birds were released from this location. Some have since been observed nesting in the Ottawa Valley region. At Cap Tourmente, Québec, 22 young peregrines were hacked between 1982 and 1984. In 1986 a pair, of which the male was one of the locally released birds, nested there successfully, fledging two young, while another pair, including a female hacked in 1984 from a site in Toronto, raised at least one chick in Québec City.

In the Maritimes, peregrine falcon releases were begun in 1982 from cliff locations at Fundy National Park, New Brunswick, and overlooking the Minas Basin in Nova Scotia. By 1987, a total of 90 birds had been released from these sites. Although no successful nesting attempts were recorded in 1987 or 1988, birds hacked from these locations were observed in the area, engaging in apparent courtship behaviour. In 1989 the patience of the Maritime peregrine recovery team was rewarded, as at least two pairs nested in New Brunswick, one in Fundy National Park and one on a bridge crossing the Saint John harbour. Indeed, across the eastern part of the *anatum* range, more returns and more nestings are being reported yearly. Encouraged by these signs, the co-ordinators of Canada's peregrine recovery effort have accelerated the rate of release to as many as 30 birds per year in selected areas, in the hope that larger concentrations of returning birds will increase the probability that self-sustaining subpopulations will be established.

Piping Plover
(*Charadrius melodus*)

Piping Plover

Vacationers enjoying a picnic on the low sand dunes that stretch along the shores of the Gulf of St. Lawrence might spend an entire day within 100 metres of a piping plover's nest and never be aware of it. So well does the thrush-sized shore bird's white, beige, and black plumage blend with the background of the beach that the adult is virtually invisible until it moves. The four ivory-coloured eggs speckled with spots of dark brown or black are equally well camouflaged. Lying among bits of shell in a shallow depression in the sand just above the high-tide line, they can scarcely be distinguished from smooth oval pebbles.

Let the family dog or an exploring toddler wander too near the nest site, though, and there will be no doubt of the tiny plover's presence. Before a potential marauder can get too close, the bird is off the nest and running in a wide arc to intersect the line of approach. If the intruder is not distracted into following, the protective parent will feign injury, fluttering in the sand and peeping forlornly to draw attention away from its precious eggs.

Nowadays, those eggs really are precious. The piping plover is a widely distributed shore bird across north-central North America, but a rare one as well — so rare that in 1985 its official status was upgraded by COSEWIC from Threatened to Endangered. Extensive surveys since the early 1980s indicate that the Canadian population now stands at about 2,000 individuals, and that a more or less similar number is found in the United States. In the Great Lakes region the piping plover has almost disappeared. In recent years, there have been only two probable breeding records on the Canadian side of the lakes, in 1981 and 1988. An American report in 1987 referred to 17 breeding pairs on the U.S. side, barely enough to constitute the base for restoring a viable population. Barring an unexpected change for the better, the species would seem to be on the verge of extirpation in the area that was once at the centre of its range.

About a quarter of the piping plovers in Canada — some 450–485 birds — are found in the Maritimes; the remaining three-quarters are in the Prairie Provinces. Data from recent census activities suggest that for the moment the distribution in both these areas is reasonably stable, and that there may even be slight increases at some locations. The species is vulnerable to such a variety of threats, however, that it would be misleading to interpret short-term, local gains as reliable indicators of long-term recovery.

In one sense, the piping plover could be accused of being its own worst enemy. Whether on the seacoast or at the margin of fresh-water prairie lakes, it consistently selects nesting sites located just above the normal high-water mark, on exposed sandy or pebbly beaches. As a matter of course, seasonal storms, sometimes coupled with high spring tides in coastal areas, produce waves large enough to wash over these sites, often scattering the eggs beyond recovery. Although the first nesting, usually in May, is early enough that a second and, on occasion, even a third

attempt may be undertaken, there is no certainty that these, too, will not be wiped out. Moreover, high water levels over a period of years have been known to result in the permanent abandonment of some lakeside sites along the shores of the Great Lakes and in parts of western Canada.

Predation is another natural hazard facing the plover — one that is amplified by the exposed locations of their nests. Gulls, crows, skunks, and raccoons, inveterate beachcombers all, will make short work of plover eggs when they find them.

Foxes and, in vacation areas, feral cats can be a threat to young and adult birds alike.

The threat that has seemingly tipped the balance against the survival of the piping plover in many areas is human activity. The same beach conditions that attract the breeding plover are those that also attract Canadian holiday-makers intent on enjoying the short summer season to the fullest. There appears to be a direct correlation between the recreational use of beaches and the reproductive success of the birds. Pairs at isolated sites produce, on average, more than twice as many surviving young as those nesting on beaches frequented by vacationers. Although picnickers may be oblivious to the presence of plovers, the birds may be sufficiently disturbed by the unwelcome company that they will abandon their nests long enough for the eggs to chill and die. The tire of a dune buggy or even a careless footstep can crush an entire clutch in an instant. The irony is that the danger comes from people who, by and large, enjoy the outdoors and would not willingly contribute to the disappearance of any wildlife species.

Since the problem became more widely known, government and nongovernment organizations in Canada and the United States have initiated piping plover recovery schemes. The national goal of the Canadian plan is to increase the population by about 50 percent, to a self-sustaining level of at least 3,170 individuals in the Prairie and Atlantic provinces, and to restore a breeding population to the Great Lakes when and where conditions permit. In order to achieve this goal by the mid-1990s, it will first be necessary to conduct additional detailed surveys to determine actual populations, breeding status, productivity, and rates of recruitment, and then to monitor progress toward the target figures. Then, meaningful protective measures may be undertaken.

Because piping plovers are so specific in their selection of nest sites, the identification and preservation of nesting habitat are vitally important elements of the plan. It may not be feasible to control the weather during the May-July nesting period, but removing eggs to temporary incubators during storms, and replacing them after the storm has calmed, is an experimental technique that shows some promise. Site preservation will also undoubtedly mean protection against human disturbance, perhaps by posting warning signs, by requiring domestic pets to be leashed in nesting areas, or by declaring specific nesting sites to be sanctuaries and restricting public access to them.

In Atlantic Canada, a significant portion of the piping plover population nests at sites that are within the boundaries of federally controlled national parks, and here, enforcement of protective measures is comparatively easy. Elsewhere, in both Maritime and prairie regions, an important part of the recovery effort will be devoted to public education and to enlisting the active support of landowners whose properties include good nesting habitat.

Roseate Tern
(Sterna dougallii)

One hundred years ago, vanity and the millinery industry came perilously close to extirpating many North American bird species. In the latter part of the nineteenth century, fashion decreed that ladies should wear extravagant and fanciful displays of plumage on their heads. Birds by the tens of thousands fell to the fowlers' guns to supply an insatiable market for fine feathers, and among the favourite targets were the terns.

Terns are a world-wide group of small, gull-like birds that nest in colonies on low sandy islands. Built for speed and maneuverability, they are the aerial acrobats of the coastal zones, darting and hovering, plunging into the waves to seize small fish in their stiletto bills, or wheeling and diving fearlessly to mob and drive off intruders to their nesting grounds.

Among these, the roseate tern was a favourite target of the feather hunters, its brilliant white plumage offset by pale blue-gray back and wings and a black cap, its underside accented by a delicate blush of seashell pink. Indeed, in the 1880s it is possible that the dead specimens of this graceful sea bird that adorned ladies' hats in Montréal, Toronto, New York, and Philadelphia outnumbered the live ones nesting in Nova Scotia and New England. To compound the problem, the depredations of egg collectors, who regularly visited tern and gull colonies throughout the summer months, effectively forestalled new generations from replacing the birds that were being sacrificed in such numbers for their beauty.

Fortunately, protective legislation and enforcement in the early twentieth century did allow the roseate tern to make a comeback, especially in the Massachusetts/Long Island area. Recovery was even noted on Sable Island and on a number of inshore islands along the Nova Scotia coast. Nevertheless, roseate terns have never become

numerous in Canada in this century. Colonies in Nova Scotia, and in recent years on the Magdalen Islands, appear to be at the outer limits of the species' range. Since about 1960 the breeding population in Canada has been in decline to such a degree that in 1986 COSEWIC designated the species as Threatened.

The roseate tern is primarily a bird of tropical and subtropical zones, more common to the shores of Africa, Asia, and the South Pacific than to the temperate and boreal climates of northwest Europe and eastern North America. In Atlantic Canada, the most recently published census figures, from 1985, indicate fewer than 5 pairs in Québec's Magdalen Islands, and be-

tween 102 and 122 pairs in Nova Scotia. There is a single record of breeding success in New Brunswick, at Machias Seal Island, in 1982.

A total of 23 Canadian breeding sites for roseate terns have been identified at various times, but of these, only 8 were found to be in use between 1982 and 1985. Although terns are known to change their nesting locations readily, it seems probable that the entire current breeding population can be accounted for at these sites, and that it amounts to no more than 100–130 pairs, or about 3–4 percent of the total population in eastern North America. Some sense of the population decline in recent years can be derived from the fact that as recently as 1970, the Sable Island

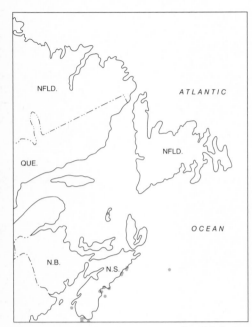

Roseate Tern

colony alone numbered 130 pairs.

Roseate terns often nest in close proximity to common tern colonies, the common terns laying their two to four eggs in open depressions in the sand, while the roseates choose the partial shelter of tall beach grass, beach pea, poison ivy, or other herbaceous plants. Each pair produces one or two cream, yellowish, buff, or olive-coloured eggs that are incubated, primarily by the female, for about three weeks.

The degree of additional cover under which the roseate tern conceals its nest may offer some protection against natural salt-marsh marauders such as crows, marsh hawks, and short-eared owls, none of which would hesitate to take young terns. However, now that exploitation by feather hunters and egg collectors is no longer a serious problem, predation on eggs and young by herring and great black-backed gulls, and loss of breeding habitat to these larger, more aggressive gull species, have become the principal threats to the roseate tern at its few remaining nesting sites in Canada. Gull numbers are on the rise because garbage is providing them with year-round food supplies.

Another danger, also related to human activity, is pollution. Once their eggs have hatched, both adult terns participate in caring for the downy young, feeding them on sand lance and other small fish, which they catch in fast-flowing tide rips near the shore. As marine predators, they are extremely vulnerable to concentrations of toxic chemicals in the fish on which they feed. This risk is not merely hypothetical. PCBs and DDE have been found in the tissues of congenitally deformed roseate tern chicks in Massachusetts and New York.

When numbers of a species fall to low levels, even minor, isolated pressures can pose major problems. This truth was brought home during the 1970s by the discovery that a surprisingly large proportion of the leg bands from roseate terns nesting in Nova Scotia and New England were being returned by a single respondent. On investigation, the individual was found to be a commercial market hunter on the Guyanese coast of South America; he had been trapping terns intensively on their wintering grounds all through the late 1960s and 1970s. Although this particular operation appears to have stopped by about 1980, it is certainly possible that other trappers, located elsewhere in the birds' South American winter range, anywhere from Colombia to Brazil, are taking enough birds to threaten the survival of the species.

Under the pressures of predation, pollution, competition for habitat in the breeding grounds, and probable human predation in the wintering areas, the northeastern North American population of the roseate tern has declined by about 70 percent in the past 50 years. In view of these negative factors, its designation as a threatened species is unlikely to be lifted for a long time to come.

Atlantic Whitefish
(*Coregonus canadensis*)

"You don't know what you've got until you've lost it," says an old proverb handed down through generations of country folk. The words may turn out to be a fitting epitaph for the Atlantic whitefish, one of half a dozen known fish species unique to Canadian waters. Its fate provides a clear-cut example of how easily a narrowly distributed wildlife species can be devastated through lack of knowledge.

The Atlantic whitefish, sometimes also called the Acadian whitefish, is streamlined and silvery, shaded a dark blue-green on the back, with white below. It grows to an average length of 380 millimetres and a maximum of at least 500 millimetres. Its known distribution is restricted to a few lakes and streams in southern and southwestern Nova Scotia, where it was long recognized by local anglers and commercial fishermen alike as a desirable edible and game species. Catches of whitefish in Milipsigate Lake, Lunenburg County, were reported by sport fishermen at least as early as the 1920s, and for many years, large numbers were netted in the Tusket River, Yarmouth County, during the October spawning runs.

To be known by the local inhabitants of an area and to be known to science are not necessarily the same thing. The field of fish studies is vast, and the resources available to support collection, description, and systematic field study are limited. It is not entirely surprising, therefore, that as recently as the 1960s this whitefish was assumed to be a common species such as the lake whitefish, which is widely distributed across Canada. In fact, it was not until 1967 that an account was published describing the Atlantic whitefish as a new and distinct species, endemic to parts of the Tusket and Petite Rivière watersheds. In 1983 it was featured, as an endangered species, on a Canadian postage stamp. Regrettably, the recognition came almost too late.

Few details of the natural history of this fish are known, but the two populations that have been identified do seem to differ in at least one significant way. Those in the Tusket River system and the adjoining Annis River are, or were, anadromous: i.e., they follow an annual migratory cycle from the brackish waters of the Tusket estuary to fresh-water locations upstream where they spawn, and then move downstream again to the sea. In fact, they are known to have travelled considerable distances in salt water, as specimens have been caught in the harbour at Yarmouth, Nova Scotia, several kilometres around the coast from the mouth of the Tusket, and at Halls Harbour, a small Nova Scotia port on the upper Bay of Fundy. By contrast, the Lunenburg County stock appears to consist of small breeding populations landlocked in a number of lakes in the upper reaches of the Petite Rivière system. Perhaps the ancestors of these fish were once anadromous too, but if so, they must have adapted to year-round life in fresh water, since the Petite has been blocked by dams for more than 150 years.

Unrecognized as a separate species, the Atlantic whitefish became endangered without anyone being aware of the fact. The first serious blow was struck against it in 1929, with construction of the Tusket River hydroelectric dam. Although a fish ladder was included in the structure to accommodate not only the whitefish but a stock of Atlantic salmon that also spawned there, it was poorly designed, providing neither an effective means of attracting the attention of the fish to its presence, nor adequate protection from poachers. Fish heading upstream to spawn were exposed to a gauntlet of men armed with dipnets and even, reportedly, pitchforks. Those making the return journey frequently missed the entrance to the ladder and were killed by the blades of the generator turbines. A further risk was posed by occasional, radical fluctuations in the water level of the reservoir, in connection with operation and maintenance of the dam. Whitefish spawning in the Annis River, a tributary that flows into the Tusket below the power dam, were spared these pressures. As recently as the 1970s it was reported that 50–100 whitefish were being taken each year as a by-catch in nets set for gaspereau, a common anadromous species in many Maritime rivers.

Atlantic Whitefish

Once they realized that the Atlantic whitefish was a rare new species, Nova Scotia officials acted quickly, amending the Fishery Regulations in 1970 to prohibit its capture in any and all waters of the province by any method, at any time of the year. A further safeguard has been afforded in the Petite Rivière watershed by the fact that the lakes where the whitefish survives supply water for the town of Bridgewater, and have therefore been designated as a Protected Water Area.

By this time, unfortunately, another stress factor, unseen but deadly, was taking its toll. During the late 1970s, owing to acidification from acid rain, the Tusket had become one of seven Nova Scotia river systems that no longer supported successful reproduction by Atlantic salmon. In 1982, its average pH level had sunk to 4.7, and that fall, no Atlantic whitefish were taken in a trap net monitored by the Department of Fisheries and Oceans at the Tusket powerhouse. On the Annis River the pH level that same year was 5.0, and a survey recorded two speci-

mens. The Petite Rivière system had a more acceptable pH of 5.5, reflecting the fact that it occupies an area where soil and rock conditions buffer the water somewhat against the effects of acid precipitation.

There are grounds to fear that the Atlantic whitefish has been extirpated in the Tusket River. In the mid-1980s, a large-scale, open-pit tin mine was opened in the East Tusket drainage area. Although corrective actions were later taken, effluent initially discharged from this site introduced high levels of suspended solids, copper, and zinc into the stream. If any whitefish were still breeding there despite acidification, the impact of heavy siltation, turbidity, and metal content in the water might well have dealt the final blow to a population already so heavily stressed.

A remnant population of Atlantic whitefish may still be present in the Annis River, and the population in the Petite Rivière system appears at present to be relatively safe from immediate dangers other than poaching. Continued acidification is a source of concern in this area too, however, and there are very few large, unobstructed watersheds with good acid-buffering capacity left in Nova Scotia where an attempt might be made to transplant fish, as one means of building new stocks.

The lack of specific knowledge is a major handicap in any effort to take corrective action. It is even conceivable that extensive field research could result in the discovery of other locations where the Atlantic whitefish survives. However, in view of its extremely limited distribution, its low numbers, and the threats to its habitat, the species seems for the time being to merit the designation assigned by COSEWIC in 1983: Endangered — facing immediate risk of extinction.

Eastern Mountain Avens
(*Geum peckii*)

Sometimes, a slightly different population of a species is found in an isolated region. This is the case with eastern mountain avens, a lovely, bright-

yellow wildflower of the rose family that grows near sea level on tiny Brier Island in western Nova Scotia. Peculiarly, the species also occurs in alpine habitats high in the mountains of New Hampshire. These populations are similar to other mountain avens of eastern North America, but botanists consider them to be sufficiently different to recognize them as a distinct species.

On Brier Island, over a dozen small populations are known in habitats including sphagnum

bogs, wet depressions along the coast, and exposed mineral soil. The most significant populations occur on a raised bog between the towns of Westport and Pond Cove. But here, drainage has not only destroyed key habitat and caused an invasion of weeds, but has also provided suitable drier habitat for a major gull rookery. The gulls trample the mountain avens and provide significant amounts of fertilizer for surface vegetation, allowing an invasion of competing species and weeds in the nesting areas, and leading to the gradual elimination of the avens in the rookery.

Additional drainage, expansion of the gull colony, sheep grazing, and cottage development remain potential threats, and for these reasons the Brier Island colonies are considered endangered.

Eastern Mountain Avens

Left: Eastern Mountain Avens – Endangered

Furbish's Lousewort
(Pedicularis furbishiae)

Furbish's lousewort is a perennial herb confined to narrow strips of shaded, steeply sloping, eroding river terraces along both sides of a 45-kilometre stretch of the St. John River in New Brunswick and Maine. The species was made famous when it became known that dams proposed by the United States Army Corps of Engineers would drown virtually all of its known wild populations.

The latest census of this species, taken in 1983, established three separate populations on the Canadian side of the river, totalling about 531 plants. Over 5,000 plants grow on the American banks of the river, but these are low numbers considering that extensive searches have taken place.

Furbish's lousewort reproduces entirely by seed and is regularly pollinated by bumblebees. A peculiar feature of the seedlings is that they must rely on the roots of other plants for nourishment. Adult plants, however, can grow independently.

By far the greatest threat to the survival of the Furbish's lousewort in New Brunswick is from additional dam proposals being considered by both American and New Brunswick governments. For this reason, the plant continues to be listed as an endangered species.

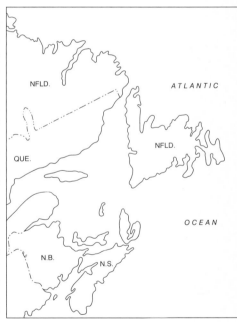

Furbish's Lousewort

Left: Furbish's Lousewort – Endangered

Pink Coreopsis
(*Coreopsis rosea*)

Pink Coreopsis

Pink coreopsis, a colourful perennial member of the aster family, is a species of the American Atlantic coast from Massachusetts southward. In Canada it grows only at the edges of a few lakes and streams along the Tusket River in extreme southern Nova Scotia, where it is considered to be endangered.

The bright, showy flowers are about two centimetres in diameter, with lovely pink petals and yellow centres. Grass-like leaves growing on thin shoots blend into the background greenery, making the pink coreopsis hard to find unless the plants are in bloom. Flowering takes place from mid-July to September and reproduction is mainly by seed, although new shoots are also produced vegetatively from existing plants.

A fascinating aspect of the biology of this rare species is that it grows intermixed in shoreline habitats with two other, entirely unrelated flowering plants, Virginia meadow-beauty (not a rare species) and Plymouth gentian. From a distance, flowers of the three are deceptively similar — all have pink petals and yellow centres. Ecologists speculate that these plants may share one or more pollinators attracted by this colour arrangement, and that over long periods of time, the three species gradually evolved to look similar in response to the activities of the same set of pollinators.

Right: Pink Coreopsis – Endangered

Any activity that disturbs the fragile open shoreline habitat of this species could lead to its extirpation. Dams to stabilize lake levels, cottage and other recreational development, and the destructive effect of all terrain vehicles are all potential threats to the survival of pink coreopsis. A recent review of the species, in fact, revealed that half the original known populations along the Tusket River have already disappeared.

Water Pennywort
(*Hydrocotyle umbellata*)

The survival story of the water pennywort in Canada is similar to those of the endangered pink coreopsis and the threatened Plymouth gentian, although the water pennywort prefers somewhat wetter sites along the shoreline and, indeed, often grows at or below water level.

The main range of this species extends along the Atlantic coastal plain from Massachusetts south, across the southern United States and into Central America. Only two lakes are known to harbour populations — Wilson's Lake on the Tusket River and Lake Kejimkujik, some 70 kilometres to the east in Kejimkujik National Park. There are two separated populations at Wilson's Lake and four in the park.

An important feature of water pennywort leaves is their shape. They look like miniature nasturtium leaves: the slender stem is attached to the centre rather than to the edge of the leaf blade. Because of this, they provide special hiding and loafing places for invertebrates and fish. An added characteristic of this species is that plants occur in a dense band several metres wide running parallel with the shoreline, creating a protective strip of matted growth — a rich habitat for aquatic invertebrates and small fish. These animals, in turn, provide essential food for other

species higher on the food chain. Diversity is enriched, and life is better for all species within the habitat.

Little is known about the water pennywort's method of reproduction. Vigorous spread by runners is clearly an important method of proliferation at the colony level, and is the cause of the matting so characteristic along some shores. A small modest cluster of white flowers is occasionally produced, but seed set has not as yet been recorded in Canadian populations.

At Wilson's Lake, the threats to the survival of this species are identical to those described for the pink coreopsis and the Plymouth gentian. The threats have recently been reduced by the establishment of a nature reserve on the lake. At Kejimkujik, however, the entire lake is protected from development, and it would appear that survival here should not be an item of concern. There may be some indirect threats within the park, however: eutrophication, which would increase competition from other plants, could be caused by activity in nearby campgrounds, and heavy boat and visitor traffic may affect the populations in future.

Water Pennywort

Left: Water Pennywort – Endangered

Golden Crest
(*Lophiola aurea*)

The threatened golden crest is of unusual interest in that its closest relatives are found in Australia,

South America, and South Africa. It is a small plant of the Atlantic coastal plain, where it is abundant on the New Jersey Pine Barrens. In Canada, it is known today from only three localities in western Nova Scotia — a small single population on Brier Island, four or five around Ponhook Lake, several at Little Ponhook Lake, and a thriving population of dense stands at Fancy Lake. A previously known colony has been extirpated from the Little River on Digby Neck. In Nova Scotia its typical habitat is sandy shorelines, peat, and floating bog mats, and its presence at some sites is to some degree dependent upon fluctuating water levels.

Plants are low, with pinkish-gray, branching stems topped by numerous bright, golden-coloured flowers that emerge in late summer and

Golden Crest

Left: Golden Crest – Threatened

early fall. Single plants may go unnoticed, but larger colonies offer expanses of colour to passing pollinators.

Threats to the survival of the species in Nova Scotia come from cottage developments, with their attendant destruction of natural ecosystems; mining operations aimed at the removal of commercially useful, calcium-rich mud; and from possible dam construction on lakes where golden crest lives.

The northwest shore of Wilson's Lake is particularly valuable because of the many rare species found there, and the loss of this unique ecosystem could mean that many species might vanish from the region. It is hoped that people living in the area will come to realize the fragile nature of the ecosystem in which golden crest and other species thrive, and take action to ensure that the shoreline habitat receives permanent protection.

The Nova Scotia government has begun to recognize the importance of preserving habitat for these shoreline species. In April 1988, the Tusket River Nature Reserve was established to protect 22 hectares of land where pink coreopsis, plymouth gentian, and water pennywort are found. None of the golden crest's habitat, however, is protected to date.

Golden Crest – Threatened

Plymouth Gentian
(Sabatia kennedyana)

Right: Plymouth Gentian – Threatened

This threatened species occurs in only a few spots along the lower Tusket River in southern Nova Scotia, where it shares the unique shoreline habitat with the endangered pink coreopsis and water pennywort. The nearest other populations of this bright-coloured member of the gentian family are far to the south — in Massachusetts, Rhode Island and the Carolinas.

People generally think of gentians as being

purple-flowered. But the petals of the Plymouth gentian (sometimes called marsh pink) are a lovely pink with a splash of yellow at the base. The plants are perennial and vegetative spread takes place by runners — as in strawberries. Where a runner touches down, a fresh rosette of leaves develops, and in time, a shoot emerges bearing as many as 10 showy flowers.

Botanists have found this species to be readily self-pollinated, but small bees are sometimes seen visiting flowers, suggesting some cross pollination. Whether or not the plants spread by seed dispersal is not known.

As this species is absolutely dependent upon the annual fluctuations in water levels to maintain open shorelines, any water-control struc-tures that stabilized lake levels would certainly result in its extirpation.

Another threat comes from picking for decorative purposes. In a normal season, fortunately, some rosettes do not bear flowers, and hence picking may not immediately wipe out a colony.

The greatest threat to the survival of both Plymouth gentian and pink coreopsis is cottage development and off-road vehicle impact. Within the last decade, some meadows where colonies were abundant have been completely lost to bulldozing.

Plymouth Gentian

Sweet Pepperbush
(Clethra alnifolia)

The swampy shrub zone along the shoreline of Belliveau Lake in southwestern Nova Scotia is the only Canadian home of the sweet pepperbush, a two-metre-high deciduous shrub that ranges from Texas to Florida and up the Atlantic coastal plain to Maine. The single pop-ulation in Nova Scotia occurs intermittently over several kilometres along the lakeshore, in association with such wetland species as sweet gale, huckleberry, chokecherry, winterberry, and red maple.

Flowers of the sweet pepperbush are showy, white, and pleasantly fragrant. For reasons unknown, the Canadian plants produce no seed, maintaining themselves solely by vegetative means.

No protection is currently provided for this species. All parts of the shoreline where it grows are privately owned, and the habitat is threatened by cottage development, the advent of which has been made easier by new roads to the lake. A serious potential threat would arise if a major dam were ever built at the lake's exit.

Left: Sweet Pepperbush – Threatened

Sweet Pepperbush

Recovery Programs: Pulling Species Back from the Brink

◆

*Wildlife in wild places is inextricably
linked with the identity of Canada. . . .
And Canadians continue to treasure
the presence of thriving populations
of wildlife species, despite the development
of an increasingly industrial
and urban society.*

Wildlife in wild places is inextricably linked with the identity of Canada. Plants and animals have occupied a central role in the cultures of the native peoples of this land. The promise of wealth to be gained through whaling and the fishery, the fur trade and forestry, was a principal incentive for European settlement from the seventeenth to the nineteenth centuries. And Canadians continue to treasure the presence of thriving populations of wildlife species, despite the development of an increasingly industrial and urban society.

We are constantly presented with evidence of the abundance of wildlife, in our backyards and city parks, around our farms and cottages, and in our spectacular national parks and vast northern wilderness. Through films and television, paintings and books, the image of nature as an essential ingredient of our culture is reinforced daily. It may come as an unwelcome surprise to many Canadians, therefore, to learn that the abundance of wildlife so intrinsic to the nation's character is being seriously threatened. Canada's flora and fauna may still be rich in numbers, but they are poor in diversity of species, and getting poorer.

One reason for the lack of diversity, as has already been noted, is a straightforward fact of geography. In the mere 10,000 years since the last ice age, there has not been time for the life zones of this northern land to develop the ecological complexity that is characteristic of biologically older regions of the planet. North-south comparisons reveal this dramatically. Canada has 512 species of native birds; Mexico, over 1,500. Canada's 3,300 species of plants are eclipsed by Mexico's 30,000.

Another reason for the precarious status of species diversity in Canada, sadly, is more immediate and less easy to rationalize. As the species accounts in this book document, our wildlife is being victimized by human apathy and ignorance. A relatively short list of species is becoming shorter. The biological richness of the nation is being diminished, its future smothered under a thickening burden of human exploitation, pressure, and waste. Most unsettling, perhaps, is the realization that this loss is occurring in spite of our having the knowledge, the technology, and the concepts of stewardship that would enable us to prevent it.

The loss of any species anywhere in the world is disturbing for both ethical and utilitarian reasons. But it is most disturbing for the plainest and most pragmatic of these: the irrefutable evidence that ecological conditions are deteriorating as a direct result of human actions. We are responsible.

As historical and current catastrophes clearly show, when ecosystems deteriorate, human welfare suffers. Each of our threatened or endangered species, then, is a warning posted along our uncertain road into the future, telling us not only that we should heed the twists and turns, but that we need to ponder where the road is taking us. Perhaps there is a better route.

How have Canadians managed to ignore the mounting evidence of ecological damage? In fairness, as a society we are only now becoming aware of the existence of many species and of our profound stake in maintaining the ecological conditions in which they can survive. For a long time, we naively assumed that the resources of nature were limitless, and for most people there was not much reason to think otherwise. Little specific information on endangered native species and ecosystems was available outside the circles of a few scientists and naturalists. Indeed, this book provides the first really comprehensive national treatment of the subject in a readily accessible, popular form.

Still, there were signs, and there were actions taken that might have led us to a more conserving viewpoint had we chosen to consider the implications. Almost a century ago, Canadian society took decisive steps to save bison, antelope, migratory waterfowl, beaver, and other game and fur-bearing species that were being decimated by uncontrolled commercial hunting. The question now is, will we act collectively in an equally decisive fashion to save today's endangered species by curbing the far more insidious threats posed by habitat destruction? The answer is that we must, for we share with these species a common future, be it survival or extinction.

The task will be difficult and costly, especially because the situation has been deteriorating for so long. It will involve making fundamental choices and changes in our society's values and institutions. But we do know what must be done. We must act to assure the recovery of species now endangered and to prevent the endangerment of others. Our operating strategies must be aimed at forestalling further ecological destruction, and at preserving and enhancing natural ecosystems and habitats. The sooner we act, the more successful we are likely to be.

In the midst of discouraging news, there are some grounds for optimism. Small groups of wildlife professionals and motivated lay people have already succeeded in rescuing several endangered species. Recovery programs that receive the active support of the whole society will have an even greater chance of success. The formula has generally been quite straightforward: prevent killing and disturbance; restore the species' habitat. The beleaguered plant or animal will usually respond almost immediately, driven by the imperative in all living things that says the best hope of survival lies in taking advantage of favourable opportunities.

We are fortunate that the crisis of species extinction in Canada is not yet as gravely advanced as elsewhere in the world, where whole ecosystems containing thousands of interdependent species have already been damaged beyond reasonable hope of recovery. Here, by and large, the problem is still relatively manageable. We only occasionally encounter species that have already been reduced below that population required for continued viability, or habitats that have been degraded beyond our ability to restore them. The whole point of the COSEWIC program has been to identify species that are at risk before it is too late to help them.

The following accounts review species that have been brought back from the brink, at least for the foreseeable future. One of these, the swift fox, has actually been retrieved from beyond the brink, after having been extirpated from its Canadian range for many years. Such reports are heartening indications that we can do something effective to arrest the process of decline and extinction. It would be irresponsible to suggest, however, that they represent an adequate national or global conservation strategy.

American White Pelican

The white pelican is the only species to date that has recovered sufficiently to justify its removal from COSEWIC's classification as a Threatened species. Once common on inland lakes from northwestern Ontario west to British Columbia, the large white waterfowl began to decline in numbers early in the twentieth century. One of the main pressures on the pelican came from hunters. With evident concern, a Canadian ornithologist wrote:

"All large birds suffer from thoughtless persecution by careless men. It would seem as though size alone were regarded as crime sufficient to turn every gun against its unhappy possessor. This has been true of the pelican, as it has been of other large birds of greater sporting or food value. Pelicans are never eaten and their carcasses serve no other purpose than to befoul the air, yet gunners are all too few who can withhold their shot when such striking targets come in range."
P. A. Taverner, *Birds of Canada,* 1937

Hunting was not the sole threat to the species. Pelicans nest in colonies on remote islands where, apart from the danger posed by poachers, they are easily disrupted by any human or animal intruders. Many eggs and chicks will die if a site is disturbed by boaters or landing parties, and entire colonies may be abandoned if disturbances are frequent. By 1978, only about 16,000 pairs remained in Canada, and COSEWIC determined that it was appropriate to designate the species as Threatened.

About half the breeding population of the white pelican nests in Canada, mainly in the three Prairie Provinces. To combat the problem of disturbance, the governments of Alberta, Saskatchewan, and Manitoba began to protect pelican colonies in the mid-1970s. Many islands became sanctuaries, off-limits to visitors; public education messages addressed the need to protect the birds. The response of the species was almost immediate. By 1987, when COSEWIC declared the pelican to be no longer threatened, its numbers had increased to 50,000 pairs, nesting at nearly 70 colonies across western Canada.

A number of factors may have combined to bring about this remarkable recovery. There were suspicions, for instance, that chemical pollutants concentrated in the pelican's diet of fish and other aquatic life might have reduced the bird's reproductive capacity. Although this hazard was never confirmed, the banning of DDT in the early 1970s removed at least one important pesticide from the list of potential environmental threats. Another positive influence on habitat has been a marked increase in populations of the small, coarse fish species on which the pelican feeds. Fishing has reduced the numbers of larger predatory fish from many prairie lakes, while farm run-off has enriched the waters to produce a food bonanza for the birds.

The case of the pelican illustrates how simple a recovery project can be under the right circumstances. A few protective and educational measures were sufficient to reverse the balance and re-establish a species that is now likely to remain secure, barring unforeseen new pressures. The task is seldom that easy.

Wood Bison

The recovery of the wood bison, the first species to have its status downlisted by COSEWIC from Endangered to Threatened, has taken far longer than that of the white pelican, and has involved many setbacks. As described in the account on page 65, protective measures for this largest of North American grazing animals were first initiated near the end of the last century, when only a scant 300 individuals of the subspecies remained in an isolated area near the Alberta/Northwest Territories border.

Protection eventually meant not only a ban on hunting, but the creation of a national park to safeguard the bison's habitat. At first the recovery program was quite successful and the herd grew steadily to about 1,200 animals. The gain was nearly lost, however, when close to 7,000 of the closely related plains bison were introduced to Wood Buffalo National Park in the late 1920s. The two subspecies interbred and the proportion of pure wood bison in the mixed herd steadily declined. Twenty years later, the wood bison was considered to be extinct as a genetically distinct race.

Fortunately, a small, isolated herd had escaped the hybridization process. Discovered in 1957, this group became the source for unmixed wood bison stock. In 1967, 18 animals were relocated near the northwest shore of Great Slave Lake, in an area now known as the Mackenzie Bison Sanctuary. A further 23 animals were placed in an enclosed section of Elk Island National Park in Alberta. As the latter herd grew, surplus animals were dispersed among zoos to protect the bloodline and provide insurance against disease. The latter consideration was important, as both bovine tuberculosis and brucellosis had infected herds of plains and hybrid bison, and the risk of contagion was a constant threat to the small wood bison herds as well. So far, both the founder herds have prospered. The Mackenzie herd now numbers over 2,000

free-ranging animals and is securely established in excellent habitat. The Elk Island herd, which is fenced, is maintained at 250 animals, and has provided more than 200 others as foundation stock for re-introduction to other locations. This has resulted in the establishment of a small unfenced herd in the Nahanni region of the Northwest Territories, and three small fenced herds in Alberta, Manitoba, and the Yukon.

Since active propagation was begun in 1967, the population has increased elevenfold and is now dispersed widely enough to ensure that neither disease nor natural catastrophe can wipe out the entire stock. Although the recovery of the wood bison will not be considered complete until two more herds are securely established and threats of disease and hybridization are minimized, there is now every reason for optimism.

Peregrine Falcon

If any species has popularized Canadian efforts to reverse the slide to extinction, it is probably the peregrine falcon. Over the past decade, the news media have carried many stories about the peregrine, illustrated with pictures of sharp-taloned, fierce-eyed chicks glowering from their cages, or of released birds soaring above cliffs and city rooftops. The saga of re-establishing the *anatum* peregrine has been re-enacted in major cities and in wilderness areas from Alberta to Nova Scotia.

The pesticide DDT is blamed for the eradication of the peregrine from its extensive range in eastern North America. After most uses of DDT were banned in Canada and the United States in the early 1970s, toxic residues in the peregrine's food chain declined to the point where re-establishment appeared to be possible.

Rather than waiting for years to see if the few surviving wild *anatum* peregrines would be able to repopulate their former vast range, wildlife agencies decided to try re-introduction, using captive-bred birds. They obtained breeding stock from nests that were still active in the wild, and from birds that had been captured years before by falconers. For centuries the peregrine had been a preferred species for the sport of falconry, and its basic husbandry was well known. It had been bred in captivity, though not on a large scale. The old lore even told how to release young, captive-bred birds, using the medieval technique of "hacking." Fledging chicks would be set free and fed at an artificial nest site till they learned to fly and forage on their own. At this point, the falconer would recapture the birds to train them for hunting; the wildlife biologists simply let them go to migrate southward, hoping they would return to breed in future years. Without the knowledge acquired over generations of human fascination with the peregrine, re-introduction would have taken much longer, and might never have been attempted.

In the early 1970s the Canadian Wildlife Service developed techniques for breeding peregrines at a facility in Alberta, and later, two university-affiliated breeding centres became involved. The first birds became available in 1976, and over the next 12 years, more than 800 young peregrines were released at over 15 sites across eastern Canada.

Losses were very high. As is normal for wild peregrines, only about one in four returned from the first winter in Central or South America. Even more perished before reaching adulthood at two or three years of age. Gradually, however, single adults and then breeding pairs appeared at widely separated sites in Alberta, Manitoba, eastern Ontario, and Québec. Some of these birds had drifted in from the northeastern United States, where a release program had begun several years earlier. The American experience prompted a change in Canadian strategy. Scientists decided to release larger numbers of peregrines at fewer sites. Their intention was to saturate an area with released birds until a pair became established, then move the release site elsewhere. An upsurge in pairs nesting along the St. Lawrence and Ottawa river valleys in 1987 and 1988 was likely a response to this new approach.

If peregrines in Canada follow the pattern observed in the eastern United States, Great Britain, and Spain, they should now be on the verge of expanding rapidly to re-occupy most of their traditional range within the next five to ten years. Government wildlife agencies would like to see the *anatum* peregrine population increase to a minimum of 60 breeding pairs by 1993. If a breeding population of that size were to produce an average of 75 fledged young per year, then by 1998 the recovery of the species to a sustainable level would be considered largely complete. The target does not seem to be unrealistic. Already, a dozen pairs are known to be established in south-

ern Canada, and evidence suggests the presence of more hidden in the vast northern wilderness areas of Ontario, Québec, and Labrador. To monitor the population trend, wildlife agencies will conduct surveys in 1990 and 1995. In addition, they will continue to measure levels of organochlorine pesticides (e.g., DDT) in peregrines and their prey, since these harmful products are still widely used in countries where the birds winter.

Government and private conservation organizations will continue to collaborate on this project for several more years. Although the final outcome is unknown, the fact that pesticide residues have declined to the point where peregrines are able to reproduce successfully in the wild is reassuring evidence that environmental damage can be reversed and affected species restored to their former habitats.

Whooping Crane

In retrospect, the decision to attempt to save the whooping crane required considerable courage. There was so little to work with. The species had been reduced to one small flock, which was exposed to many natural and manmade hazards along the 4,000-kilometre annual migration route between summer breeding grounds in northern Canada and winter range in the southern United States. Males and females did not pair until five or six years of age, and then produced only one chick per year.

When officials in the United States and Canada decided in 1966 to begin a joint effort to recover the crane, the wild flock numbered 44 birds and had limped along for years with little increase. The two governments agreed to joint ownership of all birds and eggs, full consultation on natural events and human activities that might harm the birds, and complete sharing of information on research and management activities. This international wildlife agreement, perhaps unique in its depth of commitment, allowed scientists to plan their strategy without political interference. Each government assigned biologists to work on the project full time.

The first step was to provide maximum physical protection for the wild flock. Key parts of its wintering and breeding grounds and many of its favourite migration stops were enclosed in parks and refuges. A telephone hotline was established so the public could report crane sightings. A network of experts was established in each state and province visited by the birds, to deal with any emergencies or accidents that might befall them during migration. Instructions were made available on what to do when birds were found sick, injured, or threatened by pesticides, disease, and waterfowl hunting. Any cranes found dead were studied to learn how to eliminate the cause of death. In some areas of the United States, electrical transmission towers and lines were modified after cranes had flown into them.

Despite these precautions, it was obviously not possible to protect the whooping crane from uncontrollable disasters such as storms, oil spills, or epidemics of disease. The best insurance against these hazards was to disperse the birds geographically. Using eggs from the wild flock, and sandhill cranes as foster parents, a captive flock was created at the Patuxent Wildlife Research Center in Maryland. The growth of the wild flock was not hindered. Because each pair normally produced two eggs but fledged only one chick, one egg was surplus and could be safely removed. After five years, the captive flock at Patuxent also began producing eggs for further restoration efforts. Meanwhile, biologists checked the nests of wild cranes each year, replacing infertile eggs with good ones from other pairs, and giving priority to pairs known to be the best parents.

Establishing a second, separate wild flock was the next step. The recovery team chose to do this with the help of wild sandhill cranes that nested in Grays Lake National Wildlife Refuge in Idaho and wintered at another refuge in New Mexico. Starting in 1975, eggs from captive and wild flocks were placed under selected sandhill cranes. The sandhills were good foster parents, hatching and rearing the whoopers and leading them on migration. The one disappointment is that the adopted whoopers have so far failed to reproduce, perhaps because they remain dispersed by migration and may not recognize their own kind.

The lack of reproductive success with the adoption program has led to interest in another option, that of establishing a nonmigratory flock of whooping cranes using a "soft" release of captive-raised birds. With this technique, birds would be allowed to become accustomed to the site before being set free, and provided with some supplementary care afterwards until they appeared to be fully self-sufficient. The flock would be confined to a single area and there would be no migration to disperse it. Florida has been selected as the likely site for this attempt. Biologists are considering several release strategies. Immature birds could be held at the site for a year or more and then released, or flightless adults could be held permanently, with their young being released gradually.

A second captive flock will also be established. The sole captive flock at Patuxent has suffered serious losses three times since 1984, twice from disease and once because of impure food. A separate captive flock will offer further insurance against such mishaps.

Considering the sorry plight of the whooping crane 40 years ago, progress to date is very encouraging. The population has grown to almost 200 cranes, and current goals are to boost the original wild flock to 40 pairs by the year 2,000; to create one or two more wild flocks of 25 pairs each; and to maintain several captive flocks. The whooping crane recovery program has been characterized by a careful husbanding of assets, risking only the "interest" (i.e., the eggs), while always safeguarding the "capital" (the wild flock). The story illustrates how much can be achieved against high odds when governments and the public become deeply committed to a cause.

Swift Fox

The swift fox, a denizen of the mixed-grass prairie, is back in Canada after an absence of 50 years. Originally ranging from the Manitoba-Saskatchewan border west to the Alberta foothills, and from the American border north to about the latitude of Calgary, the shy, nocturnal little fox was well known to early settlers. It supplied about 1,000 pelts per year for the fur trade between 1850 and 1870.

As agriculture developed and other changes occurred, however, the swift fox slowly disappeared from the Canadian prairie. Its last known sighting in Canada occurred in 1928. Over roughly the same period it also disappeared from most of the American prairie, persisting in only four states.

Why the swift fox vanished is unclear. The sweeping ecological changes that accompanied human settlement certainly had an impact. More specifically, the swift fox was an unintended

157

victim of poisoning campaigns aimed at the wolf and coyote. The fox's curious nature and ready attraction to bait made it particularly vulnerable. Other factors, such as disease, may also have played a role.

Unverified sightings of the swift fox were reported in Saskatchewan in the late 1960s. The United States fox population, recovering naturally, had extended to within a few hundred kilometres of the international border, and some animals may have strayed northward. The first certain return of the swift fox to Canada occurred in 1977, however, when the late Beryl and Miles Smeeton obtained government approval to import two pairs to their ranch near Cochrane, Alberta. The foxes had pups, and the Smeetons suggested to authorities that they be used to help re-establish the extirpated species on its former range. Starting in the early 1980s, scientists from the University of Calgary, the Canadian Wildlife Service, and provincial wildlife agencies conducted a captive-breeding and re-introduction program. They proceeded cautiously because little was known about this rare fox and how it would fare on the changed prairie landscape.

An area of unbroken prairie was located on a private ranch in southeastern Alberta in 1983, and 25 swift foxes were released there. These animals had been paired and given a prior orientation of one year at the release site. Their cage walls were simply removed, giving the foxes continued access to established burrows and food. By 1988, almost 100 animals had been released using this soft technique. Despite all the care, only 5 percent survived for more than a year. Most were killed by predators, especially coyotes, while some starved or were victims of road traffic. The release technique appeared to have backfired by attracting predators to the foxes without giving the foxes enough time to learn escape tactics.

While the soft releases were occurring in Alberta, a semihard technique was being tried in Saskatchewan. Here, paired foxes were held in cages at the release site, but no food was provided after the cages were removed. Survival improved to about 20 percent; because the hungry foxes dispersed more rapidly, they were apparently less vulnerable to predation. Some of these animals survived for several years and produced litters of pups in the wild.

Encouraged by this success, scientists next tried a hard release. In the fall of 1987, a total of 57 captive-bred swift foxes were liberated in small groups at scattered sites in both provinces. Transported to the release sites, these animal were turned loose immediately, 18 of them wearing radio collars to permit them to be traced. Two months later, 13 of the 18 were still alive and had selected home sites. In view of this, scientists propose to go one step further and release foxes obtained directly from the wild. The idea is attractive because wild foxes already possess survival skills. But collecting enough wild foxes at one time to justify field costs is difficult. Because they must be imported from the United States, they must be held in quarantine for a month to ensure that they are disease-free. Nevertheless, this option is now being explored.

The captive breeding stock, which provides the most reliable source of foxes for future releases, is being managed to produce individuals with the best physical and behavioural traits for survival in the wild. Because the released foxes have not survived long enough to reveal which traits are most important for survival on the Canadian prairie, the population is being managed to maintain the greatest genetic diversity possible. All foxes are registered in a stud book, or pedigree record, and matings are selected to preserve the different blood lines represented. The fate of progeny in the wild should reveal the best stock for future releases.

Whether the swift fox will regain a secure foothold in Canada remains an unanswered question. Scientists are steadily assembling the complex puzzle of original prairie ecology from the fox's point of view, and can only hope that no essential pieces have been irretrievably lost. Releases will be continued until several generations of foxes have been born in the wild. At that time, COSEWIC will likely change the status of the swift fox from Extirpated to Endangered, giving it a tentative but sincere welcome home.

Recovery So Far: A Patchwork Solution

The danger of accounts like the foregoing, which focus attention on the successful rescue of single species, is that they can provoke a heady overconfidence in the ability of our good intentions, coupled with money and technology, to set the world right. There is a temptation to embellish the accomplishments, and to distort the humbling truth: namely, that a recovery scheme is nothing more than a last-ditch struggle to prevent a failure from becoming a permanent disaster. If we are not careful, we may be seduced onto a "recovery treadmill" of actions marked by increasing expense and diminishing effectiveness. We must never lose sight of the fact that recovery programs are only short-term fixes — first-aid treatment for the symptoms of endangered species — not lasting cures for the root causes of environmental damage. A long-term solution will depend on the adoption of preventive measures to preserve and rehabilitate whole ecosystems.

Although recovery programs have scored some encouraging victories, the COSEWIC list grows longer every year, and to date only one species, the white pelican, has qualified for removal. By 1989 a total of 44 animals and 35 plants had been designated as Threatened or Endangered in Canada; yet specific recovery efforts had been initiated on behalf of only about 1 in 5 of these. Tables I and II provide scorecards of what attention the animals are receiving; too little is being done about the plant species to warrant a detailed summary.

The tables show that of 44 endangered and threatened animal species, 33 are protected by federal or provincial laws against killing or deliberate disturbance. However, measures have been taken to secure key habitat for only 12 of them. Eleven species have been successfully bred in captivity, and re-introduction methods have been developed for 6. Recovery plans have been devised for 7 species, and are being developed for 7 more.

Of 17 endangered plants, 7 are protected from disturbance on all or a portion of their range. Four (Furbish's lousewort, eastern prickly pear, small whorled pogonia, and heart-leaved plantain) occur within parks or special reserves. The Ontario Endangered Species Act protects 3 more (large whorled pogonia, cucumber tree, and small white lady's-slipper) from "willful destruction" on public and private lands. In Nova Scotia, some populations of the pink coreopsis and water pennywort are protected in a reserve. None of the 17 threatened plants is protected by legislation, and the habitat of only 2 (bluehearts and sweet pepperbush) has been partially set aside. No formal recovery plans exist for any of the plants on the COSEWIC list, with the possible exception of Furbish's lousewort.

In short, action on behalf of species officially recognized as threatened or endangered has been highly selective. Only 5 mammals, 7 birds, 1 fish, and 1 plant are receiving adequate attention. The remaining 61 species, about 80 percent of the total, are still waiting for recovery programs to begin.

Furthermore, the status of many species has not yet been determined. This is especially true of the invertebrates — animals without backbones, such as insects, worms, and shellfish — which are estimated to number more than 100,000 species in Canada, compared with 1,800 vertebrates and 3,300 species of plants. Many of them play essential roles in the decomposition of animal and plant matter, creating new organic soils, recycling nutrients, and supporting food chains. At present there is no system for identifying invertebrates that may be at risk. COSEWIC's mandate addresses only vertebrates and plants. Of all the invertebrate species in Canada, only one is protected: the West Virginia white butterfly in Ontario.

RENEW:
A National Strategy for Species Recovery

In COSEWIC, Canadians have established a mechanism for identifying plants and animals that are at risk of extinction. COSEWIC's role, however, is only to evaluate and list or de-list species; it has no authority for wildlife or environmental management, and the list of species it publishes has no legal status. In other words, there is nothing to compel wildlife agencies to devote special attention to a species just because it has been designated by COSEWIC as Threatened or Endangered. Over the past several years it has become evident that a more active approach is required to ensure that the needs of listed species will be addressed, and that action for recovery will be undertaken where feasible.

Dealing with this requirement has not been made easier by the complexities of the Canadian confederation. Care of nondomestic flora and fauna in this country is a concern of all ten provinces, two territories, and the federal government. Provincial and territorial authorities are responsible for terrestrial plants and animals, for example, except for those bird species named in the Migratory Birds Convention, a treaty signed with the United States in 1916 to give protection to a wide range of birds including waterfowl, shore birds, sea birds, and passerines (perching birds). These species fall under the jurisdiction of the Canadian Wildlife Service of Environment Canada. All marine species, including whales, seals, and other sea mammals, as well as fish, invertebrates, and plants found in salt-water, are the concern of the federal Department of Fisheries and Oceans (DFO). Jurisdiction over freshwater fish is also vested in DFO, but in certain instances particular aspects of fisheries management have been delegated to the provinces. Consequently the responsibility for endangered fish varies across the nation.

Finally, protection and management of wildlife species on federal lands (national parks, wildlife refuges, military reservations, etc.) are the responsibility of federal agencies such as Parks Canada, the National Capital Commission, the Canadian Wildlife Service, and the Department of Public Works. The end result? More than 25 government departments and agencies have some degree of involvement with wildlife and habitat protection in Canada, not to mention the voluntary programs of dozens of nongovernment conservation organizations.

In 1988, the government agencies responsible for the management of land mammals, birds, reptiles, and amphibians (i.e., the terrestrial vertebrates) took an important step toward simplifying and co-ordinating their collective task. They established an organization and strategy to deal at least with the recovery of species in those biological groups. The objective — Recovery of Nationally Endangered Wildlife — gave rise to the name RENEW. (The French name is *Rescapé*, meaning "one saved from danger," an acronym for *Rétablissement des espèces Canadiennes en péril.*) The organization is a committee like COSEWIC, composed of the directors of provincial, territorial, and federal wildlife agencies, and the heads of the three major national wildlife organizations: Canadian Nature Federation, Canadian Wildlife Federation, and World Wildlife Fund Canada. The goal of RENEW is to enable its members to work as a team to preserve endangered and threatened species from extinction, and to prevent vulnerable species from becoming threatened or endangered.

One of RENEW's first priorities will be to set up a recovery team for each vertebrate species listed by COSEWIC. Composed of experts on the species in question, each team will prepare a recovery and management plan based on the best knowledge and methods available. Once approved, plans will be carried out by the appropriate agencies in co-operation with universities and conservation groups. The creation of RENEW is an important development, not least because it will provide a more orderly framework of co-ordination for what has hitherto been a rather ad hoc range of responses from the various government organizations.

Because it deals only with terrestrial vertebrates, RENEW is by no means a complete answer to the problem of species recovery. To achieve what is needed even for the other species now acknowledged to be at risk, the team-response concept will have to be extended to include plants, fish, and marine mammals. This will require the active collaboration of provincial agencies in fields such as fisheries, forestry, parks, heritage, and environment, and at the federal level, the Department of Fisheries and Oceans. Many of these organizations have had very little occasion to work closely together in the past, and new relationships will have to be forged. The important point will be to ensure that the recovery needs of any species do not get lost in a bureaucratic shuffle, but are addressed immediately once a designation of risk has been assigned by COSEWIC.

The urgent need to adopt an active, co-operative strategy such as RENEW becomes clear when one considers the realities of the COSEWIC list. Four out of every 5 species currently listed receive little or no attention, and the list is growing. Very few reptiles or amphibians have been reviewed as yet, although it is expected that between 5 and 10 species could qualify as threatened or endangered. Added to them will be additional species or populations of fish, plants, birds, and mammals, which have been listed at an average rate of about 7 per year since COSEWIC was founded. In the meantime, only 1 species has been de-listed, and only about 5 others appear to be likely candidates for removal in the next five or six years. At this rate even a conservative projection would suggest that the list is likely to surpass 100 species by the year 2000. And if real progress is to be achieved, it will

Table I: Level of Canadian protection and recovery effort currently in place for each ENDANGERED vertebrate species (1989).

Species or Population	Killing/ Disturbance Regulated by Law	Key Habitat Protected	Species Bred in Captivity	Re-introduced Successfully	Recovery Plan Begun	Recovery Plan Complete
Beluga (St. Lawrence)	X	X	X	-	X	-
Beluga (Ungava Bay)	X	-	-	-	-	-
Bowhead Whale	X	-	-	-	-	-
Eastern Cougar	X	-	X	-	-	-
Eastern Wolverine	X	-	X	-	-	-
Right Whale	X	-	-	-	-	X*
Sea Otter	X	X	X	X	X	-
Vancouver Island Marmot	X	X	X	-	X	-
Eskimo Curlew	X	-	-	-	-	-
Greater Prairie-chicken	X	-	X	-	-	-
Kirtland's Warbler	X	-	-	-	-	X*
Mountain Plover	X	-	-	-	-	-
Peregrine Falcon (anatum)	X	-	X	X	-	X
Piping Plover	X	X	-	-	X	-
Spotted Owl	X	-	-	-	-	X*
Whooping Crane	X	X	X	X	-	X
Atlantic Whitefish	X	-	-	-	-	-
Aurora Trout	X	X	X	-	-	X
Salish Sucker	-	-	-	-	-	-
Leatherback Turtle	-	-	-	-	-	-

(X* indicates a U.S. plan for an adjoining population)

Table II: Level of Canadian protection and recovery effort currently in place for each THREATENED vertebrate species (1989).

Species or Population	Killing/ Disturbance Regulated by Law	Key Habitat Protected	Species Bred in Captivity	Re-introduced Successfully	Recovery Plan Begun	Recovery Plan Complete
Beluga (Eastmain)	-	-	-	-	-	-
Humpback Whale (Pacific)	X	-	-	-	-	-
Maritime Woodland Caribou	X	X	-	-	-	-
Peary Caribou	-	-	-	-	-	-
Pine Marten (Nfld.)	X	-	X	X	X	-
Prairie Long-tailed Weasel	-	-	-	-	-	-
Wood Bison	X	X	X	X	-	X
Baird's Sparrow	X	-	-	-	-	-
Burrowing Owl	X	X	X	X	X	-
Ferruginous Hawk	X	-	-	-	X	-
Henslow's Sparrow	X	-	-	-	-	-
Loggerhead Shrike	X	-	-	-	X	-
Peregrine Falcon (tundrius)	X	X	X	-	-	-
Roseate Tern	X	-	-	-	-	-
Blackfin Cisco	X	-	-	-	-	-
Black Redhorse	X	X	-	-	-	-
Copper Redhorse	-	-	-	-	-	-
Enos Lake Sticklebacks	-	-	-	-	-	-
Gt. Lakes Deepwater Sculpin	X	-	-	-	-	-
Lake Simcoe Whitefish	X	X	-	X	-	-
Margined Madtom	-	-	-	-	-	-
Shorthead Sculpin	X	-	-	-	-	-
Shortjaw Cisco	X	-	-	-	-	-
Shortnose Cisco	X	-	-	-	-	-

also be important to extend the RENEW strategy to species in the Vulnerable category (the classification designated as Rare up to the 1989–90 list) before their status becomes more critical.

The Costs of Recovery vs the Costs of Extinction

So far, little attention has been given to rehabilitation costs for endangered species; yet it is becoming increasingly important to know this, not only to help determine how much we need to do the job, but also to provide a better idea of the cost of developments that may contribute to species endangerment. Living species have value, not just according to some system of planetary ethics but, from a human viewpoint, for their contribution to the economic and ecological diversity of the world on which we depend for our own well-being.

Species and ecosystems are the world's most precious resources — beyond price, in fact, for while they are renewable, they are irreplaceable if pushed to extinction. Seen in that light, the cost of losing a species will always be greater than that of saving it. Therefore, if the construction of a power dam jeopardizes the survival of a species of fish, then the cost of protecting that fish should be calculated and paid as an essential part of the project. If logging, or the dumping of industrial wastes, or the expansion of a residential suburb endangers the habitat of a threatened bird, or mammal, or plant, then it is reasonable to insist that the cost of habitat preservation is a legitimate and necessary expense that should be guaranteed by the developer before permission is granted to proceed with the project. To do anything less is to squander the natural capital of the entire biosphere on activities that at best can return only short-term benefits to a few individual human beings.

Estimating the costs of species protection and/ or rehabilitation is difficult because of the many unpredictable factors that affect the course of recovery programs, and because very little effort has been devoted to developing a predictive ability based on past experience. The crude cost estimates available allow us to put the recovery investment into perspective. In 1986, an informal survey by the Canadian Wildlife Service came up with an estimate of $3 million spent on endangered species in Canada during that fiscal year, with the federal government, the provincial and territorial governments, and the private sector each contributing about $1 million. Other than the federal government, the largest single contributor was World Wildlife Fund Canada, which provided about $1,160,000 in 1987 and $1,460,000 in 1988 — a remarkable achievement for a group whose revenues come from voluntary contributions.

The Canadian share in the international project to rescue the whooping crane has resulted in the actual expenditure of about $2.2 million, $1 million in operating costs and $1.2 million in salaries, over a period of 21 years. Far more has been spent in the United States. The current peregrine falcon recovery program in Canada operates on an overall budget of about $400,000 per year. If extended over a 20-year period, such an undertaking to restore a species would cost about $8 million. Crude as such figures are, they reveal two facts. First, relative to other areas of expenditure, public spending on endangered species has been extremely modest. Second, if real gains are to be made in the struggle against extinction, significant increases in financial commitment will be essential.

Meanwhile, in order to make the most effective use of available funding, the allocation of resources may have to be made according to the "triage" principle used by battlefield physicians. That is, species at risk may have to be categorized according to whether they can survive without immediate help, whether they must be helped at once, or whether they are already beyond all hope of saving. Once these divisions are determined, the greatest share of effort and resources can then be devoted to the second category, where it is hoped it will do the most immediate good.

To some extent this practice is already unwittingly in operation. Little or no effort is being invested in the future of species like the Eskimo curlew or the eastern cougar, creatures so rare and imperilled that their survival seems most unlikely. Likewise, little attention goes to the prairie long-tailed weasel, the *tundrius* peregrine, and other species or subspecies that do not appear to be in serious or immediate danger. What triage can do, by focussing limited resources on those situations that offer the best odds for success, is help to avoid costly, well-meaning, but biologically irrelevant gestures. As an example of the opposite extreme, consider the expenditure of millions of dollars during the winter of 1988–89 to free two migrating gray whales trapped in ice off Point Barrow, Alaska. The effort revealed a commendable depth of human concern for the plight of other creatures, but the loss of two whales in that manner was a natural event that the population could sustain. The same dollars could have accomplished far more had they been spent on developing technology to avoid oil spills or plastics pollution along the Pacific coast, two problems that pose far more serious threats to the gray whale and to a wide variety of other rare and threatened marine wildlife.

In 1988, the amount of funding for species recovery in Canada got a 20 percent boost when the federal government and the World Wildlife Fund Canada, aiming to promote interest in endangered species, created an Endangered Species Recovery Fund (ESRF). Over a four-year period from 1988 to 1992, the ESRF will provide $2 million for recovery projects undertaken by nongovernment organizations such as universities, conservation organizations, and private consultants. To encourage at least partial self-sufficiency, the ESRF offers $2 for every $1 provided by the applicant. Several provincial governments have also established funds for work on endangered species. Alberta, through its Prairie for Tomorrow conservation fund, will include endangered species in the projects that it supports, and the governments of Manitoba and Saskatchewan have also set up special funds. Such allocations are encouraging indicators that there is a growing awareness of how important it is to back our good intentions with dollars. Nevertheless, the few millions we devote annually to species preservation fall far short of meeting the urgent need for action by a society that earns tens of billions annually from direct and indirect uses of the natural environment.

Technical Challenges of Species Preservation

As the uneasy awareness spreads that the world may be experiencing an unprecedented episode of mass extinction, the scientific community has

begun to respond in some very creative ways. Specialists from widely separated disciplines — animal and plant ecologists, population geneticists, zoo-keepers, herbarium managers, and the like — have joined forces to develop a new branch of life science known as conservation biology. Defined as the "biology of scarcity," it has been described by one expert as a study to be applied "when an ecosystem, habitat, species, or population is subject to some kind of artificial (man-induced) limitation — usually reduction of space and numbers." This new field is providing insights into the process of extinction, as opposed to the event itself, and developing new tools for salvaging species headed for extinction. It is also forcing a reappraisal of traditional concepts of what constitutes a secure population, and what may be the role of the zoo, aquarium, or herbarium in species survival.

Past recovery programs in Canada have relied on game-management techniques: protective regulations, sanctuaries, habitat improvement, capture and relocation of specimens, and releases of captive-bred stock. In the case of game species with large populations, these methods could be applied on a trial and error basis. Extensive knowledge of the biology of each species and its ecological requirements was desirable but not essential.

When dealing with endangered species, trial and error must be minimized, for the simple reason that failure means extinction. In the United States, captive breeding programs have recently been undertaken with the last few California condors and black-footed ferrets in existence. Both programs are under tremendous and unenviable pressure to succeed. In each case, the last few wild individuals have been taken into captivity in a desperate gamble that it will be possible to breed them in captivity and produce descendants in sufficient numbers that they might one day be re-introduced to their natural habitat.

Intimate knowledge of the biology and ecology of a species is obviously crucial to the success of such exercises, yet it is rarely available. Small populations are hard to study in the wild. For one thing, subjecting a remnant population to too much attention courts the risk of disrupting it. In addition, small populations may no longer exhibit critical traits of migration, reproductive behaviour, antipredator strategies, and the like, that would be normal in large populations of the same species. The situation presents all the elements of a crisis. The more we learn about endangered species, the more we realize that important information is missing. Meanwhile, the number of endangered species continues to grow, and populations already endangered are edging ever closer to extinction.

Undoubtedly the most revolutionary concept to emerge from conservation biology is that of the "minimum viable population." Referring to genetic fitness and diversity, it assumes that for each species there is a threshold number of individuals, or combination of individuals of differing sex and age, that will ensure the persistence of a population in a viable state for a given period of time. Below that threshold, inbreeding and other anomalies cause the loss of genetic qualities that affect survival, and the population begins an accelerating decline. In the words of one observer, "gene pools shrink to gene puddles," and finally disappear altogether. In reality, extinction occurs not when the last representative of a species dies, but when reproduction ceases.

The theory of minimum viable population holds many implications for the way in which we approach the rescue of endangered species. For one thing, it must be addressed in existing recovery programs. Although there has not been time enough to test it fully, we have little choice, where extinction is involved, but to take all reasonable precautions. The population targets that have been stipulated in recovery plans for bison, peregrine, piping plover, and other species, must take into account not only the density and distribution of historical populations, but also their genetic diversity. These plans must strive to maintain not just numbers, but a high proportion of the diversity that existed in the original gene pool. We ignore the genetic aspect of species preservation at our peril. The north Atlantic population of the endangered right whale, for example, has remained stable at about 250 individuals, despite decades of protection. This may be an indication that its numbers have fallen below the minimum viable population level that would ensure the genetic variety for long-term survival.

In other words, the designation of species at risk must take into account the population's genetic qualities as well as gross trends in number and distribution. A population of hundreds of individuals of one species may be secure; another species may need to number in the thou-

sands before the danger is averted. COSEWIC must now obtain genetic profiles that will reveal the degree of variability among individuals, and RENEW will have to make recovery plans that attempt to restore not only the numbers of a species but also its genetic diversity.

In Yellowstone National Park, Montana, there live some 200 grizzly bears. The bears had been thought to be stable and safe within the protected area of the park, but recent analyses have revealed that only about one-quarter of the bears participate in breeding, a number so small that the population is likely to develop breeding problems and die out within the next century if no preventive measures are taken. To cope with this threat, park managers now have the option of trying to introduce genes from other grizzlies into the Yellowstone population. The most promising techniques, artificial insemination and the implantation of fertilized ova from other bears, represent levels of intervention far more intense than has been considered practical in the past.

Reliance on captive stocks for genetic material to bolster wild populations of threatened species will undoubtedly increase as time goes on. One can visualize a world in which many species will be confined to small remnants of habitat and sustained by artificial exchanges of genes from captive populations. This is hardly an image calculated to please those who would prefer to see sustainable wild populations, but it is probably a better solution than extinction for species that, because of their inability to adapt to human presence or survive without vast areas of wilderness, will be the most vulnerable to human population pressures.

Some experts are now proposing that captive breeding of a species should begin as soon as it is judged to be in jeopardy. While this may be clearly necessary when dealing with species that have been reduced to the last few individuals, such as the California condor, the proposal has been criticized for suggesting to the public that there is no need to maintain natural habitats because survival in a zoo will be good enough. This, of course, is the wrong message. The goal of conservation biology is not to create living museums, but to preserve species so that, once sufficient habitat has been protected and restored, stock will be available for the re-establishment of self-sustaining populations in the wild.

Prevention: The Ultimate Cure

Despite the undeniable importance of recovering species that are in trouble, the single most important message of this book concerns the need to prevent wildlife species from becoming endangered in the first place. Clearly, to put off dealing with species until they are already endangered is folly. Not only is it more difficult and more expensive; it is far less likely to succeed. The only sane approach to environmental protection is to conduct our affairs so that entire ecosystems, with their communities of many thousands of species, are preserved in a healthy state. The following argument, put forward by Canadian ecologist Stan Rowe, bears repeating: *"Endangered organisms per se cannot be preserved. Ecosystems of which organisms are interesting ingredients can, however, be preserved — as long as the ecosphere of which they are parts continues to function in the old, natural, and healthy way. This realization turns attention more and more to the absolute necessity of preserving wilderness and natural areas, ecological reserves and animal sanctuaries, endangered places before endangered species. Unless natural ecological systems are preserved, the native flora and fauna will not be preserved. Organisms will still exist in the truncated environments fashioned by people, but only as cultivars [plants in captivity], zoo freaks, the living dead."*

> J. Stan Rowe, "On Saving Flora and Fauna," *Canadian Plant Conservation Programme Newsletter* (Vol.3 No.2)

One practical step toward adopting a strategy of preventive conservation would be to monitor species and habitats known to be sensitive to human activities, and to take precautionary steps to ensure that they would never be stressed to the point of endangerment. In effect, this would mean gradually converting endangered species programs to vulnerable species programs, parallel in all respects except that the threat of immediate extinction would no longer be a prerequisite for protective action.

The adoption of a truly preventive approach to environmental conservation will require some profound changes in the way our society views its relationship with nature and natural resources. For one thing, it will be necessary to broaden our view of resource management from the level of products to that of whole systems. Most agencies deal largely with those species or resources that provide a commercial product: wood fibre, fish, crops, energy, recreation, minerals. The resulting narrow compartmentalized focus means that no one is responsible for the overall integrity of ecosystems from which those products are extracted. If the endangerment of species is to be forestalled, then resource agencies will have to shift their emphasis from production to the maintenance of healthy productive systems.

Secondly, economic decision-makers will have to accept a much greater responsibility for preserving the well-being of the environment on which our economic prosperity has been based. The integration of economic and environmental decision-making was one of the recommendations of the National Task Force on Economy and Environment. To this end, both federal and provincial governments have established round tables of business leaders who will be advised by environmental experts on the most effective means of implementing a strategy of environmental and developmental harmony. Increasing numbers of politicians and business people appear to recognize the urgency and validity of the blunt message presented by the World Commission on Environment and Development: "Development cannot subsist upon a deteriorating environmental resource base; the environment cannot be protected when [economic] growth leaves out of account the costs of environmental destruction."

It is a message worthy of promotion at every opportunity, both among Canadians and in Canada's dealings with other nations. The endangerment of species and ecosystems is an unacceptably high cost for development; developments that will result in endangerment should not be undertaken.

In a modern democracy, it is ultimately the role of the public to challenge the political leadership to prepare an agenda of solutions to problems. At present, many of the most pressing problems are environmental, including the recovery of those species now known to be in imminent danger of extinction, and the prevention of further endangerment. So far, however, the issue has not received as much public attention in Canada as it must if many of the currently endangered species are to be rescued. Definite and drastic action is needed; yet no comprehensive national program has been devised to truly cope with the problem. Without such a program, Canada will have great difficulty doing its part to prevent what British ecologist Norman Myers has described as " . . . a mass extinction episode that is surely accounting for several species per day already, and [will] eventually eliminate at least one quarter and conceivably one third or even more of all species extant." In Canada, it is not yet too late to act.

The Power of Public Participation

The belief that wildlife is important to many Canadians is supported by the existence across the country of literally hundreds of private organizations dedicated to conservation, wildlife-related recreation, appreciation of natural history, and the welfare of animals. They form part of what British conservationist Lee Durrell calls "Noah's Army." According to her, there are about 5,000 international and 50,000 national and regional nongovernment organizations worldwide, representing many millions of individual supporters. There are at least 19 national, 84 provincial, and 205 local conservation and sportsmen's organizations in Canada.

Most citizens' organizations are societies or clubs with a general membership and elected volunteer officers. Less common is the registered nonprofit association or federation with a professional staff. Both may conduct activities supported by the dues of members and donations solicited from individuals and corporations. The memberships of these groups, like the activities and issues in which they become involved, range from the community level to the provincial, national, and international levels. Conservation groups have contributed immensely to raising public awareness and concern for the environment in general, and for the plight of endangered species in particular. Some of the major groups are highlighted below.

A number of organizations produce magazines, journals, and newsletters that present information on endangered species. Examples are *Nature Canada*, by the Canadian Nature Federation; *Seasons*, by the Federation of Ontario Naturalists; *International Wildlife*, by the Canadian Wildlife Federation; *Working for Wildlife*, by the World Wildlife Fund Canada; *Franc Nord*, by the

Union Québécoise pour la Conservation de la Nature; and the *Canadian Field-Naturalist*, by the Ottawa Field-Naturalists' Club.

An effective approach to creating an environmentally aware society is through the education of children. Several organizations have addressed this target by creating resource kits for elementary school teachers and students. The best known are the World Wildlife Fund's "Operation Lifeline" and the Canadian Wildlife Federation's "Project Wild." The federation also produces a series called "Learning about Wildlife," issued each year just before National Wildlife Week in April. Other groups, such as the Union Québécoise pour la Conservation de la Nature, have prepared wall posters on various endangered species, for classroom and general use.

Citizens' groups have organized and held important conferences on endangered species. The first major national symposium on the subject was held in 1976 by the Canadian Nature Federation and World Wildlife Fund. A recommendation made at this meeting resulted in the creation of COSEWIC by the provincial and federal governments. In 1986 and 1989, workshops on prairie conservation and endangered species were arranged by the Federation of Alberta Naturalists, the Saskatchewan Natural History Society, and the Canadian Plains Research Centre. In 1988, the Fondation pour la Sauvegarde des Espèces Menacées organized an international forum on the endangered St. Lawrence beluga whale. Besides reviewing scientific information on endangered wildlife, these conferences encourage a dialogue among scientists, industry representatives, politicians, and concerned citizens, on the most effective means of dealing with the species in question.

Some organizations raise money for work on endangered species. The World Wildlife Fund is the major force here, having provided nearly $1 million each year for the past several years, in funds solicited mainly from private companies and corporations. Its role in creating the new Endangered Species Recovery Fund has already been described (p. XX). Several other organizations, like the Nature Conservancy of Canada, Ducks Unlimited Canada, and Wildlife Habitat Canada, also raise money for projects that preserve or improve habitat, and thus benefit endangered species.

Each year private citizens probably donate as many hours to wildlife projects as are worked by the employees of government agencies. Universities, taken together, contribute the most. Notable examples include the University of Calgary, with its work on the swift fox, and the University of Saskatchewan and McGill University's MacDonald College, for their work on birds of prey.

Other organizations have conducted major projects, a particularly impressive example of which is the *Ontario Breeding Bird Atlas*, a creation of four organizations — the Federation of Ontario Naturalists, the Nature Conservancy of Canada, the Ontario Field Ornithologists, and the Long Point Bird Observatory. To gather data for the atlas, province-wide surveys were conducted by hundreds of volunteer naturalists. The atlas revealed that 24 species of birds were rare and/or declining in the province. A follow-up project, the Rare Breeding Bird Program, has been proposed to monitor these species. Labour-intensive efforts such as these are beyond the reach of government wildlife agencies, but they are essential if we are to detect and help species *before* they become endangered.

Another good example is Operation Burrowing Owl, a joint effort of the World Wildlife Fund and five provincial conservation groups. The program publicizes the plight of the owl and provides incentives to farmers to preserve breeding colonies that occur on their land.

In addition, many zoos and aquaria in Canada are operated by public societies dedicated to encouraging projects that both help endangered species and educate visitors about the nation's conservation programs. The Calgary, Assiniboine Park (Winnipeg), and Toronto zoos provide important support to the swift fox and bison recovery programs.

Collectively, nongovernment organizations play a major role in shaping the nation's environmental policies, speaking out on all sides of public debates on how we use or treat wild animals and plants. Subjects like wilderness preservation, sport hunting, subsistence hunting, trapping, game management, pest and predator control, whaling, commercial use of wildlife, and humane treatment of animals have received attention over the past few years. By bringing new information and various ethical points of view to the public forum, they have helped society contemplate the consequences of its actions, and encouraged progress toward a more enlightened treatment of natural resources.

Unfortunately, the core of concerned citizens represented by these conservation groups has not been enough to prevent the environmental deterioration to which the endangered species in this book are testimony. According to a 1981 survey conducted by the Canadian Wildlife Service (*The Importance of Wildlife to Canadians*, 1985), only about 6 percent of the Canadian population is actively involved with conservation organizations, and they constitute an insufficient rear guard for society's steady destructive march. In the vanguard are the proponents of political and socio-economic issues like sovereignty over natural resources, employment, industrial growth, and today's standard of living — issues that have always taken precedence over concerns for the long-term costs of environmental degradation. But the existence of conservation-minded organizations is immensely important; they are the nucleus of the informed public that will be essential in helping to solve our environmental problems.

What You Can Do

The message of this book is intended to be one of optimism. Many species are indeed on the brink, but it is not too late to save a good number of them. It is certainly not too late to prevent others from joining the list of species threatened with extinction. One thing is clear, however; if we are to succeed in preventing species from becoming endangered, if we are to begin to live in a world where ecosystems are not faced with imminent collapse, more people will need to become active in conserving and protecting the environment. Most Canadians are concerned about the environment, but too often they don't know how to act on their concerns, or what to do to help. The following are but a few suggestions for actions that will directly benefit endangered species, and some examples of what can be achieved when people decide to act.

STEP 1.
Congratulations! By reading this book, you have taken the first step in helping endangered species. You now know more about endangered species and what it will take to prevent their disappearance from Canada.

STEP 2.
Speak up. Now that you know something about endangered species, let your concerns be known. Write letters to your government representative and to heads of business and industry. Let them know that you think endangered species are worth saving.

Leone Pippard: Getting Recognition for the Beluga Whale

When Leone Pippard set out from Toronto in the summer of 1972 on a camping trip to Québec with her friend Heather Malcolm, she had no suspicion that she was about to discover the commitment of a lifetime. The wooded hills and headlands at the mouth of the Saguenay River simply seemed like a good spot for a wilderness vacation. Nobody warned her that she might be captivated by the snow-white beluga whales of the lower St. Lawrence.

When she sought to learn more about them, she was surprised to discover that government sources had very little published information available. Pippard and Malcolm, both photographers, decided to undertake a most unusual project. Supplementing their own funds with donations solicited from conservation organizations and other supporters, they spent the entire summer and fall of 1975 and 1977 following the amiable cetaceans. Not only did they acquire unequalled pictorial records of beluga; they also gained unprecedented knowledge of how the whales travelled, ate, slept, and interacted with each other in the wild.

As their knowledge of the animals grew, so did their realization that the St. Lawrence belugas were in trouble. Although large-scale hunting of belugas had ceased in the 1950s, the population had continued to decrease. Leone wanted to know why.

Pippard and Malcolm submitted a report detailing their suspicions in 1978, but government authorities hesitated to act on their observations and were reluctant to respond to their concerns. Pippard refused to be brushed aside. She continued to campaign for some action on the beluga. In 1979 the St. Lawrence River beluga was given protected status by the Canadian government, and Leone Pippard was commissioned by COSEWIC to prepare a report on the whale's status. In 1983, mainly as a result of her efforts, it was listed by COSEWIC as Endangered — faced with immediate danger of extirpation.

But there was no answer to Leone's question of what was causing the beluga population to decline. Pierre Béland, a marine ecologist, and Daniel Martineau, a veterinarian, were interested in the whales, and they began to study the dead whales that washed ashore. They performed autopsies and had the tissue analyzed for chemical contamination. What they discovered was alarming. The whales were afflicted with a diverse assortment of disorders, some never before seen in toothed whales, including pneumonia, hepatitis, and abscesses. Even more alarming were the levels of contaminants in the belugas' tissues. Every animal sampled had exceptionally high levels of PCBs, DDT, and other complex synthetic chemicals. Twenty-four potentially toxic chemicals have been identified in the tissues of the St. Lawrence River beluga. Obviously, the whales were highly contaminated and pollution in the St. Lawrence River was to blame.

This finding brought the beluga whale into the

forefront of the campaign to clean up the St. Lawrence. Pippard, Béland, and Martineau have been joined by others who want to save both the whales and the river. A major focus now is the need to clean up pollutants at their source. The years of research and lobbying are beginning to pay off. In 1988, the federal and Québec governments unveiled a St. Lawrence River Action Plan, aimed primarily at controlling the discharge of pollution into the river, and funding research into habitat requirements of belugas and other river species.

Meanwhile, after a decade and a half of tireless effort, international recognition and support are coming to Leone Pippard. In January 1988 her picture appeared on the cover of *Ms.* magazine as one of the periodical's "Women of the Year." An article in the same issue quoted her in a statement that sums up the depth of her feelings about what turned a summer holiday into a full-time vocation: "[The belugas] are as much a part of the river as the whitecaps. And yet we're only now starting to learn how curious and intelligent and gentle they are. If we lose them, we'll lose a part of our history — and worse, it'll be a case of wiping something out before we've even begun to know it."

STEP 3.
Volunteer your time and energy to assist conservation efforts in your area.

Winifred (Cairns) Wake: The Piping Plover

In the mid-1970s, few people even noticed the piping plover. It was not a common bird, and for a number of years had appeared on the "Blue List" of rare species published by *American Birds,* the magazine of the Audubon Society. In Canada, the shy little shore bird's breeding range included the Gulf of St. Lawrence and southern Nova Scotia, as well as the shores of the Great Lakes and many smaller bodies of water on the Prairies.

To Winifred Cairns (now Winifred Wake), a graduate biology student at Dalhousie University in Halifax, the bird seemed like an ideal research subject for her master's thesis. Her field studies, conducted in 1975–76, revealed a lot about piping plover behaviour. It also left her wondering just what its status might really be in

Atlantic Canada.

Returning to her native Prince Edward Island, she began to survey nesting sites, spending much of the summers of 1977 and 1978 searching for the inconspicuous birds, aided by a $500 subsidy from the provincial government to offset travel costs. The grant set something of a precedent. As one official was later to remark wryly: "It may have been the first time the government funded research on a species that you couldn't shoot!" As a matter of fact, Winifred did do some shooting, with a camera, while preparing a slide talk and a plover puppet that she used in presentations to visitors at Prince Edward Island National Park where she was employed as a naturalist in 1977. Subsequently, she worked with another islander, Dan McAskill, to prepare an educational videotape, which is still used in the province's schools.

The outcome of her survey was a clear indication that the piping plover was indeed a rare species, even in relatively isolated sections of beach along the north shore of P.E.I., the gulf coast of New Brunswick, and Québec's Magdalen Islands. Summarizing their research in a paper published by *American Birds* in March 1980, she and Ian A. McLaren estimated the total Atlantic Canadian population at 220–250 breeding pairs.

By the beginning of the 1980s, Winifred Cairns's persistence started to pay off, as wildlife agencies took a more systematic approach to assessing the plover's status. Her work undoubtedly contributed to COSEWIC's approval of the Endangered designation, and to the formation of a North American piping plover recovery plan.

Meanwhile, although she has since married and moved to London, Ontario, Winifred's interest in the plovers has not waned. She has presented talks on the species and its plight to many naturalists' clubs in eastern Canada, and has promoted its cause with the Canadian Nature Federation. In addition, she has given freely of her time during vacations on Prince Edward Island in recent years, assisting in the production of a television documentary on the bird, and appearing before a provincial land use review board to oppose shore developments that would threaten nesting habitat. Ever modest when discussing her part in the establishment of a recovery program, Winifred Wake insists on diverting credit to co-workers in the field such as McLaren, McAskill, and Roland Chiasson. It remains for others to insist that without her initial interest and continued involvement over the past 15 years, the piping plover might now be in far worse straits than it is.

STEP 4.
Help raise money for conservation.

Fundraising for the Rain Forest

In the fall of 1988, concern about the destruction of South American rain forests was at an all-time high. In Newmarket, Ontario, people decided to translate their concern into action. Maria Brunati is a member of World Wildlife Fund Canada and a teacher at Sacred Heart Secondary School in Newmarket. When she received information in the mail about WWF's campaign to protect the rain forest, she wanted to help. She assembled a group of enthusiastic students, and they set about developing a fundraising plan.

At about the same time, Newmarket District High School students, Sarah Faulkner and her friends, Tammy Barclay and Lisa Philips, were reading about rain-forest destruction in the newspaper. They wanted to know more. They contacted Raymond Perkins of Roots Canada, who gave them more information and told them about WWF's campaign to buy hectares of rain forest. For each $25 donated to the fund, one hectare of rain forest would be conserved in its natural state. The girls were keen to help. A challenge from Sacred Heart high school to raise money for the "Guardian of the Rain Forest" campaign during the month of November was the incentive they needed.

Students at both schools began separate fundraising efforts. At Sacred Heart, students were stopped on their way into the cafeteria and asked to donate some of their lunch money; classes challenged their teachers to match whatever money was raised by the class; videos on the rain forest were shown; students went home and asked their parents for donations.

At Newmarket high school, groups of students made short presentations to each home room and then asked for donations, which were recognized by a paper leaf placed on an artificial tree in the hall. Contributions of $25 or more were marked by a gold leaf. Art students designed tropical boxer shorts with a rain-forest theme and these were auctioned off, one pair fetching as much as $70.

When the month came to an end, everybody at both schools knew a lot more about the problems facing the rain forest, and together had raised over $4,000 — enough to protect 163 hectares of rain forest. Although the campaign had started as a competition, everyone was a winner.

STEP 5.
Help protect the habitat of endangered species. Get your family and friends involved.

Frederick W. Tribe: The Furbish's Lousewort

Some may see a gentle irony in the fact that the Furbish's lousewort was rediscovered in New Brunswick because the United States Army Corps of Engineers wanted to build a dam in the state of Maine. The rare wildflower, which is endemic to the upper Saint John River Valley, was described in 1882 and originally bore the name Miss Furbish's wood betony in honour of the lady who found it. Up to the mid-1940s it had been collected in a number of locations in the Saint John watershed. Then it disappeared, and by 1975 it was assumed to be extinct or very nearly so.

In 1976 a few specimens were discovered growing on the site where the Corps of Engineers was planning to build the Dickey-Lincoln dam near Dickey, Maine. This posed a dilemma, as the dam could not be built if it would threaten an endangered plant or its habitat. The corps engaged scientists to search for other stands of the lousewort, or, failing that, to investigate means of transplanting it successfully to other locations. Hal Hinds, curator of the University of New Brunswick, and George Stirrett, retired chief naturalist of Parks Canada, were commissioned to conduct the search in Canada, and Dr. Stirrett invited Frederick W. Tribe, a friend and keen amateur naturalist and horticulturist from Andover, New Brunswick, to join him.

The plant turned up on both sides of the border at a total of 44 stations — 18 in Maine, and 26 concentrated in three population areas in New Brunswick. In all, the world population of the species was estimated to consist of some 1,100 specimens — encouraging, but not a large number on which to depend for long-term survival of the species. To make matters worse, it grows in a moist, unstable riverbank habitat that is highly susceptible to erosion during the spring run-off.

Furthermore, two of the three known New Brunswick locations will be drowned if the provincial power corporation implements plans for raising the water behind its dam at Grand Falls by some 20 feet, and carries out the proposed construction of the new Morell dam further downstream.

Considerations such as these provide a strong incentive to extend the distribution of the Furbish's lousewort as rapidly as possible. In the United States, Dr. L. W. Macior of Akron, Ohio, has been propagating the plants under greenhouse conditions. In Canada, Frederick Tribe has taken an active interest in this aspect of species survival work, collecting seed from mature plants and germinating it in his home greenhouse. At first his crops failed, germinating well, but then turning yellow and dying. On learning that the young plants are somewhat parasitic on other species, he tried seeding clover with the lousewort, and met with success. He has raised plants to maturity and gathered seed from them at home. He has also nursed seedlings through their first year in flats, and then set them out in wilderness locations that offer appropriate habitat conditions.

Aside from his horticultural efforts, he keeps a close eye on local stands of Furbish's lousewort and does what he can to educate people about its scarcity and importance. When the owners of one site started developing a riverside picnic spot right where the plant was growing, he drew their attention to the fact and secured their cooperation in protecting it. Such close personal concern is almost essential. High spring floods in 1987 reduced the population at one site from about 200 plants to 40. It is fortunate indeed that Frederick Tribe's reserve stock was available to help replace them.

STEP 6.
If you are a landowner, think about saving some space for wildlife.

Ontario Natural Heritage Stewardship Program

Even a casual reader of this book will notice how many endangered, threatened, and rare species live in southern Ontario. This small area, some of the best agricultural land in the country, is home not only to many species of flora and fauna found nowhere else in Canada, but also to almost half

our human population. For most of the species in this region, the threats come mainly from loss of habitat. Demands for land in southern Ontario are high; the species simply have no place to live.

The Ontario Heritage Foundation is a group devoted to preserving Ontario's heritage. This includes preserving some of the natural environment that early settlers to the area would have known. In 1982 the foundation formed the Ontario Natural Heritage Stewardship Program, a coalition of nongovernment and government groups, to find innovative ways of conserving natural areas. The major objective of the coalition was to convince landowners to set aside valuable agricultural and/or development land as nature reserves. The coalition originally thought that landowners would be opposed to the idea, but in early interviews, researchers discovered that the majority of the landowners were enthusiastic about it.

The coalition developed an award system whereby landowners who agreed to protect special natural features on their land would receive a plaque signed by the premier of Ontario and the chairman of the Ontario Heritage Foundation.

The real value of the award is the education that comes with it, for those giving as well as for those receiving. Landowners learn about the special characteristics of their land, and the Natural Heritage Program researchers learn about the pressures facing landowners in a changing rural landscape. Some landowners may be eligible for small management grants to encourage participation, and a proposed Conservation Tax Rebate may provide a partial rebate of property taxes for those making stewardship agreements.

The stewardship program has been extremely successful in its few years of operation. Concentrating on unique aspects within the Carolinian life zone, it has given stewardship awards to more than 450 landowners and managed to conserve over 5,000 hectares of precious habitat.

Programs similar to the Ontario Heritage Stewardship Program exist across Canada. Wildlife Habitat Canada acts as a national focus for many provincial and regional habitat conservation plans. The aim is to integrate activities in areas of critical wildlife habitat for the benefit of all species. More information on stewardship programs in your area can be obtained from Wildlife Habitat Canada, 1704 Carling Avenue, Ottawa, Ontario, K2A 1C7, (613) 722–2090.

STEP 7.
Think about ways in which your business or company could help endangered species. Many companies are discovering that activities that are good for the environment are also good for business.

Canada Life and the White Pelican

The white pelican has graced Canada Life's corporate logo since 1847. Chosen because of its fierce devotion to its young, the large white birds are an ideal symbol for the insurance company. It was with some shock, then, that Canada Life's public affairs director, Dan Needles, learned of the bird's status as a threatened species during a 1984 canoe trip. Needles returned to Toronto determined to persuade his company's management to invest in the future of the pelican. At first he met with some resistance, but his perseverance and sincerity were rewarded when he convinced Canada Life to sponsor the World Wildlife Fund's White Pelican Program.

The program involved co-operation from the Manitoba, Alberta, and Saskatchewan governments and the Canadian Wildlife Service. It included surveying the prairie lakes where pelicans nested and a major public awareness campaign. It has been an unqualified success. In 1987 the white pelican became the first species to be removed from COSEWIC's Threatened category.

The success of the White Pelican Program was not the end of Canada Life's involvement with endangered species. The company discovered that protecting wildlife was good for business. The publicity generated by the pelican program was better for Canada Life's image than any advertising campaign. Dan Needles even helped to develop a new slogan for the company: "Bringing protection to life." Canada Life is now involved in several endangered species recovery programs, including those of the peregrine falcon and the swift fox. Directors at Canada Life have even, on occasion, relinquished their dining room so that young peregrine falcons can be released from its windows.

Canada Life is just one example of a company that has realized that the aims of conservation and business are not mutually exclusive. These companies recognize that their customers care about protecting the environment, and that good environmental policy is also good for business. The role of corporations like Canada Life is becoming increasingly important in the battle to save both species and their habitats.

STEP 8.
Know the laws regarding wildlife and abide by them. Try to go a little further. Be conscientious about your impact on the environment, and urge your friends to do the same.

STEP 9.
Join an environmental group. There are hundreds in Canada, from political lobby groups, to naturalist groups, and heritage leagues. Some form around a single issue while others are devoted to general nature interests. There is something for every preference. The Canadian Nature Federation can provide listings of many provincial and local environmental groups.

Some National Organizations Doing Work on Endangered Species

Canadian Nature Federation
453 Sussex Dr.
Ottawa, Ontario
K1N 6Z4
(613) 238–6154

World Wildlife Fund
Suite 201, 25 St. Clair Ave. E.
Toronto, Ontario
M4T 1N5
(416) 923–8173

Fondation pour la Sauvegarde des Espèces Menacées
8191 Avenue du Zoo
Charlesbourg, Québec
G1G 4G4
(418) 622–0595

Canadian Wildlife Federation
1673 Carling Ave.
Ottawa, Ontario
K2A 3Z1
(613) 725–2191

Photographers/Illustrators

The authors and publishers gratefully acknowledge permission to include the illustrations, paintings, and photographs, many of which were provided free of charge by the following individuals and organizations.

14 Beedell/Department of External Affairs
19 Tim Fitzharris/World Wildlife Fund
20 Rob Tuckerman
21 World Wildlife Fund
22 Rob Tuckerman
23 Laurie Manson/World Wildlife Fund
24 Rob Tuckerman
25 Maryanne Collins
27 Rob Tuckerman
28 World Wildlife Fund
29 World Wildlife Fund
30 Peter Buerschaper
32 George Hunter/SSC Photo Centre
37 Robert Milko
39 Herbert Pikl
40 Peter Buerschaper
42 Peter Buerschaper
44 Peter Buerschaper
45 Donald R. Gunn
46 Donald R. Gunn
47 Suzanne L. House
48 K. H. Raach/SSC Photo Centre
52 Michael Cobus/ Canadian Parks Service
54 Terry Gregoraschuk
57 Tom Duncan
58 Mia and Klaus/ Department of External Affairs
62 Esther Schmidt/Valan Photos

64 Bruce Wood
66 David Campbell
67 Herbert Pikl
69 Peter Buerschaper
71 left and right: Suzanne L. House
72 F:11 Photographic Design
76 Brian Milne/First Light
78 Dwayne Harty
80 Kiyomi Shoyama
82 Dennis Fast
84 Gary Seib
86 Dan Wood
88 David Brynaert
90 Brian Williams/SSC Photo Centre
94 Kiyomi Shoyama
96 J. R. Graham
98 Peter Buerschaper
99 Peter Buerschaper
100 Peter Buerschaper
101 Peter Buerschaper
103 Peter Buerschaper
105 Peter Buerschaper
106 Peter Buerschaper
108 Peter Buerschaper
109 left: John D. Ambrose; right: Suzanne L. House
110 J. R. Graham
111 Michael J. Oldham
112 top: Suzanne L. House; bottom: Donald R. Gunn
113 top: Donald R. Gunn; bottom: Suzanne L. House
114 top: Suzanne L. House; bottom: John D. Ambrose
115 J. R. Graham
116 left: Suzanne L. House; right: John D. Ambrose
117 P. Allen Woodliffe
118 top: Donald R. Gunn; bottom: John D. Ambrose
119 Suzanne L. House

120 Donald R. Gunn
121 Donald R. Gunn
122 top left: Suzanne L. House; top right: John D. Ambrose; bottom; J. Ross Brown
123 top and bottom: Ontario Ministry of Natural Resources
124 Suzanne L. House
125 Donald R. Gunn
126 Jane K. Hugessen/ Valan Photos
129 Donald R. Gunn
130 S. Homer/SSC Photo Centre
134 Herbert Pikl
136 Terry Gregoraschuk
139 David Brynaert
141 Bruce Wood
143 David Brynaert
145 Peter Buerschaper
147 top: Suzanne L. House; bottom: Erich Haber
148 Donald R. Gunn
149 top and bottom: Donald R. Gunn
150 top and bottom: Donald R. Gunn
151 Suzanne L. House

Government Agencies Responsible for Endangered Species

Federal

Environment Canada
Canadian Wildlife Service,
Ottawa, Ontario K1A 0H3

Administers Migratory Birds Convention Act, Canada Wildlife Act, Convention on International Trade in Endangered Species of Wild Fauna and Flora, and National Registry of Pesticide Residues in Wildlife Tissues. Carries out research throughout Canada on migratory birds, endangered species, and other wildlife of national and international importance.
Headquarters (819) 997–1301

Regional Offices

Atlantic:
Canadian Wildlife Service,
Environment Canada,
31 West Main Street,
P.O. Box 1590,
Sackville, N.B. E0A 3C0
(506) 536–3025

Ontario:
Canadian Wildlife Service,
Environment Canada,
1725 Woodward Drive,
Ottawa K1A 0E7
(613) 998–4693

Pacific and Yukon:
Canadian Wildlife Service,
Environment Canada,
5421 Robertson Road,
P.O. Box 340,
Delta, B.C. V4K 3Y3
(604) 946–8546

Québec:
Canadian Wildlife Service,
Environment Canada,
1141 Route de l'Église,
P.O. Box 10100,
Sainte-Foy G1V 4H5
(418) 648–3914

Western and Northern:
Canadian Wildlife Service,
Environment Canada,
Twin Atria No. 2,
4999-98 Avenue,
Edmonton, Alberta
T6B 2X3
(403) 468–8919

Parks Service
Ottawa, Ontario K1A 0H3

Responsible for acquiring and developing representative areas of the country for use by the public, consistent with the preservation of such areas in their natural state; also for preserving, restoring, and operating sites and structures of importance to Canadian history, including historic canals.
Assistant Deputy Minister (819) 997–9525

Regional Offices

Western:
220 Fourth Avenue SE,
P.O. Box 2989, Station M,
Calgary, Alberta
T2P 3H8
(403) 292–4444

Prairie:
457 Main Street,
Winnipeg, Manitoba
R3B 3E8
(204) 983–2127

Ontario:
111 Water Street E,
Cornwall K6H 6S3
(613) 938–5866

Québec:
3 Rue Buade,
C.P. 6060, Haute-Ville
Québec City G1R 4V7
(418) 648–4042

Atlantic:
Historic Properties,
Upper Water Street,
Halifax, Nova Scotia
B3J 1S9
(902) 426–3405

Fisheries and Oceans

200 Kent Street,
Ottawa, Ontario K1A 0E6

Responsible for fisheries development and management, including marine mammals on both coasts, fisheries research, oceanography, hydrography, and the administration of small-craft harbours.
Fisheries Research (613) 990–0287

Provincial

Alberta

*Department of Energy
and Natural Resources,*
Fish and Wildlife Division,
Main Floor, North Tower,
Petroleum Plaza,
9945-108 Street,
Edmonton T5K 2C9

The overall responsibilities of the division are to manage the fish and wildlife resources of the Province of Alberta for the benefit and enjoyment of the people, and to promote legislation and programs in support of this goal.
Assistant Deputy Minister (403) 427–6749

British Columbia

Ministry of Environment,
Parliament Buildings,
Victoria V8V 1X5

Responsible for the preservation of a quality environment for all living resources, including man. Its mandate involves several management activities, many of which are interrelated, as well as co-operation with other provincial and federal agencies. Under its legislation, the ministry is responsible for the management of water resources (quality and quantity), air quality, fresh-water sport fisheries, aquaculture, and wildlife. It also regulates waste disposal and pesticide use. Government-wide services for surveys and resource-map production, organization of emergency responses to disasters, and the operation of an environmental laboratory are other ministry responsibilities.
Fisheries Management Branch (604) 387–9507
Wildlife Management Branch (604) 387–9731

Manitoba

Department of Natural Resources,
Room 314, Legislative Building,
Winnipeg R3C 0V8
(204) 945–3730

The department's purpose is to encourage wise use of the province's natural resources and preserve them for future generations.
Fisheries Branch P.O. Box 20, 1495 James Street, Winnipeg R3H 0W9 (204) 945–7808
Wildlife Branch P.O. Box 20, 1495 James Street, Winnipeg R3H 0W9 (204) 945–7775

New Brunswick

Department of Natural Resources and Energy,
P.O. Box 6000,
Fredericton E3B 5H1
(506) 453–2440

Wildlife Management Division (506) 453–2440
Fish Management Division (506) 453–2440

Newfoundland

Department of Culture, Recreation, and Youth,
P.O. Box 4750, St. John's A1C 5T7

Objective is to maintain the ecosystems upon which wildlife and people depend, and to do so recognizing the values of the diversity and

abundance of species; to provide for the safe and sustainable use of wildlife, both consumptive and nonconsumptive; and to help create a social environment conducive to effective wildlife conservation.
Wildlife Division,
Building 810, Pleasantville,
P.O. Box 4750,
St. John's A1C 5T7
(709) 576–2817

Northwest Territories
Department of Renewable Resources,
Government of the Northwest Territories,
Yellowknife X1A 2L9

Has broad responsibility for wildlife management and environmental protection in the Northwest Territories, and provides guidance and assistance to people dependent on these resources, encouraging them to harvest wildlife in a manner that will ensure continued availability of the resource.
Wildlife Management Branch (403) 873–7411

Nova Scotia
Department of Lands and Forests,
1701 Hollis Street,
P.O. Box 698,
Halifax B3J 2T9
(902) 424–5935

Charged with the administration of the Lands and Forests Act and various other statutes. Inherent in the legislation and incumbent upon the department are responsibilities pertaining to the productivity of the forests generally, the supply of forest products, the conservation of wildlife, and the enhancement of recreational areas.
Wildlife Branch (902) 678–8921

Ontario
Ministry of Natural Resources,
Whitney Block, Queen's Park,
Toronto M7A 1W3

The ministry's programs are concerned with the use of the physical resources of land, water, trees, fish, animals, and certain minerals for resource utilization and recreation.

Outdoor Recreation Group,
Whitney Block, Queen's Park,
Toronto M7A 1W3

Responsible for managing Ontario's resources of fish, wildlife, provincial parks, and recreation areas, in addition to planning and providing the wide variety of recreational opportunities afforded by these resources.
Fisheries Branch (416) 965–5947
Wildlife Branch (416) 965–4254

Field Offices
North-central Region:
Ontario Government Building,
435 James Street South,
P.O. Box 5000, Station F,
Thunder Bay P7C 5G6
(807) 475–1231

District Offices:
Thunder Bay (807) 475–1521
Terrace Bay (807) 825–3205
Nipigon (807) 887–2120
Geraldton (807) 854–1030
Atikokan (807) 597–6971

Northwestern Region:
810 Robertson Street,
P.O. Box 5160,
Kenora P9N 3X9
(807) 468–3111

Northern Region:
140 Fourth Avenue,
P.O. Box 3000,
Cochrane P0L 1C0
Fisheries (705) 272–7038
Wildlife (705) 272–7044

Northeastern Region:
199 Larch Street,
Sudbury P3E 5P9
(705) 675–4120

Southern Ontario:
P.O. Box 7400,
Maple L6A 1S9
(416) 832–2761

Algonquin Region:
Brendale Square,
P.O. Box 9000,
Huntsville P0A 1K0
(705) 789–9611

Leslie M. Frost Natural
Resources Centre,
Highway 35,
Dorset P0A 1E0
(705) 766–2451

Eastern Region:
Provincial Government Building,
Concession Road,
Kemptville K0G 1J0
(613) 258–3413

Central Region:
10670 Yonge Street,
Richmond Hill L4C 3C9
(416) 883–3227

Southwestern Region:
659 Exeter Road,
P.O. Box 5463,
London N6A 4L6
(519) 661–2749

Niagara Escarpment Commission,
232 Guelph Street,
Georgetown L7G 4B1
(416) 877–5191

Maintains the Niagara Escarpment and
land in its vicinity as a continuous natural
environment, and ensures only such
development as is compatible with that
environment.

Prince Edward Island
*Department of Community
and Cultural Affairs,*
P.O. Box 2000, Charlottetown C1A 7N8

Objectives are to conserve and manage
wildlife, fish, and habitats on which they
depend. Objectives are approached through
co-ordinated biological, enforcement,
education, and public relations programs.
Fish and Wildlife Division
(902) 892–0311 ext. 268

Québec
Department of Recreation,
Fish and Game, Place de la Capitale,
150 East, St-Cyrville Blvd.,
Québec City G1R 2B2
Fish and Game Branch (418) 644–9376

Saskatchewan
*Department of Parks and
Renewable Resources,*
3211 Albert Street,
Regina S4S 5W6
Fisheries (306) 787–2884
Wildlife (306) 787–2309

Yukon
Department of Renewable Resources,
P.O. Box 2703,
Whitehorse Y1A 2C6
Fish and Wildlife (403) 667–5460

References

General

Brown, Lester R., et al. 1988. *State of the world 1988*. New York: W. W. Norton.

Diamond, Anthony W., et al. 1987. *Save the birds*. Cambridge: Cambridge University Press.

Durrell, Lee. 1986. *State of the ark*. London: Gaia Books Limited.

Ehrlich, Paul and Anne. 1981. *Extinction: The causes and consequences of the disappearance of species*. New York: Ballantine Books.

Fitter, Richard. 1986. *Wildlife for man: How and why we should conserve our species*. London: Collins.

Fitzharris, Tim, and John A. Livingston. 1988. *Canada: A natural history*. Markham: Penguin.

Goudie, Andrew. 1986. *The human impact on the natural environment*. 2d ed. Cambridge: The MIT Press.

Livingston, John A. 1981. *The fallacy of wildlife conservation*. Toronto: McClelland and Stewart.

Luoma, Jon R. 1987. *A crowded ark: The role of zoos in wildlife conservation*. Boston: Houghton Mifflin Company.

Mowat, Farley. 1984. *Sea of slaughter*. Toronto: McClelland and Stewart/Bantam Limited.

Myers, Norman. 1978. *The sinking ark: A new look at the problem of disappearing species*. New York: Pergamon Press.

Passmore, John. 1980. *Man's responsibility for nature*. 2d ed. London: Duckworth.

Rolston III, Holmes. 1986. *Philosophy gone wild*. Buffalo: Prometheus Books.

Soulé, Michael E., ed. 1986. *Conservation biology: The science of scarcity and diversity*. Ann Arbor: University of Michigan School of Natural Resources.

Stone, Christopher D. 1987. *Earth and other ethics*. New York: Harper and Row.

Suzuki, David, and Peter Knudtson. 1988. *Genethics*. Toronto: Stoddart.

Wilson, Edward O. 1984. *Biophilia*. Cambridge: Harvard University Press.

Mammals

Ad hoc committee for the conservation of the St. Lawrence Beluga. 1987. *Statement of problems of the St. Lawrence belugas*. Department of Fisheries and Oceans.

Banfield, A. W. F. 1974. *The mammals of Canada*. Toronto: University of Toronto Press.

Braham, Howard W., and Bruce D. Krogman. *Population biology of the bowhead* (Balaena mysticetus) *and beluga* (Delphinapterus leucas) *whale in the Bering, Chukchi and Beaufort seas*. Northwest and Alaska Fisheries Centre Report.

Dauphiné, T. Charles, Jr. 1975. The disappearance of caribou reintroduced to Cape Breton Highlands National Park. *Canadian Field-Naturalist*. 89(3):299–310.

——. 1987. *Status of the wolverine* (Gulo gulo) *in Canada*. Report to the Canadian scientific authorities for the Convention on International Trade in Endangered Species (CITES).

de Jong, G. G. van Zyll, and E. van Ingen. 1978. *Status report on the eastern cougar* (Felis concolor couguar) *in Canada*. Ottawa: COSEWIC status report.

Farr, A. C. M., and F. L. Bunnell. 1980. *The sea otter in British Columbia — problem or opportunity*. Victoria: Fish and Wildlife Branch.

Gamble, R. L. 1981. Distribution in Manitoba of *(Mustela frenata longicauda)* the long-tailed weasel, and the interrelation of distribution and habitat selection in Manitoba, Saskatchewan, and Alberta. *Canadian Journal of Zoology*. 59(6):1036–39.

——. 1982. *Current status of* (Mustela frenata longicauda) *long-tailed weasel in Canada*. Ottawa: COSEWIC status report.

Gaskin, David E. 1987. Updated status of the right whale *(Eubalaena glacialis)* in Canada. *Canadian Field-Naturalist*. 101(2):295 ff.

Gerson, H. 1986. *The status of the cougar* (Felis concolor linnaeus) *in Ontario, with an overview of the status in Canada*. Toronto:

Ontario Ministry of Natural Resources.

Gunn, A., F. F. Miller, and D. C. Thomas. 1979. *Status report on Peary caribou* (Rangifer tarandus pearyi) *in Canada*. Ottawa: COSEWIC status report.

Hoyt, Erich. 1983. Great winged whales. *Equinox*. (10):24–47.

——. 1984. *The whales of Canada*. Camden East: Camden House.

Kelsall, John P. 1983 (rev. 1984). *Status report on woodland caribou* (Rangifer tarandus caribou) *in Canada*. Ottawa: COSEWIC status report.

MacAskie, Ian B. 1987. Updated status of the sea otter, *Enhydra lutris*, in Canada. *Canadian Field-Naturalist*. 101(2):279–283.

Mansfield, A. W. 1985. Status of the bowhead whale, *Balaena mysticetus*, in Canada. *Canadian Field-Naturalist*. 99(3):421–24.

Miller, M. D. 1930. Vancouver Island Marmot. In*Threatened and endangered species and habitats in British Columbia and the Yukon*. Victoria: B.C. Ministry of Environment.

Moisan, G. 1959. The caribou of Gaspé — III. *Le Naturaliste Canadien*. 84(1):5–27.

Munro, W. T., et al. 1985. *The Vancouver Island marmot: Status and management plan*. Victoria: B.C. Ministry of Environment.

Nero, Robert W., and Robert E. Wrigley. 1977. Status and habits of the cougar in Manitoba. *Canadian Field-Naturalist*. 91(1):28–40.

Novak, M., et al. 1987. *Wild furbearer management and conservation in North America*. Toronto: Ontario Ministry of Natural Resources.

Novakowski, N. S. 1978. *Status report on the wood bison*. Ottawa: COSEWIC status report.

Pippard, L. 1985. Status of the St. Lawrence River populations of the beluga. *Canadian Field-Naturalist*. 99(3):438–50.

Reynolds, H. W., and A. W. L. Hawley, eds. 1988. *Bison ecology in relation to agricultural development in the Slave River lowlands, Northwest Territories*. Ottawa: Canadian Wildlife Service.

Sergeant, D. 1986. Present status of white whales in the St. Lawrence estuary. *Le Naturaliste Canadien*. 113:61–81.

Snyder, Joyce. 1985. *The status of the pine marten* (Martes americana) *in Newfoundland*. Ottawa: COSEWIC status report.

Watson, Lyall. 1981. *Sea guide to the whales of the world*. Scarborough: Nelson Canada Limited.

Whitehead, Hal. 1987. Updated status of the humpback whale *(Megaptera novaeanglise)* in Canada. *Canadian Field-Naturalist*. 101(2):284–94.

Wright, Bruce S. 1972. *The eastern cougar: A question of survival*. Toronto: Clarke Irwin.

Birds

Adam, Christopher I. G. 1987. *The status of the loggerhead shrike* (Lanius ludovicianus excubitorides) *in Saskatchewan: The 1987 surveys*. Regina: Prepared for World Wildlife Fund Canada and Canadian Wildlife Service.

Anweiler, Gary G. 1977. *Saskatchewan greater prairie chicken reports 1965–1977*. Regina: Unpublished Province of Saskatchewan report.

Banks, Richard C. 1977. The decline and fall of the Eskimo curlew. *American Birds*. 31(2):127–34.

Bent, A. C. 1929. *Life histories of American shore birds, part II*. Washington: Smithsonian Institute, U.S. Nat. Mus. Bull. 142 (Dover ed. 1962).

——. 1921. *Life histories of North American gulls and terns*. New York: Dover Publications, 1963.

——. 1976. *Life histories of North American marsh birds*. New York: Dover Publications, 1963.

Blankinship, David R., and Kirke A. King. 1984. A probable sighting of 23 Eskimo curlews in Texas. *American Birds*. 38(6): 1066–67.

Cadman, Michael D. 1985. *Status report on the loggerhead shrike in Canada* (Lanius ludovicianus). Ottawa: COSEWIC status report.

Cadman, M. D., P. F. J. Eagles, and F. M. Helleiner. 1987. *Atlas of the breeding birds of Ontario*. Waterloo: University of Waterloo Press.

Campbell, E. C., and R. W. Campbell. 1984. *Status report on the spotted owl*, Strix occidentalis caurina, *in Canada*. Ottawa: COSEWIC status report.

Chamberlain, Debra. 1978. *The status of the Kirtland's warbler* (Dendroica kirtlandii) *in Canada*. Toronto: COSEWIC status report.

Cramp, Stanley, et al. 1985. *The birds of the western Palearctic*. Vol. IV. Oxford: Oxford University Press.

De Smet, K., and Michael Conrad. 1987. *The status of the loggerhead shrike* (Lanius ludovicianus) *in Manitoba during 1987*.

Report to Manitoba Department of Natural Resources, World Wildlife Fund Canada, and Canadian Wildlife Service.

De Smet, Ken D., and Wayne S. Miller. 1988. *Status report on the Baird's sparrow* (Ammodramus bairdii) *in Canada*. Ottawa: COSEWIC status report.

Erickson, Gary. *Status of burrowing owls in Alberta*. In Holroyd, G. L., et al. 1987. *Endangered species in the prairie provinces*. Edmonton: Provincial Museum of Alberta.

Gochfeld, Michael. 1983. The roseate tern: World distribution and status as a threatened species. *Biological Conservation*. 25:103–25.

Godfrey, W. Earl. 1986. *The birds of Canada*. Ottawa: National Museum of Natural Sciences.

Gollop, J. G., T. W. Barry, and E. H. Iverson. 1986. *The Eskimo curlew: A vanishing species?* Regina: Saskatchewan Natural History Society, Spec. Pub. No. 17.

Gollop, J. B., and C. E. P. Shier. 1978. *The status of the Eskimo curlew*. Ottawa: COSEWIC status report.

Haig, Susan. 1987. *Piping plovers in Manitoba. In* Proceedings of the Workshop on Endangered Species in the Prairie Provinces: Occasional Paper No. 9. Edmonton: Provincial Museum of Alberta.

———. 1985. *The status of the piping plover in Canada*. Ottawa: COSEWIC status report.

Hanrahan, Christine. 1987. The loggerhead shrike: Status report for the Ottawa district. *Trail and Landscape*. 21(3):154–68.

Harrison, Colin. 1984. *A field guide to the nests, eggs, and nestlings of North American birds*. Toronto: Collins.

Howie, Richard. 1980. The spotted owl in British Columbia. *In Threatened and endangered species and habitats in British Columbia and the Yukon*. Victoria: B.C. Ministry of Environment.

Johns, B. W. 1987. *Whooping crane sightings in the prairie provinces, 1979–85*. Ottawa: Canadian Wildlife Service.

Johnston, A., and S. Smoliak. 1976. Settlement of the grasslands and the greater prairie chicken. *Blue Jay*. 34(3):153–56.

Kirkham, Ian R., and David N. Nettleship. 1987. Status of the roseate tern in Canada. *Journal of Field Ornithology*. 58(4):505–15.

Knapton, Richard W. 1982. *The Henslow's sparrow* (Ammodramus henslowii) *in Canada: A status report*. Toronto: Ontario Ministry of Natural Resources.

Kuyt, E. 1981. Population status, nest site fidelity and breeding habitat of whooping cranes. In Lewis, J. C., and H. Masatomi. 1981. *Crane research around the world*. Proceedings of the International Crane Symposium, Sapporo, Japan.

Lewis, Charles. 1987. No home on the range. *Nature Canada*. 16(4):41–44.

McKeating, G., and T. Charles Dauphiné, Jr. 1987. *National recovery plan for piping plover*. Ottawa: Canadian Wildlife Service.

Marchant, J., T. Prater, and P. Hayman. 1986. *Shorebirds: An identification guide to the waders of the world*. Boston: Houghton Mifflin Co.

Murphy, Julia E. 1987. *The 1985–86 Canadian peregrine falcon survey*. Ottawa: Canadian Wildlife Service report.

Noble, D. G., J. E. Elliott, and D. B. Peakall. 1987. *Environmental contaminants in Canadian peregrine falcons: A toxicological assessment*. Ottawa: Canadian Wildlife Service draft report.

Porter, R. D., M. A. Jenkins, and A. L. Gaski. *Working bibliography of the peregrine falcon*. Washington: National Wildlife Federation, Scientific and Technical Series No. 9.

Province of Saskatchewan. 1978. *The status of the greater prairie chicken* (Tympanuchus cupido pinnatus) *in Canada*. Ottawa: COSEWIC status report.

Ratcliff, Brian D. 1986. The Manitoba burrowing owl survey 1982–84. *Blue Jay*. 44(1):3–37.

Schmutz, Josef K., and Sheila M. Schmutz. 1979. *Status of the ferruginous hawk* (Buteo regalis) *in Canada*. Ottawa: COSEWIC status report.

Squires, W. A. 1976. *Birds of New Brunswick*. Saint John: New Brunswick Museum, Monographic Series No. 7.

Tufts, Robie W. 1986. *Birds of Nova Scotia*. 3rd ed. Halifax: Nimbus Publishing/N.S. Museum.

Wallis, Clifford A., and Cleve R. Wershler. 1981. Status and breeding of mountain plovers(Charadrius montana) in Canada. *Canadian Field-Naturalist*. 95(2):133–36.

Wallis, Clifford A., and Cleve R. Wershler. 1986. *Status report on the mountain plover* (Charadrius montana) *in Canada*. Ottawa: COSEWIC status report.

Wedgwood, J. A. 1976. Burrowing owls in

south-central Saskatchewan. *Blue Jay.* 34(1):26–44.

——. 1978. *Status report on the burrowing owl* (Athene cunicularia) *in Canada*. Ottawa: COSEWIC status report.

Wershler, R. 1987. *Loggerhead shrike survey of southern Alberta.* Edmonton: Prepared for Canadian Wildlife Service, Alberta Fish and Wildlife, and World Wildlife Canada.

Fish

Campbell, R. R. 1987. Status of the longjaw cisco*(Coregonus alpenae)* in Canada. *Canadian Field-Naturalist.* 101(2):241–44.

Evans, D. O., J. J. Houston, and G. N. Meredith. 1987. *Status report on the Lake Simcoe whitefish* (Coregonus clupeaformis). Ottawa: COSEWIC status report.

Goodchild, Cheryl D. 1988. *Status report on the margined madtom* (Noturus insignis) *in Canada*. Ottawa: COSEWIC status report.

Houston, J. J. 1987. *Status report on the shortjaw cisco* (Coregonus zenithicus) *in Canada*. Ottawa: COSEWIC status report.

McAllister, Don E., Brad J. Parker, and Paul M. McKee. 1985. *Rare, endangered and extinct fishes in Canada*. Ottawa: National Museum of Natural Sciences, Syllogeus Series No. 54.

McPhail, J. D. 1988. *Report on the status of the Enos Lake stickleback species pair* Gasterosteus spp. Ottawa: COSEWIC status report.

——. 1987. Status of the salish sucker *(Catostomus sp.)* in Canada. *Canadian Field-Naturalist.* 101(2):231–36.

Mongeau, J.-P., P. Dumont, L. Cloutier, and A.-M. Clément. 1987. *Status of the copper redhorse* (Moxostoma hubbsi) *in Canada*. Ottawa: COSEWIC status report.

Parker, B. 1987. *Status report on the deepwater sculpia* (Myoxocephalus thompsoni). Ottawa: COSEWIC status report.

——. 1987. *Status report on the shortnose cisco* (Coregonus reighardi). Ottawa: COSEWIC status report.

Parker, B., and C. Brousseau. 1987. *Status report on the aurora trout* (Salvelinus fontinalis Mitchill). Ottawa: COSEWIC status report.

Parker, B., and E. Kott. 1988. *Report on the status of the black redhorse* (Moxostoma duquesnei) *in Canada*. Ottawa: COSEWIC status report.

Peden, A. E., and G. W. Hughes. 1984. Status of the shorthead sculpin, *Cottus confusus,* in the Flathead River, British Columbia. *Canadian Field-Naturalist.* 98(1):127–33.

Peden, A. E., W. E. Roberts, and G. W. Hughes. 1989. Morphologically distinct populations of the shorthead sculpin, *Cottus confusus,* and *C. bairdi* in British Columbia. *Canadian Journal of Zoology.* In press.

Scott, W. B., and E. J. Crossman. 1973. *Freshwater fishes of Canada.* Ottawa: Fisheries Research Board of Canada, Bulletin 184.

Reptiles

Forsyth, Adrian. 1984. On the Beach. *Equinox.* 14(2):29–49.

Froom, Barbara. 1976. *The Turtles of Canada.* Toronto: McClelland and Stewart.

Goff, Gregory P., and Jon Lien. 1988. Atlantic leatherback turtles, *Dermochelys coriacea,* in cold water off Newfoundland and Labrador. *Canadian Field-Naturalist.* 102(1):1–5.

Threlfall, William. 1978. First record of the Atlantic leatherback turtle, *Dermochelys coriacea,* in Labrador. *Canadian Field-Naturalist.* 92(3):287.

Plants

Allen, Gary M. 1986. *Status report on purple twayblade* (Liparis liliifolia L.) *in Canada.* Ottawa: COSEWIC status report.

Ambrose, John D. 1983. *Status report on Kentucky coffee tree* (Gymnocladus dioica). Ottawa: COSEWIC status report.

——. 1987. *Status report on red mulberry* (Morus rubra L.), *a threatened species in Canada.* Ottawa: COSEWIC status report.

Ambrose, John D., and Steven W. Aboud. 1987. *Status report on chestnut* (Castanea dentata). Ottawa: COSEWIC status report.

——. 1983. *Status report on the blue ash* (Fraxinus quadrangulata). Ottawa: COSEWIC status report.

——. 1984. *Status report on the cucumber tree* (Magnolia acuminata). Ottawa: COSEWIC status report.

Argus, George W. 1981. *Status report on* Armeria maritima ssp. interior, *a rare Canadian endemic.* Ottawa: COSEWIC status report.

——. 1981. *Status report on* Salix planifolia spp. tyrrellii, *a rare Canadian endemic.* Ottawa: COSEWIC status report.

Brownell, Vivian. 1985. *Status report on the bluehearts* (Bunchnera americana). Ottawa:

COSEWIC status report.

——. 1985. *Status report on the heart-leaved plantain* (Plantago cordata). Ottawa: COSEWIC status report.

——. 1984. *Status report on the pink milkwort* (Polygala incarnata). Ottawa: COSEWIC status report.

——. 1981. *Status report on the small white lady's slipper* (Cypripedium candidum). Ottawa: COSEWIC status report.

——. 1982. *Status report on the small whorled pogonia* (Isotria medeoloides) (Pursh.) Raf. Ottawa: COSEWIC status report.

Brunton, Daniel. 1984. *Status report on the giant helleborine* (Epipactis gigantea). Ottawa: COSEWIC status report.

——. 1984. *Status report on the mosquito fern* (Azolla mexicana). Ottawa: COSEWIC status report.

——. 1984. *Status report on the southern maidenhair fern* (Adiantum capillus-veneris). Ottawa: COSEWIC status report.

Canne-Hilliker, Judith M. 1987. *Status report on Gattinger's purple false foxglove* (Agalinis gattingeri), *an endangered species in Canada.* Ottawa: COSEWIC status report.

——. 1987. *Status report on Skinner's purple false foxglove* (Agalinis skinneriana), *an endangered species in Canada.* Ottawa: COSEWIC status report.

Crins, William J. 1986. *Status report on hoary mountain mint* (Pycnanthemum incanum). Ottawa: COSEWIC status report.

Gauvin, Claire. 1984. *Status report on the American water-willow* (Justicia americana). Ottawa: COSEWIC status report.

Keddy, Cathy. 1986. *Status report on eastern mountain avens* (Geum peckii). Ottawa: COSEWIC status report.

——. 1987. *Status report on golden crest* (Lophiola aurea). Ottawa: COSEWIC status report.

——. 1987. *Status report on pitcher's thistle* (Cirsium pitcheri). Ottawa: COSEWIC status report.

Keddy, Cathy, and Paul Keddy. 1984. *Status report on the pink coreopsis* (Coreopsis rosea).

Ottawa: COSEWIC status report.

——. 1984. *Status report on the Plymouth gentian* (Sabatia kennedyana). Ottawa: COSEWIC status report.

Kirk, Donald A. 1987. *Status report on colicroot* (Aletris farinosa) *in Canada.* Ottawa: COSEWIC status report.

——. 1987. *Status report on spotted wintergreen,* Chimaphila maculata (L.) Pursh, *an endangered species in Canada.* Ottawa: COSEWIC status report.

Klimas, J. E., and J. A. Cunningham. 1974. *Wildflowers of North America.* New York: A. E. Knopf.

Klinkenberg, Brian, and Rose Klinkenberg. 1985. *Status report on the eastern prickly pear cactus* (Opuntia humifusa). Ottawa: COSEWIC status report.

Klinkenberg, Rose. 1986. *Status report on the large whorled pogonia* (Isotria verticillata). Ottawa: COSEWIC status report.

Pratt, P.D. 1986. *Status report on slender bush clover,* Lespedeza virginica (L.) Britt. (Fabaceae), *an endangered species in Canada.* Ottawa: COSEWIC status report.

Taschereau, P. M. 1986. *Status report on sweet pepperbush* (Clethra alnifolia). Ottawa: COSEWIC status report.

White, David J. 1988. *Ecological study and status report on American ginseng* (Panax quinquefolium). Ottawa: COSEWIC status report.

Wilson, Scott. 1985. *Status report on the water pennywort* (Hydrocotyle umbellata). Ottawa: COSEWIC status report.

Woodliffe, P. Allen. 1986. *Status report on the nodding pogonia* (Triphora trianthophora). Ottawa: COSEWIC status report.

COSEWIC status reports can be obtained by writing to:

COSEWIC Secretariat
Canadian Wildlife Service
Environment Canada
Ottawa
K1A 0H3

Index